GW00382938

CAMBRIDGESHIRE

The King's England

A New Domesday Book of 10,000 Towns
and Villages

Edited by Arthur Mee

Complete in 41 Volumes

Enchanted Land (Introductory volume)

Bedfordshire and	*Lincolnshire*
Huntingdonshire	*London*
Berkshire	*Middlesex*
Buckinghamshire	*Monmouthshire*
Cambridgeshire	*Norfolk*
Cheshire	*Northamptonshire*
Cornwall	*Northumberland*
Derbyshire	*Nottinghamshire*
Devon	*Oxfordshire*
Dorset	*Shropshire*
Durham	*Somerset*
Essex	*Staffordshire*
Gloucestershire	*Suffolk*
Hampshire with the	*Surrey*
Isle of Wight	*Sussex*
Herefordshire	*Warwickshire*
Hertfordshire	*Wiltshire*
Kent	*Worcestershire*
Lake Counties	*Yorkshire – East Riding*
Lancashire	*Yorkshire – North Riding*
Leicestershire and Rutland	*Yorkshire – West Riding*

NOTHING like these books has ever been presented to the
English people. Every place has been visited. The Com-
pilers have travelled half-a-million miles and have prepared
a unique picture of our countryside as it has come down
through the ages, a census of all that is enduring and worthy
of record.

King's College Chapel   **The Crowning Glory of Cambridge**

THE KING'S ENGLAND

CAMBRIDGESHIRE

The Country of the Fens

EDITED BY
ARTHUR MEE

With 150 Places
and 106 Pictures

THE KING'S ENGLAND PRESS
2001

First published 1939

This edition published 2001 by
The King's England Press,
Cambertown House, Commercial Road,
Goldthorpe, Rotherham,
South Yorkshire, S63 9BL.

© The Trustees of the Estate
of the late Arthur Mee

ISBN 1 872438 31 8

Printed and bound in Great Britain by
Woolnough Bookbinding, Irthlingborough, Northants.

The Editor is indebted to

*ERNEST BRYANT, E. S. GREW, and
CLAUDE SCANLON*

for their help with this book

For the pictures to

SIDNEY TRANTER, ART EDITOR

and to the following :

The Architect and Building News, The Architectural Press, Edgar Bull, Brian Clayton, Country Life, Fred Crossley, J. Dixon-Scott, H. Felton, Humphrey Joel, A. F. Kersting, W. F. Taylor, The Times, and F..R. Winstone

PICTURES OF CAMBRIDGESHIRE

When the pictures are not on or facing the pages given
they are inside the set of pictures beginning on that page

PICTURES OF CAMBRIDGESHIRE

The Country of the Fens

IF we look at the map of Cambridgeshire we may think it not unlike the shape of the island of which it is a small 100th part; in shape the part is not unlike the whole. But in fact they are anything but similar, for, while our island rests securely in the sea which serves it in the office of a wall, the county lies so low that it must be protected from the sea. We must think of Cambridgeshire as we think of Holland, fighting for its life against invading waters, and with ceaseless effort and invigorating spirit winning the fight and conquering Mother Nature.

It is a romantic story that these 864 square miles tell, for much of it has been snatched from swampy ground and made fair to see and profitable to cultivate, and on this soil so unpromising have been built up two of the wonders of our English world—the marvellous cathedral of Ely and the unparalleled city of Cambridge. From the county have come men famous for the qualities of these two unique places, men of spirit and men of mind—Milton, Cromwell, and a countless host of Cambridge men, while if we think of our own time this small county gave 5421 men to die for English freedom.

It is a characteristic physical feature of Cambridgeshire that it lies so low. It is only in the southern regions to the west and east of Cambridge that we find the land rising as much as 400 feet on the range of chalk hills that sweep like a bow across England from Dorset, through Wiltshire and Buckinghamshire and across South Bedfordshire, to enter Cambridgeshire where it runs with Hertfordshire, passing then through East Anglia to where Hunstanton's cliffs gleam white at the rising sun. Known to the mapmen as the East Anglian Heights, these small hills have at least one boast, for there is nothing higher due east in all Europe until the boundary with Asia is reached. The ridge with this distinction has been important in the ancient story of our island, for along it ran the prehistoric trade route known as the Icknield Way; and who dare say how much of our earliest civilisation did not enter by it?

With fens to the north and dense forests to the south, the Icknield Way was for centuries the only route for trade across the heart of England. Newmarket just over the border in Suffolk and Royston just across the Hertfordshire boundary (not long ago Cambridgeshire towns) are linked by it, and, to judge by the dykes or the ramparts we find straddling between them, many a fierce resistance to oversea invaders must have taken place in this region when men fought only with stones and primitive weapons. We know that the entrenchments we see were for the defence of the route, for they extend in one direction to where dense forests stood, and in the other downhill to where primeval marshes made any advance impossible.

There were British Camps along this route, and pottery has been found mingled with the bones of animals on which men fed, as in the war ditches near Cherry Hinton. Some of the dykes have been used for roads, notably the Worsted Dyke, which was once the Roman Via Devana, having acquired its present name from the wool carried along it to Stourbridge Fair. Another long rampart has the name of Devil's Dyke and can be seen between Newmarket Racecourse and the village of Reach. In Burwell Fen near Reach was found the skull of an ox extinct in our island before Caesar came, and still imbedded in it was the stone axe which killed it.

The best known camp in the county is on the best known hills, the Gog Magogs, outliers of the range toward Cambridge, and rising to 300 feet. The camp is called Wandlebury, and in its day consisted of a triple ring of ramparts about a mile round, difficult to trace now, but actually traceable in the shrubberies of the great house here. The Gog Magogs are one of the best viewpoints in the county, Ely's wondrous towers alone surpassing it, and as we look west across the River Cam we see the county's only other group of hills over 200 feet, the greensand range which forms the southern boundary of the Great Ouse Valley. These rocks are older than Gog Magogs, but as we go north we walk above rocks that are older still, the Oxford Clay.

But the most striking things to the eye from our vantage point on the Gog Magog Hills, and much more pronounced from Ely's great tower, is the network of waterways which cover most of Cambridgeshire. Those that are straight are man's, those curving are Nature's. Man's work has marvellously changed the face of Cambridgeshire. The volume of the water in the natural waterways is not what it was. Man's energy from Roman days till now has driven the sea back from the northern boundary as it was 2000 years ago; Wisbech is now ten miles from the coast, whereas in Roman days it lay at the head of an estuary.

Centuries ago the combined waters of the Great Ouse and the Nene made their way through Wisbech to the sea. Today the Great Ouse reaches the sea at King's Lynn, having joined the Little Ouse, once a separate and much narrower river. Now, therefore, we must call the Little Ouse a tributary, coming in at Brandon Creek after having formed the boundary with Norfolk. Part of the county's boundary with Suffolk is formed by the River Lark, the next tributary of the Great Ouse as we come inland. Down the valleys of the chalk hills forming the Essex boundary in the south flow the Bourn, the Granta, and the Rhee, losing their clarity and their chattering speed as they merge to form the Cam, which flows through Cambridge at the Backs of the Colleges, coloured by the lowland mud and so perhaps a little unworthy of the lovely lawns. From Cambridge the Cam runs north to join the Great Ouse (here known as the Old West River), where Ely's towers begin to dominate the north horizon. This Old West River has come meandering east across the county from St Ives over the border, at first forming the border with Huntingdonshire as far as Earith, a vital spot in the story of this river. To complete the tale of Nature's waterways we must add the River Nene, the old course

3

of which wanders across the county to Upwell before taking its slight waters to Wisbech, whither the new Nene has come by a direct route from Peterborough.

The work of men in controlling sea and river here has been so vital to the county and its neighbours that it is well worth while to consider what it means. The problem is as old as the earth itself—the unceasing contest between land and sea. The Atlantic tide sweeps down the North Sea, often enough with a gale driving the waves against the coast. The rivers pour back into the sea the rain that has fallen on nearly 6000 square miles of our island, for that is the area of the basins of the four rivers which flow into the Wash, the Great Ouse and the Nene being the two rivers in Cambridgeshire. The greater part of the county lies low, so that the rivers flow slowly in normal times, but after a long spell of rain much water comes along, meeting the tides as they make their way up the estuaries. With a high spring tide at this time the river banks will burst and the rivers seek new channels, flooding the country and making it a perpetual fen, to penetrate farther and farther inland as the sea eats into the coast.

We may conceive the fen country, as Nature fashions it, as a vast low-lying flat area covered with water plants, bog myrtle, and those trees (like the willows and the alders) that are always to be found in watery areas. Winding waterways link together shallow lakes which vary in size according to the season. In prehistoric times the land was at a higher level, with oaks and firs and birches, and the trees which once clothed this countryside now lie buried in the peat which formed as the earth sank down. The silting-up of the estuaries and the inrushing tides prevented the outpouring of the rivers into the sea and added to the marshy nature of the land, which, however, was richly fertile if it could be drained.

The Romans from their long experience at home knew what needed to be done, and photographs from the air have revealed that much of this area was cultivated in small fields. In Saxon times, however, things became very different, possibly because

4

any artificial drainage introduced by them fell into a state of neglect, but more probably owing to subsidence of the land. For five centuries the fenland deteriorated rapidly and its very remoteness attracted to it bands of monks. Thus Ely, Crowland, Thorney, Chatteris, and Ramsey became centres of reclamation; but before the end of the 13th century the silting up of the Wisbech estuary caused the rivers flowing through the Middle Level to change their courses, the Ouse having begun to flow out to sea at Lynn, flooding reclaimed marshland.

Artificial channels on a big scale seemed the only solution, and Bishop Morton cut a 40-foot dyke twelve miles long to take the Nene direct to Wisbech. With the Dissolution of the Monasteries half a century later the greater part of fenland fell into the hands of laymen who sought to get rich quick from sheepwalks for which dry pastures are essential. Consequently in the reigns of Elizabeth and James the First laws were passed for the draining of the fens on a big scale, Cornelius Vermuyden, a Dutch engineer, being called in. He was promised 93,000 acres as a reward, and Charles Stuart, who fostered the scheme, was to get 12,000 acres, a company of Gentlemen Adventurers led by the Earl of Bedford being the promoters.

Then came the Civil War, bringing the work to a standstill, but it was resumed under Cromwell by the first Duke of Bedford, again with Vermuyden as chief engineer, and the work was completed by 1653. The fenland was divided into the North, Middle, and South Levels, and long straight channels were dug to replace the rivers, one named the Old Bedford River and one the New. The Old River ran from Earith to Salter's Lode, 21 miles long and 70 feet wide. Channels were cut to feed the two rivers and smaller drains to collect the waters in the marshes. Windmills were built to raise the water from level to level, a task which is now performed by steam pumps. Sluices regulate the flow and height of the artificial rivers, and their banks have to be kept in perfect repair. Since the main task was finished small lakes have been drained in the past hundred years, while Telford and Rennie directed the outfall of the waters, whether from the artificial or natural waterways, into the sea, and also modified the effect of the tidal bore by vast engineering works on the shores of the Wash, at a cost of £200,000.

And yet these fens have not been altogether evil. They have indeed been a sure anchor of security, for they have provided sanctuary for lovers of peace from marauding conquerors, and there are even those who claim that to the shelter afforded by the fens we owe the new learning of the Mind and the new valuation of things of the Spirit which we call the Reformation. If Cambridge gave us our greatest Reformers, it was to Ely and Fenland in very great part that we owe Cambridge University.

After the passing of the Romans, who had built a bridge at Cambridge for roads linking Colchester and Godmanchester, and had skirted the Fen Country with their great Ermine Street (which enters this county from Royston and leaves it just before it reaches Godmanchester), the sea-rovers from over the North Sea found their way up the Ouse and the Cam and destroyed the civilisation the Romans had established. The descendants of the British tribe of the Iceni seem to have taken refuge in the island among the swamps of Ely.

We can only guess whether the Christian faith survived in that fifth century, but we do know that a hundred years later the eastern part of the county formed part of the kingdom of East Anglia, which became Christian early in the seventh century. King Anna fell in battle against the heathen Penda, King of Mercia, but his family was famous, and four of his daughters became abbesses. His daughter Etheldreda had already been married two years, receiving the Isle of Ely as her wedding gift, and a few years after the death of her lord the King of Northumbria demanded her hand for his son of 14. Etheldreda went to the Northumbrian Court desiring to unite the two kingdoms, but later fled to a monastery, where she took the veil. Her husband pursuing her, she fled to her inaccessible Isle of Ely, and there founded the monastery which became famous for centuries, ruling over her first husband's subjects and establishing a tradition of government which has left its mark on the county to this day.

From being a camp of refuge, Ely became for 1000 years the dominant centre of a wide area. It is true that the island fell on troubled times, but Canute looked with friendly eyes on Ely and rebuilt Cambridge. Before his century was out Ely became a city of refuge against another warrior of northern blood, the Conqueror. Truth vies with legend in the story of Hereward the Wake, but here the Saxons made their last stand before the monks settled down with Norman knights, and the magnificent shrine we see today began to lift its towers above the fens. The monks continued the work of reclaiming the fens and spread their teaching as far as Cambridge, probably laying down the nucleus of the University. The Bishop of Ely had exceptional powers long after the Reformation, appointing magistrates and having a voice at the Assize, which was held in his name and at his pleasure till 1836, when a special Act of Parliament brought to an end the extraordinary powers which had persisted from the saintly Etheldreda's day.

If Ely's monks had their part in establishing learning at Cambridge, it was Oxford which sent there some of its earliest students when its schools were closed in 1209. In 20 years another group from Paris arrived, and in 20 years more a further group from Oxford. With the Conqueror's castle to protect the town, religious orders settled in it, including the energetic Friars, and students became more numerous than townsmen. It was Hugh de Balsham, Bishop of Ely, who established the first College of Peterhouse in 1284. His example was soon followed, kings and commoners rivalling one another in setting up these colleges which are the pride of England now. Even Henry the Eighth is held in high memory in a statue on the great gate of Trinity, built in his reign to commemorate Edward the Third and his six sons. As the result of the wealth poured into the university town Cambridge has examples of all our great architects down the centuries, and the tale is not yet ended.

Cambridge, indeed, has examples to show of all the building periods from the Saxons until now. The fine little tower of St Benet's is an outstanding example of Saxon work. The Templars Church of the Holy Sepulchre recalls the Norman Crusaders, and remains one of the four round churches of these knights still standing and in use in England. For Norman architecture at its best we must go to Ely where the arches of nave and transepts are astounding in their strength and height and number. There is nothing like it anywhere. Begun three years before the Conqueror's Domesday Book, it was nearly a century before the timber roofs were in position 100 feet above the floor, and by this time the Norman craftsman had become so expert with his chisel that his exquisite Prior's Doorway, leading from the cathedral into the cloister, is unsurpassed for its beauty.

For other Norman work in the county we should seek out Ickleton, where the pillars of the nave are single stones, fashioned, it may be, by Romans and converted to this sacred use; their simple capitals indicate the earliest period. We find another huge stone in the double arch over the window in the round tower at Snailwell, while Hauxton has one of the small Norman churches which flourished in Becket's day and set his portrait on its walls, still to be seen. Wisbech keeps its Norman nave and there is a Norman chancel arch at Rampton. On the font in little St Peter's at Cambridge the Norman sculptor has set mermen grasping their tails.

The first English style came gloriously to Ely, with the splendid Galilee Porch and the six arches of the presbytery as a fitting sequel to the Norman grandeur of the nave. In over a dozen village churches we come across this 13th century work, and all will linger in admiration at Cherry Hinton's example in its double piscina. There is a font of those days at Witcham which has vigorous sculpture and shows the staple by which the cover was padlocked against witches; it is curious that this village is called Witcham and has this witness of witchcraft.

The work of the decorator in stone reached its highest perfection in the imitation of nature in the 14th century, and the arcaded stalls in Ely's lady chapel are exquisite, as good as any in the world. This was the age when Alan of Walsingham served his cathedral first as Sacrist and then as Prior. An appalling disaster called forth his energies, the Norman central tower crashing down in 1322, and in place of the four-sided tower he conceived an octagon, setting his piers on solid concrete and scouring England for eight great oaks to hold up his lovely lantern. We can read in the muniment room the contemporary story of this huge undertaking.

The paintings in the Octagon are not yet centenarians, but they take the place of 14th century paintings at which the monks would gaze as they sat at worship. Their seats are now in the choir, of which the three mighty arches were also raised in Alan Walsingham's day. This extraordinary man is said to have built the delightful Prior Crauden's Chapel, rich in windows and pictured tiles, and the east window of Little St Mary's in Cambridge is believed to be his. Balsham's tower proclaims the 14th century from the highest village in the county, near the Devil's Dyke, and Leverington's spire soars from a lovely 13th century tower. There are stone screens at Bottisham and Harlton, and oak screens at Chippenham and Guilden Morden, one with two of the saints painted on it in the 14th century.

In a county lying so low the towers and spires beloved of 15th century builders are prominent features of the landscape. Cambridgeshire has many that are memorable and it is hard to name the best. Among the spires Whittlesey should not be missed, if only for comparison with the steeple of its neighbour March, a great church boasting a double hammerbeam roof. The towers of Soham and Wisbech have graceful pinnacles, Haslingfield and Thorney have bold turrets, and both Burwell and Sutton have shapes of unusual designs. But the crowning glory of that wonderful age is King's College Chapel of high renown, with the fan-vaulted roof finished 70 years after Henry the Sixth laid the foundation stone. No county in England has a nobler sight to offer a traveller than this chapel which Milton and Wordsworth knew and every visitor to Cambridge loves.

The county has much woodcarving from the 15th century. The hammerbeam roof at Willingham has three tiers of angels, and so has the similar roof at March. The name and date of its maker are carved on the roof at Isleham, 1495, and the church has fine stalls of the period. At least half a dozen oak pulpits are 15th century and Fulbourn has one of the 14th, though there are only a small number of medieval pulpits left in all England. The carved panels of Landbeach pulpit are of unusual beauty. The 24 stalls with their misereres were given to Balsham Church by the rector John de Sleford, whose portrait is on the floor beside them, a brass which is one of the best in England. Both the pulpit and the stalls at Elsworth date from this century, the poppyhead stalls having linenfold backs and hinged lockers under the book-rests. Soham, which has 14th century stalls, has a fine set of 15th century benches and a small but elaborate screen which is its crowning glory.

At Swaffham Bulbeck is a chest which has only one rival in England; it was a travelling altar with paintings on the inside of the lid, which formed the reredos. Perhaps it may be because travel was difficult in this low county that there are so many St Christophers on the walls of its churches; the patron saint of the traveller is in frequent evidence. One of the best paintings is at Bartlow, with a Doom on the same wall. Both these scenes appear also at Barton, where we see a figure of St Thomas Cantelupe. Thomas Becket has been on the church walls of Hauxton since the 13th century. Chippenham, Impington, Kingston with its Seven Deadly Sins, and Willingham with its Doom, are other places with good wall-paintings. Cambridgeshire has some splendid brasses older than Balsham's, the most famous being Sir Roger de Trumpington of 1289, the second oldest in England. Very early, too (1325), is the brass of Sir John de Creke and his wife at Westley Waterless. At Hildersham Robert de Paris and his wife kneel on either side of an ornamental cross of 1379, and at Fulbourn is Willam de Fulbourn, who died in 1390 a Canon of St Paul's.

The glass in the village churches felt the fanatical hand of William Dowsing in the Civil War and one of the heavy losses must have been the Te Deum window at Little Shelford, of which only fragments of its 30 pictures remain. Trumpington has kept figures of Peter and Paul and Landbeach has portraits of the first Duke and Duchess of Somerset. We see an archbishop giving a blessing in a roundel at Fordham and a 14th century Earl of Suffolk at Wimpole. Leverington is more fortunate with a dozen of the original figures out of 61 in a fine 15th century Jesse Tree.

The windows at King's College Chapel are among the glories of England, and we may like to think that Cromwell himself, at Milton's request, preserved them from destruction. They tell the story of the life of the Madonna, and though placed here early in the 16th century were made in the century before. Milton has given immortality to this in Il Penseroso, and the poet was thinking not only of

> *that high embowèd roof,*
> *With antique pillars massy proof,*
> *And storied windows richly dight,*
> *Casting a dim religious light,*

but also of the woodwork added in the reign of Henry the Eighth, the organ screen bearing the initials of Anne Boleyn.

Many of the most pleasing sights in Cambridge took shape in the reign of Queen Elizabeth. Who can forget the charming little Gate of Honour of Caius College, or the lovely painted gateway of St John's, or the quadrangles of Sidney Sussex, about which young Oliver Cromwell would walk continually?

It was when Milton was a student at Cambridge that all the college authorities were in a fervour to convert what was medieval in their buildings into the new classical style. The Civil War stopped the change for a while, but before the war broke out the poet's own college (Christ's) had completed its lovely Fellows Building. Clare was not so lucky, only two sides of their new Court being complete when the Parliament men seized the materials to fortify Cambridge Castle. Sixteen years after that, with a king again on our throne, Sir Christopher Wren built Trinity's superb library and designed the chapels of Pembroke and Emmanuel. Wren's pupil Gibbs gave Cambridge its noble Senate House and every famous architect since his day has contributed to that grand array of Cambridge buildings which is among the wonders of the world. One of the latest of all is the noble University Library by Sir Giles Scott.

Famous buildings of many centuries greet the traveller through the county. Anglesey Abbey has a vaulted room in which the monks took their meals 700 years ago, and a new domed library panelled with elm from the piles which supported Waterloo Bridge. Another 13th century room with 14th century work above it is in the quaint rectory at Chesterton. Better known is the palace Bishop Alcock built himself at Ely at the end of the 15th century; this faces the Galilee Porch and has a fine gallery added in the 16th century. The black and white tithe house, now St Mary's Vicarage, was the home of Oliver Cromwell when he was training his Ironsides. Sawston Hall is Elizabethan, built from stones of old Cambridge Castle given by Queen Mary Tudor. The red-brick gate tower at Kirtling was built in Mary Tudor's reign; the twelfth Lord North looks out over the wide moat from its splendid two-storied oriel as the first Lord North would have done, but the great house in which his son entertained Elizabeth stands no more.

Approached by a double avenue of elms, three miles long, and with the River Cam flowing through its grounds, stands Wimpole Hall, famous for the magnificent library of books collected by Robert Harley and his son Edward, and for the gathering of poets here before the second earl sold the house for

£100,000 and his widow sold his manuscripts to the nation; they form the Harleian Collection at the British Museum, and are worth hundreds of thousands of pounds. Madingley Hall (of Tudor brick) has a legend that it sheltered Charles Stuart during one of his brief escapes.

In village and town we come across things that speak to us of the past. At Whittlesey is a market house standing on pillars of stone. At Burwell is a black towered windmill, and above the thatched barns of Bourn rises a smock mill of Cromwell's day, the oldest in the county. In Stretham we find a 14th century preaching cross. In Whittlesford a black and white inn claims to be the home of the prior of an ancient monastery. On the little green at Meldreth stand the whipping-post and stocks. In Cambridge is the conduit Thomas Hobson set up in 1614.

The famous men and women associated with the county are of two kinds, those born there and those who came to learn and teach at the university. The roll of fame of Cambridge is immense, and it may be said that as Oxford was the home of lost causes Cambridge was for the most part the nursery of the new, whether in matters of faith, learning, or affairs of State. Erasmus and Coverdale, Latimer and Ridley and Cranmer, Cromwell and Milton, Francis Bacon and Isaac Newton, Clerk-Maxwell and Kelvin and Darwin, Wordsworth and Coleridge and Byron, Tennyson and Macaulay—all had much of that spirit which urged the world forward, and all are Cambridge men.

Her natives are an interesting group. Sir John Cheke was a pioneer of the New Learning. Thomas Tenison of Cottenham was one of the Seven Bishops who defied James the Second and sounded the doom of the Stuarts. Wisbech gave to the world Thomas Clarkson who fought the slave trade and Octavia Hill who fought the slums. Jeremy Taylor, a Cambridge tailor's son, taught men how to live and how to die. Among other Cambridgeshire writers were Matthew Paris of Hildersham, most famous of all our chroniclers; Jeremy Collier of Stow-cum-Quy, who attacked a debased stage and wrote an Ecclesiastical

History; Richard Cumberland, dramatist, and William White-head, Poet Laureate, both born at Cambridge. Cambridge had a Puritan mayor who gave a phrase to the English language, Hobson's choice; he let out horses and every hirer had to take them in strict rotation, having no choice but Hobson's. Henry Cromwell, most illustrious of the Protector's sons, was born at Wicken, and another famous Puritan was Francis Holcroft, who covered the county with his preaching at the time John Bunyan was doing the same for Bedfordshire. And who, recalling the associations of men and women with this proud county, can forget Samuel Pepys, who was educated here and left to his university his immortal Diary and 3000 books?

We see how wide has been the net spread by this little county. It has caught up in its clutches a vast number of the lives that have influenced the world. And it is carrying on its intellectual sway, for it is Cambridgeshire that has set England a high example which all our counties might well follow—the example of rural colleges for bringing the best education to the villages. Already a good proportion of the youth of its countryside is within the range of this vital experiment, and it is permissible to hope that the seed being sown will bear fruit not unworthy of the harvest of the ages which has been to Cambridgeshire so great a heritage, and to England such an abiding glory.

Sixteen Sons and Daughters

ABINGTON PIGOTTS. It is pleasant with trees and orchards, quaint cottages and thatched roofs, and an old church in the meadows between the old rectory and the gabled manor house, a dignified and delightful home of Queen Elizabeth's day. Down Hall, a farmhouse on the edge of the village, hides in the trees at the end of a lane, with a moat and a watermill.

A fine avenue of lofty limes brings us to the flint and cobbled church, into which we come by a door which has opened and shut for centuries. The porch in which it hangs is dated 1382 and has bargeboards and roof beams, windows and seats, a coffin stone 700 years old, and a holy-water stoup set on a fragment of Norman carving. An ancient mass dial is on the wall. Indoors is a 15th century oak screen with delicate tracery set in a chancel arch 100 years older. In the tracery of two nave windows are fine old fragments of glass with saints and angels in black and gold, and engraved in brass is the portrait of a 15th century family, showing a civilian in a fur-lined gown with 16 sons and daughters. The two-decker pulpit is made up of Jacobean panels, the modern font has a Jacobean domed cover, there is an old chest, and quaint angels support the old roof beams. The vestry door has been hanging on its hinges for many generations.

ARRINGTON. It lies on the Roman Ermine Street, but the oldest thing it has is a crude Norman font shaped like a tub. Its neat little church stands on a hill looking over the cottages with a peep through the trees to the fine park of Wimpole Hall. It has lost its aisles but their 14th century arches are still in the walls, the windows and the old doorway set in them. Perhaps the best possession of the church is a striking 700-year-old piscina niche; though much worn and with one of its pillars gone, it has beautiful arches.

Brave Curate and Rich Adventurer

BABRAHAM. It is in the delightful wooded stretch of the valley of the Granta with the Gog Magog Hills looking down. Its

15

ways are lined with great sycamores and chestnuts, and they bring us to a green with a cross on which are sixteen names and Laurence Binyon's famous words:

> *At the going down of the sun, and in the morning,*
> *We will remember them.*

It is a pleasant walk through the meadows (especially if we come in spring when they are like a cloth of gold) to the church over the little wooden bridge across the stream. Babraham Hall, the great 19th century house, stands on the site of the old hall built in magnificent fashion for a Genoese adventurer who was rich enough to lend money to kings and grand enough for the great Elizabeth not to scorn a loan from him. He commanded a ship against the Armada, and it is said that during Mary Tudor's reign he collected Peter's Pence for the pope, giving rise to the lines:

> *Here lies Horatio Palavazene,*
> *Who robbed the pope to lend the queen.*

This very fine fellow was Sir Horatio Palavicini. He left a widow and two sons, and after his death they married Cromwell's great uncle and his two daughters.

It is said that there may be Saxon masonry in the walls of the old church, but the church is mainly 15th century, though it has an aumbry, a piscina, and stone seats for priests 700 years old. There are fragments of medieval glass in the fine windows, 15th century benches in the nave, a 15th century font, and a pulpit of the same time which has been made into a three-decker by using up the timbers of the old screen. The oak chest is 16th century, and the altar rails 17th. There are old high box-pews spreading from the north aisle into the chancel. On a mighty marble monument lie two haggard-looking brothers who were village squires during the Commonwealth, studying at the same school, university, and inn of court, and marrying two rich sisters. They were Sir Richard and Sir Thomas Bennet, and it was one of their descendants who founded the almshouses and the school. On the walls of the church is a tablet to John Hullier, a brave curate of Tudor days who walked into the fire for his faith. It is strange to read that as he came to the stake a looker-on said to him "The Lord strengthen thee," a sergeant bidding the man hold his tongue or he should be sorry for it; and it is incredible to read that he was bound with chains and set in a pitch barrel, books being cast into the fire, one of which he opened and read as the flames gathered fiercely about him.

Craftsmanship Old and New

BALSHAM. Within a mile of it is the only unbroken sector of the once mighty earthwork known as Fleam Dyke. For centuries it was used as a packhorse way, and here in 909 was a great slaughter when Danish invaders were attacked by Alfred's son. A century later another attack swept over East Anglia and left alive but one gallant defender of the village in the Saxon tower.

A memory of the Saxon church was found in the churchyard not so very long ago, a Saxon coffin stone cut with plaits and a cross in a circle; but the church we see crowning the highest bit of Cambridgeshire in a thatched roof village (with a pretty green and a wayside duckpond) was mostly built by John de Sleford, who added the clerestoried nave and the aisles to the 13th century tower and the chancel, built just before his time. He furnished the chancel with 24 magnificent stalls still here, with traceried fronts and backs, lions and faces for poppyheads, and such an array of creatures on the tops and under the seats that they are like an old bestiary in wood. We remember among them a muzzled bear tethered for baiting and a man on stilts leading a dog. From the same century comes the lovely chancel screen remarkable for having still above it the old roodloft reached by the old rood stairs. It is a rare survival, for there are very few roodlofts left in this country from the days before the Reformation. There are ancient timbers in the roof of the chancel, and an Elizabethan table in a little chapel.

We found Canon Burrell, the faithful rector here, still adding rich carvings to Balsham's rich collection of medieval woodwork grand enough for a cathedral. He has made craftsmen of his village folk, training the men at woodwork classes, and himself carved the altar rails, the almsbox, and the marvellous font cover which represents nine years of his labour. It rises 30 feet high, having a steeple of delicate tracery and pinnacles, rising in tiers from eight canopied niches, with figures in them among which we can see his far-off predecessor, John de Sleford, with two other benefactors, Thomas

Sutton, the famous founder of Charterhouse, and Hugh de Balsham, the founder of Peterhouse.

We meet John de Sleford again in the magnificent east window, a glory of colour in a grand stone setting. The rays of Christ's glory light a crescent rainbow of angel wings in the centre, and below are four medieval rectors with the founders of Charterhouse and Peterhouse and Ely, and Prior Houghton, who gave up his life during the suppression of the monasteries. Even the old sexton cutting the grass outside this church has a corner in this window, and Charterhouse boys playing cricket have another. The window is by A. K. Nicholson. In another chancel window by Christopher Webb is a charming St Nicholas with the three boys in a tub, and next to them stands St Felix, with a long candle as if he were lighting them to bed. There are fragments of old glass in other windows.

There are three brass portraits, one of an unknown 15th century knight, and the two grand ones of rectors, wonderful treasures for a village church which has already so much. Both brasses are over eight feet long. John de Sleford appears in rich vestments, his cope embroidered with canopied saints all neatly named, while on the points of his canopy are seraphim and shields, and a representation of the Trinity above two angels carrying the rector's soul upwards in a sheet. The inscription tells us that this rector, who was Edward the Third's Master of the Wardrobe, was beloved of the king to the slow sad end, and also that he opened wide his purse and wrought with bounteous and free spending hand. No less sumptuous is the brass of John Blodwell, whose inscription begins "Wales gave me birth, Bologna taught me Law, and Rome its practice," but omits what is to us the more interesting fact that he was locum tenens for the Bishop of Ely who, as Archbishop of Rouen, assisted in the trial of Joan of Arc. We see him in vestments and a skull cap, with lions' heads and saints embroidered on his cope, and more saints on the shafts of his canopy.

Kept in a case is the old hourglass and the choir's old musical instruments with some handwritten music of 300 years ago ; and still in the tower is a bell 400 years old on which is engraved in Latin the assurance that "The voice of Michael's bell thunders from Heaven." It is the only bell still in the county made by John Tonne. On the font are several figures of friends of the church, the 13th century Bishop of Ely who founded Peterhouse, and Thomas Sutton again. Nothing is left here of his old home, unless it be the 16th century doors and fireplaces in Nine Chimneys House.

One of Six Hundred

BARRINGTON. There is a window in the church in thankfulness for a happy childhood spent here, and we do not wonder, for it is a charming place, with a stream running past and fields of buttercups. Sheltered on one side by a hill, the village slopes on the other side to the meadows of the Cam, and has orchards and cottages on both sides of a green half a mile long, with the church at one end and the gables of Barrington Hall just topping the trees. The hall is the home of the Bendyshes, who came to Barrington in the 14th century. Even then they would come into the church by the very door we open, for it has been here 600 years, beautiful with flowing tracery and set in a doorway older than itself, with deep arch mouldings and carved capitals crowning its shafts.

The tower was added 500 years ago by the men who built the north porch, but the fine arcades of the nave, with richly moulded arches and clustered pillars, are 700 years old, with the light falling on them from 15th century clerestories, and crowned by a roof of massive beams and quaint figures. Little faces peep out from walls and arches. Between a pillar of the nave and the 13th century chancel arch is a spiral stairway which led to the old roodloft; the chancel itself is 14th century. There are medieval oak benches, rare for having book-rests so early as the 15th century, a canopied Jacobean pulpit, a font bowl probably Norman, and a wonderful chest latticed all over with sturdy iron bands, in which treasures have been kept for 700 years.

In the back of a niche are painted the names of Barrington's heroes, among them George Coote, a stoker on the Formidable sunk by a German submarine on the first day of 1915. He was one of six hundred men who went down.

The Weighing of Souls

BARTLOW. The Bartlow Hills from which it takes its name belong to Essex, a last resting-place of British chieftains. The small flint church is famous for its round tower and its medieval pictures, the tower perhaps 13th century, with walls six feet thick and an ancient ladder of 27 rungs climbing up to three medieval bells. The ancient door still opens and shuts for us, ancient glass is still in some of the windows, the plain font has been here 500 years, we found a small carved box of 1641 on a windowsill, and the vicar keeps in his vestry two pewter flagons from the days when the church sold ale in them to raise church funds. The pictures are on the walls of the nave, among them St Christopher, a remnant of St George and the dragon, and Michael weighing souls, with the Madonna helping to weigh down the scales on one side against a demon and a great clawed dragon on the other.

The Old Pictures

BARTON. It has in its 14th century church a very interesting collection of wall-paintings, long hidden under whitewash before they were uncovered a generation ago. They are simple pictures in red, some clear and others hard to make out, telling the stories of the Bible and the saints in the way medieval folk could understand. Adorning the south doorway is the Annunciation, and two scenes on the south wall show the Last Supper and what is thought to be the Baptism in Jordan, with bare legs showing in the water. Over the north door we see St Michael weighing a soul, with the kindly Virgin laying her rosary in the scale to help the poor sinner, while a demon sitting on the other scale is being attacked by a knight with a lance. Beside the doorway is Bishop Cantelupe who died in 1282 and was canonised as St Thomas of Hereford, and farther west is the Madonna crowned, with the Holy Child. John the Baptist is here with the Lamb in his upraised hand, and near him a horseman with birds and a dog; and there is a scene of St Anthony with his hog, reminding us that he was the patron saint of the Hospitallers, who, when others had to keep their pigs confined, had the privilege of letting theirs run loose with bells round their necks.

The oldest possessions of the church are a Norman piscina and a Norman font, the font framed by a beautiful tower arch. There is a fine canopied pulpit of 1635, a good Jacobean chair, and a 15th century screen rich with tracery, heraldry, and foliage. Two tiny brass portraits on the chancel floor show John Martin and his wife in Elizabethan costume.

Fragments of pottery found hereabouts take the story of Barton back to the New Stone Age. The Romans brought their Akeman Street this way, and where the Bourn Brook ripples by it about a mile away is a stretch of greensward where men who were to be archers at Crecy and Poitiers bent their bows in practice. It is a hundred yards wide and a third of a mile long, and in those days every village had such a range as this.

Prince of Beggars

BASSINGBOURN. Here sleeps the Prince of Beggars, the second Viscount Knutsford, who spent 30 years begging for London Hospital.

The grave he chose for himself in a corner of the churchyard tells us that "his joy was to help all in distress, and to bring happiness into the lives of others." If ever men lived joyfully he did, and he saw his hospital rebuilt and better equipped before he was carried to it in 1931, when all the skill in the world could not save him. Not a wreath was laid on his coffin, not a word was said in praise at his funeral, for he had asked that it should be like that, but few among the village folk and the men and nurses come from his hospital could hold back their tears, for they all loved him.

Old Kneesworth Hall, which we see from the Royston road, was made new for him, but the church by his grave is medieval, its 700-year-old tower topped by a tiny spire, its fine oak porch of 500 years ago sheltering a 15th century door and an ancient coffin stone; and everywhere are old and curious faces from the days when this straggling village of thatched cottages, limes, and chestnuts, had some importance as a small market town.

The faces look down at us outdoors and in, a bat and an old man stroking his beard among the gargoyles, five fair women on the 14th century arcades facing the scowls and grins of ugly fellows opposite, kings and queens and angels in the daintily niched east window of an aisle, and more odd heads staring from the roof and windows of the 14th century chancel, still complete with aumbry, sedilia, and canopied piscina. The old chancel screen has delicate tracery but a poor modern top. Some of the benches are old, and there are two old chests, a 15th century font, and an ornamented coffin stone. John Turpin, who died in 1494, is with his wife on brass, and Henry Butler, who died in 1647, is sculptured in his shroud. Many of the

Nightingale family have memorials, but it is Sir Edward Nightingale who is best remembered, for in 1717 he gave the church most of its library, an unusual possession of hundreds of old theological books on shelves in the tower. With them are some churchwardens' accounts from 1498 to 1534, telling us much about village life at that time; but they do not help to solve such a problem as that of the two wooden ploughs in the belfry. Why they were treasured here and who hauled them up nobody knows.

Knight and Lady

BOROUGH GREEN. It lives about its great green, and at one end stands the old church with so much made new, yet having still in its keeping the monuments of its great family 600 years ago. They were the De Burghs, who held the manor in the 14th century. and some of their tombs are set under three finely arched recesses. On them are figures of three knights and a lady, nameless, battered and worn. Under the finest of the three arches, carved with flowers, lie a knight and his lady, he with his legs crossed, his head on a tilting-helmet, and his body on a bed of pebbles, a thing rarely seen on a tomb. He may be Thomas de Burgh of 1345, and it is thought that perhaps his pebbled bed may represent a rock or a shipwreck, or may indicate that he was a traveller. The lady beside him, perhaps Catherine de Burgh of 1410, wears an embroidered gown and her hair is in a net. Her husband Sir John is supposed to lie on the next tomb in armour with gauntlets. On the third tomb is an armoured knight with a heart in his hands and his feet on a lion.

For 500 years two other figures have been here, now set on a big tomb made up in an aisle. They are John Ingoldsthorpe and his wife Elizabeth de Burgh; his arms are gone, but his feet are still bravely on a lion, and on his curly hair is a headdress carved with flowers. A jewelled band holds his lady's draped headdress. Under a stone in the chancel sleeps a man who was rector for 69 years of last century, Charles Wedge. It is perhaps a record of long service for the county, and one of the longest we have come upon.

The Strangers

BOTTISHAM. Halfway from Newmarket to Cambridge we come upon its overhanging cottages and the graceful tower of a church which glories in some of the finest 14th century work in the county. The tower and the gaunt chancel with its fine stone seats are 13th century but the nave and aisles and porches are all as the builders left them in the 14th. The south porch has a beautiful inner doorway through which we enter by a wicket door, to find that the rich arcading of the south wall runs along the inside as well as the outside wall. This south aisle has a stone seat for the priest, a piscina, and in its floor an ancient coffin lid. Above the stately arcades is a clerestory of fluted lancets of rare beauty, and the traceried aisle windows are richly moulded inside and out. Here is the font where the children who saw this beauty grow were baptised; and there are three old screens of the 14th century, two of oak and the rarest of stone, with three delicate open arches before the chancel. There is an ironbound chest of 1790, and some fragments of carved stones, the oldest being a Norman tympanum.

A table tomb has the mark of a vanished brass portrait of Elias de Beckingham, who was said to be with one exception the only honest judge in the reign of Edward the First. Only he and one other were acquitted when every judge was charged by the king with bribery. A sculptured monument of three centuries later shows Margaret Coningsbye kneeling behind her husband, both in black robes and ruffs. Cherubs hold back the curtains of a stone canopy to show two children asleep with flowers in their hands, Leonard and Dorothea Allington, of whom the inscription of 1638 tells:

> *These the world's strangers were, not here to dwell.*
> *They tasted, liked it not, and bade farewell.*

The east window and a tablet close by are in memory of Colonel Jenyns, who rode down the Valley of Death at Balaclava and survived. Other memorials to the family, whose home (Bottisham Hall) was rebuilt in 1797, show Sir Roger and his wife sitting on their tomb holding hands, with dressing-gowns thrown over their night things as if they had just woke from sleep. Their son Soame was for 38 years in Parliament, a keen debater, and is remembered here by angels garlanding an urn.

Bottisham is one of the group of villages in which the village colleges of Cambridgeshire are being developed. The first college was built at Sawston in 1928, and the idea of these magnificent modern buildings is to draw children over eleven from the villages round into an atmosphere in which they will develop a taste and a capacity for rural life and craftsmanship, with facilities for training themselves in whatever career they desire, and with opportunities for practising music or drama, cooking or needlework. The buildings at Bottisham are charmingly planned so that all the principal rooms run round a curve and look out on to the playing-field. The Bottisham buildings were planned by the county architect, Mr S. E. Urwin.

The Oldest Windmill

BOURN. Today Bourn windmill takes the breeze as gaily on its hill as in the days when Shakespeare wrote in Twelfth Night

I am a feather for each wind that blows,

for this is possibly the oldest windmill in the country, certainly the oldest in the county. It was bought and sold by deed in 1636, and nearly 300 years later people who care about such things came together, raised subscriptions, and put the fine old breadwinner in action again, making it a national monument. It is a post windmill with fine old timbers inside, and its white sails and tail screen have been restored. A model of it is in the Children's Gallery in the Science Museum at South Kensington.

It is one of the many ornaments of a place where every prospect pleases, woods and dales, and the brook that gives the place its name gaily rippling past the houses and below the church. Bourn Hall, not far from the church, is one of the most fascinating Elizabethan manor houses in a county which is not poor in them. It is as beautiful within as without, and its gabled red brick front is a sight to linger in the memory. The park had once a castle given to a sheriff of the county by the Conqueror, and part of its Norman moat remains.

The church stands on a slight rise above Bourn Brook, and is built in the shape of a cross with a quaint leaded spire soaring from its 700-year-old tower. The impressive west doorway has a richly moulded arch on 12 shafts, but it is a plain Norman doorway on four shafts that leads us in, through a 13th century porch. The glory of the interior is in the beautiful arches with fine clustered shafts. Three steps lead into the tower where the ancient font, surrounded by eight coloured bell ropes, is set in the middle of a floor of red and blue tiles forming a maze, of which a plan hangs on the wall. The

Burwell   **Windmill and Church and Farm**

Bourn   **The Ancient Windmill**

A Farm Road

The Windmill at Stretham

THE FLAT COUNTRY OF THE FENS

maze is very rare or perhaps unique in an English church, though familiar on the continent.

The lofty arcades set up by our first English builders are a fine spectacle, and are crowned with 14th century clerestories; they are best seen from the chancel, which has a 15th century oak screen across the arch, three canopied stone seats, and ancient stalls with poppyheads of priests and angels.

About 20 modern angels look down from the ancient roof, at the ends of the hammerbeams. There is an Elizabethan table, some Jacobean panelling, a modern oak screen across the tower with St Margaret standing on a dragon, many old bench-ends, and some ancient coffin stones in the vestry floor. In the fine medieval windows are a few fragments of the original glass.

The Blind Scholar

BOXWORTH. It has been the home of two fine scholars: John Boyse, a rector who translated the Apocrypha, and Nicholas Saunderson, who was blinded by smallpox as a child, yet grew up a university professor. He has lain under the altar here since 1739. He had a marvellously quick and active brain, mastered the classics at school, and became so learned that George the Second made him a doctor of law, and Lord Chesterfield declared that though he had lost the use of his own eyes he taught others to use theirs. He had an acute sense of hearing and a trained ear for music, he could tell the size of a room by the sound of his voice in it, and could judge his distance from a wall by the echo. His sense of touch was so delicate that it was said he could detect false medals merely by touching them.

The neat little church stands in a trim churchyard by fields and woodlands, with an old farm and thatched barns to keep it company. A pretty picture it is, with its 15th century tower and fine battlements crowning its patchwork of flint and stone. In one of the aisles is Norman masonry. The dim religious light of the interior moved the restorers last century to set windows in the roof of an aisle and a glass door in the 15th century doorway of the porch. They serve their purpose well, lighting up the 14th century arcade. The beauty of the glass makes up for the light it steals, for though it is modern it is attractive and rich in colour. We see St Etheldreda crowned, Gabriel bringing the good news to the Madonna, a fine little Nativity with the shepherds and another with the Wise Men, Christ appearing to Mary in the garden, and David with his harp. There is a plain old font, a small chest with two locks, and a pulpit 250 years old.

Two Little Ones

BRINKLEY. It lies in the meadows and hides among the trees with a simple old church from the 15th century. It has ancient glass in its windows with golden-winged angels and a medley of flowers. There is a broken old font under the tower, a battered Jacobean pulpit, a pew with Jacobean panels for the squire, and old box-pews for the people. On the wall of the squire's pew is a constable's staff of 1734, with a little crown carved at the top and gaily painted with the royal arms and the Union Jack. Here two small people are remembered, a boy of four days and a girl of four months. The boy was Richard White, who lived for four days in 1723, "a blessed little infant." He is said to have died near the font while being christened. The girl was Anne Anstey, whose memorial is carved with fruit and an angel's head, and the words, "Let no sad tear these infant relics mourn." She died in 1710.

The Splendid Roof

BURWELL. Here we must believe is sanctuary not for wild life only but for ancient memories, for the men of Burwell Fen and Wicken Fen are much as they were when Hereward the Wake held out against the Norman Duke, or when Geoffrey de Mandeville attacked King Stephen's fort here and died a rebel's death. His corpse was excommunicated by the pope and was carried to the Temple in London, where it was kept unburied for years until the pope was satisfied that his sons had made reparation for his sins. He had been unfaithful to two sovereigns, and was killed by an arrow from Burwell Castle, which stood within the earthworks and the overgrown moat still seen here.

Out of the great flats over which the wind sweeps to the windmills rises the lofty tower of Burwell's magnificent church, a landmark seen for miles. Some of its stones are probably Saxon but others are certainly Norman, and its pinnacles are 14th century, the small spire above them being worn to a skeleton of its ancient self. The 15th century church is one of the finest of its time in the county, with grand porches, one of which has five graceful niches over the entrance, a fan-vaulted roof, and St George fighting the dragon on the gable, another saint supporting him.

The nave is stately and spacious, with a flood of light from the great windows of the aisles and the clerestory. The walls above the nave arcades are richly panelled in intricate design, and pilasters rise between the arches to support a noble roof. Where a rose window lights a panelled wall above the chancel arch is an inscription of 1464 telling us to whom we owe this splendour. It asks us to pray for the souls of John Benet, of Johanna and Alice his wives, and of his parents, who had the carpentry done in this church. The roof they gave is alive with angels and animals, a dog chasing a hare, a goat, a swan, many other birds, and the winged creatures of the Evangelists; among the flowery bosses are a king and a queen, a dragon and a pelican.

But it is in the chancel that they achieved their grandest effect, for here the walls are wedded to the roof in a charming composition, the oak men holding up the beams being supported in their turn by stone angels over the windows and by the finials of canopied niches between the windows. There are niches on each side of the east window, canopied mosaics of the Annunciation, and the Visitation, and the Marriage in Cana; and there are also paintings of the Twelve Disciples. Old tracery enriches the backs of the stalls, and new heads decorate the arm-rests. St Christopher stands out in a medieval wall-painting, and there is a 15th century font. Thomas Gerard and his wife kneel on the monument he put up in 1608, both painted figures, and Sir Lee Cotton lies in armour on his canopied tomb. A most interesting brass is in the chancel floor showing Laurence de Warboys, the last Abbot of Ramsey. Made in his lifetime the portrait was found to be out of date when he died in 1542, for it represented him as an abbot and his abbey had then been suppressed. Something had to be done about it, and the brass was cut in two and one half turned over and engraved afresh, so that we see the abbot transformed into a simple cleric. The brass is interesting not only for the marks of this transformation, but because under the canopy on the other side is a fragment of a much earlier portrait showing the only known example of a deacon in vestments engraved on brass.

There is an inaccessible crypt below the chancel, and just outside the chancel lies Mary Sharpe, who is said to have inspired the song

My Pretty Jane, written by the Burwell poet, Edward Fitzball. He wrote the libretto for many of Balfe's operas, and for melodramas played at the Adelphi. A tragic stone in this churchyard tells a ghastly tale, for it marks the grave of 78 people who were burned to death in a barn here during the performance of a travelling show.

Old Door and Old Screen

CALDECOTE. It hears the rippling music of the little Bourn Brook, it looks across to the tower of Kingston from its wooded hill; and it goes to church half a mile away, its 15th century shrine half hidden by chestnuts. The old studded door still hangs on its strap hinges in the medieval doorway, and across last century's chancel stands a simple oak screen 500 years old. A niche by the chancel arch is sculptured with heads of animals. The very graceful tower arch opens from the aisleless nave and has no capitals. On a wooden tablet are the names of 17 men who went to the war and three who never came home. One was on HMS Formidable, one of 600 to go down in the first battleship of its class sunk by a submarine.

The Incomparable City

CAMBRIDGE. We may be Oxford or Cambridge on Boat Race day, changing as the wind blows, but as travellers we are Cambridge for ever. Neither of our own centuries has spoiled it; it is the pure University town. For that young Englishman whose chance in life begins here there is no better gift that the world contains. It is a marvellous thing to be young and to be learning in Cambridge.

And even for those of us who are but travelling, coming into Cambridge one day and leaving the next, there are no English acres to surpass these, no streets with such fine sights. Whenever we come these Colleges are a spectacle unsurpassed in England, but if we come in springtime we come to an enchanted land. Indoors the beauty of Cambridge stands from age to age, but out of doors it changes with the seasons, and in all our tour of England has been nothing to equal the picture of Cambridge as we glide in a boat along the River Cam, or as we saunter at the Backs and stand on the bridges. An hour like this in days like these, with the strain of the world heavy upon us all, is to be removed far from the spectre that haunts mankind, and to be lost deep in the beauty of an age that has passed away. College after college passes by, bridge after bridge, and these stone walls of the palaces of learning look down on this unchanging scene—the noble lawns, the gliding river, the delicate green willows, the majestic copper beeches, the glorious avenues, a hundred thousand daffodils, the delightful rock gardens, are a memory that never fades from the traveller's mind.

And if we walk along the streets, along incomparable Trumpington Street, even on a dull day, but best of all when the sun is high in the heavens, we are dead to the delights of the world if we are not deeply moved as there bursts upon us the dazzling skyline of King's College, the gateway and the chapel renowned to the ends of the earth. We need no great imagination to think ourselves looking at some scene of Oriental splendour.

All this has Cambridge, and more, and more. Gateway after gateway holds us spellbound, and a stone's throw apart stand a little square tower of the Saxons and a little round church of the Normans. The great and the small quadrangles are haunted by the sense of the past. The great interiors, the gallery of St John's, the library of Trinity, the noble rooms of the Fitzwilliam Museum, hold us entranced. The treasures of beauty and learning are beyond compute. We may see the manuscript of Milton's Paradise Lost, Keats's own writing of his Ode to the Nightingale, Macaulay's Diary, the manuscript of In Memoriam, Pepys's books on the shelves on which he kept them. We may walk round acre upon acre of scientific buildings, laboratories, museums, until we feel that all the learning on the earth is housed with dignity in this most spacious town. We do not tire of it, for it has an infinite variety, but again and again we seek the haunting beauty of the Backs, or walk along the fens that creep up to the River Granta, or loiter on these matchless bridges. All these centuries Cambridge has been teaching the love of beauty to our sons (and in our own century to our daughters too) and it remains unique as a city that has not thrown its beauty all away, has not allowed it to be sold for sixpences, but has kept its streets delightful, its lawns fit for kings, and its Backs a veritable treasure for the nation.

Cambridge owes its existence and its early rise to its place on the dry ground stretching from the chalk hills to the fens, and to the river by which it could draw supplies from the country round, or from abroad through the port of Lynn. For many years after the coming of the railway barges arrived almost every day to unload their cargoes by the Mill Pool and the Great Bridge, the bridge first built of wood, then stone, now iron. It is this bridge that appears from early days in all the changing names of the town, which was laid waste by the Danes in 870 and burned by them in 1010. When Danish warriors settled here for a year they knew it as Grantan-brycge. In Domesday Book it was Grantebrige. It may have been the Normans who changed it to Cantebrigge, which in time became Caumbridge and the name we know. The old name of the river was the Grant or the Granta, and it was not till Shakespeare's day that the name Cam became established.

The grassy mound on the high ground above the river, which the Conqueror raised for a castle to guard the bridge, is still here for us to see, with earthworks about it which may have marked the boundary of the fortified enclosure of the Saxons. The belief that the present town was formed by the union of the Saxon community with another across the river is supported by the fact of Saxon architecture in the churches on both banks, St Giles's and St Benedict's. King John gave the burgesses a Merchants' Guild and the right to choose their Provost. He surrounded the town with the King's Ditch, which Henry the Third strengthened and crossed by bridges near the two medieval gateways, Trumpington Gate near the corner of Trumpington and Pembroke Streets, and Barnwell Gate in St Andrew's Street.

The chief trade of the town today is in supplying the wants of the University; but it was probably due to the town's importance as an early trading centre that the growth of the University received its impetus, which was helped by monastic bodies anxious to reap benefit from this educational movement. It was helped, too, by the migration of many students from Oxford owing to trouble between that town and its University, and it grew till by 1231 it was an important centre with a chancellor of its own. It was about this time that the students began to live in hostels under the rule of a principal, instead of in separate lodgings as they pleased, and half a century later came the beginning of the collegiate system, when Peterhouse was founded by the Bishop of Ely, Hugh de Balsham.

From that time the story of the University is splendidly illustrated by the array of buildings associated with it, built of stone and brick, and standing mostly between the river and one of the two main roads running through the town. This is a fine tree-shaded road as we enter Cambridge from the south, changing its name during its narrowing journey through the town from Trumpington Road and Street to King's Parade, Trinity Street, and St John's Street, at the end of which, facing the little Round church, it joins the second main road. This comes over Gog Magog Hills and represents the Roman road, passing through the town from Hills Road as Regent Street, St Andrew's Street, Sidney Street, and Bridge Street; then, beyond the Great Bridge, going on as Magdalene Street and Castle Street. The many names of both these roads are a useful guide as to what is found along them, and linking one with the other is a network of narrow ways. Where the road from the station meets the Hills Road is the town's memorial to its heroes, a bronze soldier on the march.

Cambridge is small in compass, but so packed with interest that the traveller hardly knows how to begin to make its acquaintance. Two things he should do: he should climb the Castle Mound, 40 feet high, for the view of the neighbourhood and a survey of the town with its towers and spires; and he should walk along Queen's Road which bounds the Backs, the lovely college grounds on the west bank of the River Cam. Here the stately buildings are seen in all their majesty, and as we walk towards them, down their delightful avenues of lofty trees, rising from velvet lawns patterned at times with golden crocuses, and ending at the charming bridges crossing the stream, the crowded streets are completely forgotten in the beauty and peace of these cloistered ways. We should look long to find a happier memory to keep of Cambridge than the picture seen from the west side of the old balustraded bridge of St John's. On one hand is the 19th century Bridge of Sighs, its stone beauty enhanced by the dark old yew at one end; on the other side is Trinity's bridge of 1765; in front of us is the rich red of St John's, with the beautiful bay of the Library bearing on its gable the date 1624 and initials representing the Bishop of Lincoln who paid for most of it. No bridge of all those crossing to the Banks is lovelier than Clare's, designed by Thomas Grumbold three centuries ago. A beautiful picture seen from Queen's Road embraces the west end of King's Chapel, and the Fellows Building, its archway framing a picture of the fountain in the Great Court surmounted by the bronze statue of Henry the Sixth. Above the Backs the river flows between Coe's Fen and Sheep's Green, west of which are three of the younger colleges.

Below the Backs it flows by Jesus Green and Midsummer Common, with the boathouses on the other side. This lower part of the Cam is used for the college Bumping Races.

Though the castle was never important as a fortress, it is said to have been strengthened in medieval days, and was renovated by Cromwell's supporters; but nothing is left of it. Yet its site is one of the most pleasant in the town. The Shire Hall facing the street was built in classical style a century ago, its front adorned with columns supporting a cornice on which stand four symbolical figures. Behind it the Mound rises from a beautiful lawn, looking to the new County Hall, an imposing block with many stone windows in walls which are an attractive medley of grey, red, and blue bricks.

On the top of the Mound is a plan of the old castle and the earthworks, with the directions and distances to towns and cities and features of interest in Cambridge. The domed Observatory is seen 1500 yards to the west, rising among the trees; St Giles's with its Saxon remains is close at hand, and just beyond Castle Street are the gables of the Westminster Theological College, dignified and pleasing with its red brick walls, low tower, and imposing iron entrance gates.

At the foot of Castle Street is a rambling place which was once the White Horse Inn, with low rooms of all sizes and stout oak beams looking old enough inside to justify the date outside, 1423. Now it is a Folk Museum, its rooms furnished as in days gone by. In the fascinating nursery are countless dolls, chairs, beds, and toys. There is a zoetrope (the first form of moving picture), and a backboard to make a child sit straight. There are oldfashioned dresses, a chest with a coved lid and three locks, a town-crier's bell, tipstaffs carried by mayors, and a picture of a weird flying machine of 1877 with wings like a bird's. In the yard outside are the old hobby-horse and bone-shaker bicycles, a wooden plough, a stately coach in which the high sheriff rode, and Trinity's old fire-engine.

Where this road continues as Magdalene Street are more old houses and shops. Facing Magdalene College the old Cross Keys Inn has become a post office, but still has two overhanging storeys, brackets carved with grotesques, and gabled dormers over the timbered storey looking on to its old yard. This leads now to Magdalene's new courts—the dignified Benson Court designed by Sir

Cambridge   King's College Chapel

Market Hill and St Mary the Great

The Famous Round Church of the Holy Sepulchre

FAMOUS SIGHTS OF CAMBRIDGE

Edwin Lutyens, and Mallory Court, a happy conversion of old buildings into a tall gabled block named as a tribute to George Leigh Mallory, who walked into his immortality near the top of Everest, and has there an unknown grave. Behind these courts is what is known as the School of Pythagoras, a two-storeyed stone house of the 12th century with some original windows and one from the close of the 13th century. Built up to it is a later brick wing with curved gables, standing in a walled garden with lawns and yews. Seen from Northampton Street, it is one of the town's attractive peeps.

It is worth while strolling through the streets to look at these quaint places. Bridge Street was once full of inns, and though many of the fronts are made new there is still much old architecture in the yards and at the back. Once the Hoop Inn from which stage-coaches set off to London, Number 4 Bridge Street is now a shop of which the Georgian front still has windows with ironwork below them and stone faces above. Beyond the Round Church are more old houses over shops, some with dormers, others with storeys overhanging. Fronted by a lawn in Jesus Lane is Little Trinity, a brick house of Queen Anne's day with a pediment and vases. Between St Catharine's College and King's College in Trumpington Street is the Bull Hotel, the old home of the Bull Book Club.

Among the various almshouses is the Hospital of Saint Anthony in Panton Street, founded in the 14th century on another site; Anthony with his pig and bell and Eligius with tongs and a horse's leg are on the gables. Since John Addenbrooke, Fellow of St Catharine's, bequeathed a few thousand pounds for the founding of a hospital for the poor in the 18th century many more thousands have been given and spent in making the fine hospital bearing his name in Trumpington Street.

The marketplace, too, has greatly changed since its old days. On the south side is the new Guildhall, built of brick and stone on its older site; over shops on the north side are new chambers of Caius College; and here and there one or two old houses are left. One of the 17th century has a window with a shell hood, a wrought iron balcony, and a rich plaster ceiling within; one has a 15th century ceiling and panelling two and three hundred years old.

Behind the Guildhall is the public library with 70,000 volumes and a Shakespeare collection. Round the walls of the domed reading room are prints of Old Cambridge, one showing the coronation festival of 1838, when 15,000 people dined on Parker's Piece. Facing the library is the Corn Exchange, a plain brick building with scenes of ploughing and reaping carved in stone, and inside, by Baron Marochetti, a stone figure of Jonas Webb, a noted breeder of sheep.

The County Hall, a 20th century building with a classical front, is in Hobson Street, the name recalling the Cambridge carrier Thomas Hobson, whose memory lives on our lips, for from his rule never to let a horse out of its proper turn came the phrase Hobson's Choice, this or none. The elaborate fountain in the marketplace replaces an old conduit Hobson set up, and has an octagon with a golden pineapple crowning its domed top, and a parapet adorned with a painted shield and cherubs.

Cambridge has a group of churches well worthy of the traveller's attention. It will be convenient to visit them before going the round of the University and its colleges. We take 17 of the churches, beginning with the University church of Great St Mary.

Fringed with trees and bordered with lawn, St Mary's is a fine building in a splendid setting, befitting its rank as the University church. With its great turreted tower of gleaming stone rising high above embattled walls, it has the busy marketplace on one hand, and on the other the majestic group of Caius College, the Senate House, the Old Schools, and King's Chapel.

It comes chiefly from rebuilding on older foundations between 1478 and 1608. Though the chancel is partly 14th century, the aisle windows are 18th century (when the galleries designed by James Gibbs were erected), and the south porch was made new in the 19th. The nave was completed by 1519, and the shields in the windows of the aisles are of those who helped its rebuilding, in response to the Proctors of the University who rode through England seeking contributions. Carved in stone below these windows are the pelican of Edward the Fourth, crowns for Henry the Seventh, and plumes for Henry the Eighth as Prince of Wales. Among the stone corbels supporting the roofs of the aisles are a white hart, an angel, a jester with a bauble, a cock with a scroll, and another cock attacked by a fox, alluding to Bishop Alcock of Ely.

The nave is striking with its lofty arcades of delicately moulded arches, their spandrels filled with tracery below a band of quatrefoils.

Similar carving is over the chancel arch. The clerestory is a splendid lantern of richly glowing glass (by Powell) in the long lines of ten three-light windows on each side, illustrating the Te Deum. In this gallery of 60 figures, with saints and apostles, are portraits of Dr Hort, Bishop Lightfoot and Bishop Westcott, Dr Arnold, F. D. Maurice, and Dean Stanley. The best of the fine old roofs is the nave's, supported on arches which spring from between the clerestory windows; bosses adorn the ridge and angels the wall-plates. There are several Jacobean benches with foliage poppyheads, and the screens in the aisles are 1640. The stalls and the rest of the benches are 19th century; the font, with flowers and cherubs, is 1632.

The earlier work in the chancel is seen in remains of an arch high in the south wall, a fine double piscina, and a priest's seat. In the rich sculpture of the 19th century reredos are the Crucifixion with Mary and John, Samuel in the School of the Prophets, and Paul preaching at Athens. A floor brass tells of the reformer Martin Bucer, who was buried here in 1551, though his body was taken up in 1557 and burned in the marketplace. A wall-monument has the figure of William Butler of Clare Hall, a noted physician who died in 1618; he wears a ruff, and has his hands on a book and a skull. A beautiful chest is 15th century, and in the Tudor south doorway, adorned with the rose and portcullis, hangs an old panelled door.

The north chapel has a roof-corbel showing an ape blessing a chalice, and a stringcourse with the Bourchier and Stafford knots. Here are war flags which flew over Cambridge Military Hospital near Boulogne, and a lectern made from wreckage on the shore for use in the hospital chapel. Two windows here have more Powell glass, one with four saints and pictures of Latimer by a fire, Isaac Barrow with St John's College for a background, Thomas Bray, and Bishop Berkeley. The east window has the Crucifixion and Our Lord Risen, our four patron saints, and pictures of Rheims Cathedral, the Sphinx, Mesopotamia, and the landing at Gallipoli. Except for its modern west doorway the tower is 16th century. On its peal of twelve bells are sounded the Cambridge Quarter Chimes. Curfew is tolled every evening on the great bell.

The church of St Mary the Less has a gallery still connecting it with Peterhouse, that earliest of Cambridge colleges to which the church gave a name, serving as its chapel till 1632. It was as St

Peter's that the church was dedicated in the 12th century, and its new name came with its rebuilding in the 14th. Restoration last century included the east window, notable for the charming tracery above its six lights. The upper portion of its Kempe glass is in memory of James Hamblin Smith; the armorial panels below are a tribute to John Willis Clark, the Cambridge antiquarian, who was churchwarden here. There are coloured figures of St Mary and St Peter in niches on each side of the window. The best glass is the gallery of saints in the south windows; designed by Mr F. C. Eden, and shining on a clear ground, the figures are Stephen, Martin, Teresa, Nicholas, Francis, Monica, Andrew, and Elizabeth of Hungary.

There are traces of the Norman church in the modern north-west porch and an ancient mass dial on the walls. The old font has a cover in which new carving has been blended with the old. The oak pulpit and its sounding board were made in 1741; but inlaid are radiating strips of mahogany which was then coming into the hands of the wood carvers, and destined in the hands of Chippendale and his contemporaries to oust oak and walnut for furniture. On the site of one of the chantries founded by 15th century Masters of Peterhouse, a chapel has lately been built, entered by the original arch.

There are two 15th century brasses, one of John Holbrook, Master of Peterhouse, and a memorial to Matthew Wren, uncle of Sir Christopher. Richard Crashaw the poet was vicar here in 1639, but better known to many, because of his monument, is Godfrey Washington, vicar from 1705 till 1729. Over the inscription is a shield with bars across and stars above, and over a coronet an eagle. The resemblance to America's stars and stripes and bird of freedom is unmistakable, and many Americans come to see what they believe to be the memorial to the great-uncle of George Washington.

St Michael's is 14th century, and was built as the chapel for Michaelhouse, the college absorbed in Trinity by Henry the Eighth. We see it still as the 14th century building which accommodated both college and parish, one of its five bays the chancel, two the choir, two the nave for the parishioners, their lofty arcades opening on each side into the aisles. There is a fine little pinnacled archway which was probably part of a stone screen, a piscina and sedilia with leafy canopies, medieval stalls, a medley of old glass, a picture of Charles Stuart reading a book (given to the church at the Restoration), an

36

old painting of the Holy Family, and a print of Paul Fagius, one of the Forerunners of the Reformation, who was buried here with honour but dug up by Mary Tudor's Commissioners, who burned his body in the marketplace. The founder of the church, Hervey de Staunton, has been sleeping here since 1327.

Three martyrs of the Reformation (Thomas Bilney, Robert Barnes, and Hugh Latimer), preached in the church of St Edward the King in the heart of the town, hemmed round with old houses and small shops. The plastered tower of diminishing stages is chiefly 13th century, with older masonry in the base. The nave and its aisles, divided by slender arches, and the pleasing chancel up three steps, are 14th century; the chancel aisles are 15th, and keep their old roofs. The tilting chancel arch is held by an iron bar. The old font has rich carving of tracery and flowers, with angels round the base. There is a fine bronze portrait plaque of Frederick Denison Maurice, vicar here for a short time till his death in 1872.

St Benedict's is the oldest church in the town; indeed Cambridge has no older building than this, for its story takes us back nearly a thousand years. The fine tower of three stages, one of the delightful peeps of the city, stands almost as it stood in Saxon days, with its walls of rubble, its long and short work, and belfry windows with baluster shafts. The round-headed windows at each side of these are said to be 16th century, and over them are blocks of stone pierced with round holes. The windows in the base of the tower are modern, but the fine leaning arch opening to the nave is Saxon, springing from imposts on which sit two quaint animals. In the tall window over the arch is a figure of St Benedict.

The plan of the nave and chapel is that of the Saxon church, but both were made almost new in the 13th century, when the arcades of pointed arches and clustered pillars were built. The Saxon corner-stones of the nave are still seen inside, and the south wall of the chancel is chiefly Saxon. There are small painted angels on the beams of the nave roof, and 18 gaily coloured figures, wearing crowns and holding shields, adorn the striking roof of the north aisle.

The church has an old ironbound chest and an iron fire-hook for dragging down burning thatch, an old altar stone by the vestry door, an early gravestone carved with a cross, and a small brass portrait of Richard Billingford of 1442, Master of Corpus Christi College.

With two chained books in a case are two Bibles, one of 1635, the other of 1611, given to the church a few years before he died by Thomas Hobson, the noted Cambridge carrier. He sleeps in the chancel, but has no memorial. A still more famous man, Fabian Stedman, the inventor of change ringing, was clerk of this parish about 1650. He was a printer who printed his changes on slips of paper and taught them to the bellringers in St Benedict's Saxon tower. Every bellringer in England knows his name, for he it was who put the art of bellringing on a sure foundation. He is very nearly the patron saint of English ringers, and it was in St Benedict's that he learned about bells. Therefore it is fitting that the bellringers have restored this old tower as his memorial. They gathered here one day in 1931 and rang from morn till dusk the very bells that Stedman rang, they having till then been long silent.

The blocked doorways to the structure on the south side of the chancel remind us that the church served as the chapel of Corpus Christi College till late in the 16th century. Built in early Tudor days, it consisted originally of chapels on the first floor, where the services in the choir could be witnessed by the Master and members of the college, connected by a gallery with the north range of the old court. Below the gallery was a covered passage.

St Botolph's church stands near the site of the old Trumpington Gate. Nothing is left of the Saxon church before it; of the Norman one are left fragments in the walls of the tower, and two capitals built into the nave pillars. From about 1320 come the nave (roofed with old tiles), the lofty arcades, and the aisles, though their windows are 15th century. The tower is 500 years old with a 19th century west window; the south porch and the chapel joining it are 15th century; and the chancel is 19th.

The tower has massive buttresses, an old sundial, and a rare ring of four medieval bells, cast by John Danyell about 1460. It is one of the few towers keeping four bells that were ringing at the Reformation, made at one time by the same founder and still unaltered. Having served as a vestry for three centuries, the chapel is now furnished as a memorial to those who fell in the Great War; its 14th century east window shines with beautiful glass showing two knights. There are old stalls enriched with linenfold and fleur-de-lys poppy-heads, and here too is a monument with the quaint figure of Thomas

38

Plaifere of 1609, holding a book; he was Lady Margaret Professor of Divinity.

There are old moulded beams in the north aisle and the chapel, an ironbound chest with two big padlocks, and an old carved panel from Nuremberg showing the Betrayal, with a little church perched on a cliff for background. The medieval screen is much restored and has on it modern paintings of the Annunciation. The ancient font is hidden in a wooden case of the 17th century, its four pillars supporting the canopy, painted green and gold.

All Saints church, facing Jesus College, with Westcott House (a clergy training school) for a neighbour, was built last century from designs by Mr Bodley, and has a fine tower with a graceful spire, a nave and aisle of equal size divided by a lofty arcade, and a 15th century font from the old church which it replaced. In the pleasant enclosure marking the site of the old graveyard (opposite St John's College), an elegant memorial cross was set up in 1880, enriched with niches and dainty tracery, and serving also as a tribute to literary men, benefactors, and other folk associated with the town. Among the many names on the cross is that of Henry Kirke White, the young Nottingham poet who died and was buried at St John's in 1806. The east window (by William Morris, Burne-Jones, and Ford Madox Brown) has Adam and Eve and a score of saints, prophets, and martyrs. In a nave window we see George Herbert in front of Trinity College, with a picture of Bemerton church where he was buried in 1633; Bishop Westcott of Durham, showing him bringing together master and man in the great coal strike of 1892; and Henry Martyn translating the New Testament into Persian. The first Cambridge missionary to India, Martyn died at Tokat in 1812.

In a marble panel, sculptured in low relief, Herbert Mortimer Luckock kneels at a desk: he was vicar here and Dean of Lichfield. On the brass plate with the list of vicars are engravings of the old church and the new.

St Clement's church, not far from the river in Bridge Street, has lost much of its medieval interest, but the nave arcades with tall octagonal pillars are chiefly 13th century, and we come in by a 13th century doorway. The medieval chancel was taken down and the stone used for building Jesus College. The brick chancel is 18th century, the small tower being 19th. The old font remains. Three bays of the south aisle are enclosed by an oak screen with twisted balusters in memory of a curate who came in 1865 and stayed till 1930, one of the longest periods of service in any church in Cambridgeshire. There are figures on pedestals of the Madonna and Child, and of the two martyrs canonised in our own time, John Fisher and Sir Thomas More.

St Giles's church, sheltered by the castle mound, with Magdalene College and St Peter's church near by, was built of brick and stone in 1875, taking the place of the older church which stood close by. This had been turned into a strange place through additions earlier in the century. Three treasures from the old church are in the new. One is the massive Norman font. Another is the old south doorway, weathered and battered but still fine, leading now from the east end of the north aisle to the vestry. It frames a splendid modern door, the panels richly carved with foliage, in which are lambs, birds, and a pelican with her young. The third fragment of the old church is the arch the Saxons built between their nave and chancel, leading now from the south aisle to the chancel chapel. High and narrow and out of shape, it has "long and short" work in the sides, and imposts carved with cable and diaper of stars.

The reredos has a painting of the Wise Men offering gifts. The chancel screen, painted in medieval style, has pictures of saints on the base. A figure of St Giles with his crook and hind is under a canopy on the porch. The windows of the aisles have a gallery of saints of the centuries, from the first to our own; among them are St Clement (1st century), Bede, Alfred, and the Confessor (8th, 9th, and 11th), St Francis of Assisi (13th), Henry the Sixth holding a model of King's Chapel (15th), Charles the First (17th), Samuel Seabury, first bishop of the Church in America (18th), and Bishop Gore (20th).

A path made of gravestones leads to the quaint little church of St Peter's on Castle Hill, with a medieval cobblestone tower crowned with a short stone spire. The church was reduced to its present size (less than 30 feet long) in the 18th century, but there is Norman masonry in the walls, and we enter by a doorway built when the Norman style was passing, the round arch resting on shafts with capitals of simple leaves; one of the shafts is renewed in oak. A small doorway of the same time is blocked in the north wall. The curious square bowl of the font was made by the Normans, who carved the rim with cable, and gave the four men at the corners legs like tails, which they hold to form festoons.

Most famous of all the churches of Cambridge is the church of the Holy Sepulchre. Compelling in its modesty compared with the great pile of St John's Chapel over the way, it is unusual outside and striking within, and has its own fame as one of the few round churches of our land—four still in use, and one at Ludlow Castle in ruin. Like those at Ludlow and Northampton, it is thought to have been built not later than 1140, and was modelled on the church of the Holy Sepulchre in Jerusalem. It was at first only the nave surrounded by the vaulted aisle and a small chancel, perhaps with an apse, where the altar stood. Over the round arcade, its eight massive pillars and capitals with simple carving, was the beautiful triforium, its wide arches on short pillars framing smaller ones. Above the triforium was the clerestory, giving on to the vaulted roof. Alterations in the 15th century included the rebuilding of the 14th century chancel and its north aisle, the raising of the nave walls to make an eight-sided belfry, the insertion of new windows, and the replacing of some of the round arches by pointed ones. So it stood till the great restoration of 1841, when the Round was given its original 12th century appearance. The belfry gave place to a roof resembling the conical one of the Normans, and a bell turret was added at the corner of the north aisle which was lengthened eastward to be in line with the chancel. The fine west doorway, with zigzag ornament and six shafts, is chiefly new. It is interesting to walk slowly round the ambulatory (the aisle of the Round) and catch glimpses of the carved heads peeping from the walls between the piers. There are seven heads round the aisle and eight more inside the nave, all vivid and striking, and all different.

The tower and spire of Holy Trinity, rising over the busiest part of the town, belong to a church which has been greatly changed since its 13th century days. The aisles were added in the 14th century; from the 15th come the transepts, the clerestory, and the north porch; and the chancel is modern. It is lofty and light with walls seeming to be all windows, the beautiful glass in one of them showing Moses, Elisha, and the disciples healing. Its striking feature is the west end, where the tower, standing in the nave, is supported by two flying buttresses to the slender 14th century arcades, and by two great panelled buttresses which reach the fine old roof. This is 15th century, the time of the roofs of the transepts and the north aisle. There are three 700-year-old arches in the 13th century tower, the oldest portion of the church.

There is a memorial to Sir Robert Tabor, who has been sleeping here since 1681; a famous physician, he perfected the cure of ague by the use of quinine, two of his royal patients being Charles the Second and the Dauphin.

The church of St Andrew the Great is the third that has faced Christ's College in the last three centuries. In its walls are a few stones from Barnwell Priory, but the interest of the church is chiefly in a monument on the wall in honour of a man to whom every English boy should raise his cap. On this monument are the names of Captain Cook, his wife, and their six children, two of whom sleep with their mother in the middle aisle of the church. Captain Cook's wife, who set up this monument, was surely as lonely a mother as children ever had. She was Elizabeth Batts when she stood as a girl on the banks of the Thames to welcome back the victors from the Plains of Abraham. Wolfe had died but James Cook came back, and in three years he was married to Elizabeth Batts. They had six children, of whom three died as babies. When Captain Cook returned from his second voyage round the world his two eldest boys, James and Nathaniel, were longing to join the navy, and did so; just before he set out again the little baby Hugh was born. He was all Elizabeth had to comfort her when Captain Cook had sailed again; three babies had died, two boys were at sea, and little Hugh was growing up. It was in 1776 that they said Goodbye, but it was not till 1780 that news came to England of Captain Cook's death 20 months before. News travelled slowly then. The stricken Elizabeth was to survive him for 56 years, years of great sorrow to her, for she outlived all her children. Within 16 years of their father's death his three sons died, and their mother was to be alone for 40 years. Nathaniel was lost serving as a middy in the West Indies in the same month as the news of the death of his father came. Hugh was growing up as a scholar at Christ's College, and on the anniversary of her wedding this young scholar died. His mother and his brother James came to his funeral in St Andrew's, and here within another week or two the mother was again, this time alone, laying James beside Hugh, for he had been drowned in a high sea. The poor mother set up this memorial, with a relief of the globe and the names of all her children on it, and for 40 years more she lived alone and was then laid to rest with these two boys, she being 94 years old.

St Andrew the Less is an aisleless building of the 13th century on the Newmarket road at Barnwell. It has often been called the Abbey church, and a little to the north of it are scant remains of a monastery founded in the Conqueror's day near Cambridge Castle, and moved a little later to Barnwell. The church has a nave and chancel under one roof, and a figure of St Andrew over the modern porch; the ruins have a small block roofed with tiles, with pillars and some windows in the walls, and there is a house built out of the materials of the priory.

The 19th century St Matthew's church, more curious than pleasing, is shaped like an octagon, with four short arms giving it the form of a cross-head. Its great wooden roof is like an eight-sided pyramid over our heads, and is crowned with a lantern outside. Two trumpeting angels in oak are over the windows near the pulpit.

St Mary Magdalene is the chapel of the old leper hospital, and though it looks forlorn, standing in a field below the road (at Stourbridge), the small aisleless building is full of interest. Restored by Sir Gilbert Scott, it is almost entirely 12th century. Though its walls of stone and cobbles are patched with brick, those of the chancel have been raised, and the oak roofs of open timbering are 15th century. The stout arch dividing the nave and chancel has shafts and zigzag ornament, and zigzag enriches the arch and hood of the south doorway. The stringcourse has carving like the teeth of a saw. The side windows have shafts and carved hoods, and there are two round windows at the west end.

St Andrew's church belongs to Chesterton, the riverside village which has been swallowed up by Cambridge. But its fine old church remains from medieval days, with flint walls of the 14th and 15th centuries, gargoyles under the battlements, and a beautiful spire crowning a tower with a turret stairway half in and half out. Its fine 600-year-old arch opens on the impressive arcades of the nave, with their long line of seven bays on each side and the 15th century clerestory over them. The roofs are borne on angels and grotesques and women with draped headdresses, and there is a fine display of carving in the great array of benches, some old and some new. It is a veritable zoo, for we counted 144 animals on the arm-rests, including dogs, griffins, lions, and antelopes. On two old poppyheads are men in tasselled hats looking at each other across the nave, each with his fingers in his belt. They come from the time when Richard the First was king. On a poppyhead in the north aisle is a monk with a scourge. The low pulpit is Jacobean, the oak chancel screen is 18th century, the canopied sedilia and piscina are 15th. Above the chancel arch and continuing on the wall above the south arcade is a patch of a Doom painting with many clear figures of demons and people, one demon throwing a man into a grave. The churchyard wall has ancient coffin stones in its coping, and among the orchard trees by the vicarage are remains of a medieval building in which we found fragments of an ancient chancel screen. The old church has a new one to keep it company; it comes from last century, and has arcades with clustered piers and a few fragments of old glass. It is one of the finest of our modern churches, impressive in its simplicity, full of light and space, and with a stone statue of St George on the outer side of the west wall.

The Roman Catholic church of Our Lady and the English Martyrs is an imposing 19th century building with a fine belfry tower and a spire rising 216 feet, the most conspicuous feature of the town till the coming of the great tower of the University Library. It has a second tower over the central crossing, an embattled lantern with a staircase enclosed in a turret of pierced stonework. The walls inside and out are richly adorned. There are flying buttresses from the aisles to the nave, beautiful vaulted roofs, and richly moulded arches on clustered pillars with handsome capitals. On the west front are figures of the Madonna with St Joseph and St Anne, and a scene of her Crowning. On the north porch, under the belfry tower, is the Madonna with the English martyrs, and between the two doors stands John Fisher in his cardinal's robes. In the porch are carved portraits of the Duke of Norfolk who gave the site and Mrs Lyne-Stephens who gave the church. Among the heads on the hoods of the south aisle windows are the architects (Dunn and Hansom), Christopher Scott (pastor for 54 years), and Cardinal Newman.

Over the west doorway, within the church, the Madonna stands on the crescent moon with the vanquished serpent below, and on each side are Prior John Houghton and John Fisher, who stands also on the rich stone reredos of his memorial chapel. The glass in the west window shows two groups of martyrs, the clergy with John Fisher, the laity with Sir Thomas More, and the aisle windows have scenes of their suffering. Under a canopy in the south aisle is an oak statue of the Madonna 400 years old.

So completing the round of the town's most interesting churches, we come to the University renowned through Christendom. We will visit the colleges more or less in the order of their foundation, beginning with the oldest and coming to the youngest.

PETERHOUSE

For more than 650 years it has stood at the Trumpington Street entrance to the University, the first college founded in Cambridge, its founder being Hugh de Balsham, who in 1280 obtained a charter for introducing scholars into the Hospital of St John, and four years later separated his scholars and their Master from the brethren of the hospital by housing them in two hostels on this spot.

So was founded the House of Peter, which served as the college chapel till the time of Charles Stuart. The bishop died in 1286, leaving money with which the scholars built the hall. As the college developed the early buildings became the south range of the principal quadrangle we see today. Between 1424 and 1460 came the building of the north side (where much of the old work is still seen), the west side (keeping some of the old windows and its winding stairway), and the kitchen. The entrance court began to take shape when Dr Perne (the 16th century Old Andrew Turncoat) left books and money for a library. In 1590 the south range was carried eastward. The lodge has stood across Trumpington Street for over two centuries.

The two original hostels were destroyed to make way for the chapel of 1632, which projects into the entrance court like the middle arm of the letter E, and its classical west front, facing the main court, is a charming feature, linked with the north and south ranges by galleries on open arcading.

Panelled with old wood and still lighted by candles, the chapel has a gilded figure of St Peter in front of the organ gallery, and an east window with Flemish glass, said to be a design by Rubens for the Crucifixion, though the action is violent and the expression of the

45

actors unpleasing. More attractive is the 19th century Munich glass in the other windows, looking like oil painting with Bible scenes in rich and vivid colours.

The hall has 17th century tables and seats, and a fine gallery of portraits, some painted on wood. Among them are Bishop Law, painted by Romney, and Lord Kelvin, who even as an undergraduate was recognised as a great mathematician by the examiners, one of whom said to another that they were just worthy to mend his quill pens. The windows dimming the hall have the rich colour and interesting design to be expected from their authors William Morris, Burne-Jones, and Ford Madox Brown; we see in them the founder (Hugh de Balsham), Sir Isaac Newton with his apple, Henry Cavendish with books and instrument in hand, Thomas Gray in a churchyard, Richard Crashaw with palette and book, Bishop Cosin who followed Wren as Master, Archbishop Whitgift reading as he walks along, John Holbrook (a 15th century Master), Henry Beaufort holding a crown and staff, John Warksworth whose manuscript enriched the library, and six saints. By the handsome doorway near the high table are carved a lion and a lamb; we see them again on a wall of the pretty Gisborne Court, to which we come through an 18th century gateway in the main court.

From a small garden we come to the grove, with a lovely lime avenue. The grove is bounded on one side by the 400-year-old wall separating the college domain from Coe Fen and the river beyond. A blocked gateway still older than the wall has the arms of Bishop Hotham of 1316 on the outside, and those of Bishop Alcock of 1486 within. Beyond the grove is an enchanting garden with fine trees, a lime sweeping the ground, a superb walnut, and weeping elms. The last window of the buildings overlooking the churchyard of St Mary the Less belongs to a room used by the poet Gray, who was a Fellow Commoner in 1742, and had these bars fixed so that he might fasten a rope ladder to it in case of fire. Some undergraduates amused themselves by raising a cry of Fire, and Gray descended by the ladder in his night-shirt, only to find he had been hoaxed, being so incensed that he migrated to Pembroke.

CLARE COLLEGE

Seen at its best from the beautiful river lawn of King's, Clare's walls of mellowed sandstone, topped by balustrades and pierced by handsome windows, appear to be a noble addition to King's, though Clare is much older. It was founded as University Hall in 1326 by Richard Badew, and took the name of Clare from Lady Elizabeth de Clare, its second founder. The small quadrangle had become ruinous at the end of the Elizabethan Age, and was replaced by this splendid court. More like a palace than a college, as one admirer said of it, it took about 80 years to build, from the early days of Charles Stuart to the end of Queen Anne. It stands as a striking example of English Renaissance work. The beautiful ironwork of the gates and railings, designed by a great craftsman of Wren's day, is a fit prelude to the fan-vaulting of the entrance; and both are a courtly introduction to the grace of a harmonious quadrangle which must have been thought a triumph by the architect and the masons too.

From the quadrangle a path leads to a charming stone bridge with three round arches under parapets, 300 years old and the best known of all the bridges of the Backs. No view of the river is complete without Thomas Grumbold's bridge, and the scene from it where the willows overhang the river, closing in beyond so that the picture is like a dream, is one of the favourite sights of Cambridge. Across the bridge the path continues along an elm avenue, with Warren's gates at each end, to the new buildings of the college. Designed by Sir Giles Scott in memory of nearly 200 men of Clare who fell in the Great War, they stand on rising lawns behind great trees, a flight of steps mounting to an archway, which leads to a spacious court and frames a striking view of the great tower of the University Library.

The names of the men are written on panels in an old octagonal chapel with arcaded walls and a panelled dome. The chapel, of a fine simplicity, has its old panelling, a rich coved ceiling with floral bosses, a handsome organ resting on an imposing screen, Cipriani's Annunciation for an altarpiece, and two windows with beautiful glass. In one Richard Badew is kneeling on a sphere, offering his University Hall and its band of scholars to the Madonna, who stands on a rainbow holding the boy Jesus, cherubs about her feet; in the other are Hugh Latimer and Nicholas Ferrar, both of this college; both kneeling by a cross, Ferrar in court dress of flowing red, Latimer in the black and white garb of a priest. In the lantern beside him is a candle, reminding us of his last brave words:

Be of good comfort, Master Ridley, and play the man, for we shall this day light such a candle in England as I trust by God's grace shall never be put out.

The 17th century hall is a lofty and stately chamber with a magnificent ceiling, and panelled walls adorned at each end with richly carved pilasters. Among the portraits are Lady Elizabeth de Clare, Richard Love, Edward Atkinson, Peter Gunning, Charles Townshend, Hugh Latimer, Isaac Bargrave, Thomas Holles (Duke of Newcastle), Thomas Cecil (Earl of Exeter), John Tillotson, Lord Cornwallis, Josiah Hort, and Martin Folkes.

PEMBROKE COLLEGE

It is the younger neighbour of Peterhouse, but has stood on the other side of Trumpington Street at the entrance to the University since the 14th century, and has preserved an unbroken front. It came on the tide of scholars and colleges flooding into Cambridge in those days, and was the foundation and pride of Marie de Saint Paul, widow of Aymer de Valence, Earl of Pembroke.

Founded as the Hall of Valence Marie in 1347, it was in the early days a quadrangle modest to meagreness, barely more than 30 by 20 yards. So it remained with little change till the 17th century, when the buildings of the second court were set up and Wren's Chapel was built. The 19th century saw some of the old buildings pulled down and the erection of new ones. The old chapel is of special interest as the first college chapel in Cambridge; the new one was built at the expense of Matthew Wren, uncle to Sir Christopher. His benefaction was in fulfilment of a vow made by him when a prisoner in the Tower, and the chapel was the first work of his famous nephew. A dignified building in classical style, it has a magnificent moulded ceiling which is one recessed panel of flowers. There is rich old carving in the stalls and the charming altar rails. The altarpiece, a Descent from the Cross by Baroccio, is interesting for having belonged to Sir Joshua Reynolds. The glass of the east window is a tribute to Sir George Gabriel Stokes, who was Master of Pembroke. It shows the Crucifixion, with the Countess of Pembroke and Matthew Wren beside the Cross, and figures of Henry the Sixth (with Soham church for a background), Laurence Booth (Archbishop of York in the 15th century), William Smart by his wharf at Ipswich, William Moses (Master in the Commonwealth),

King's College Chapel   **Clare College New Buildings**

Newnham College   **Girton College**

FOUR CAMBRIDGE PORTALS

The Backs of Cambridge, with Glimpses of St John's

Sir Robert Hitcham (a 17th century benefactor), and Mrs Sarah Lonsdale.

The new hall is part of Alfred Waterhouse's architectural scheme of last century. It is a fine long chamber full of light, with rich panelling, a splendid oak fireplace by the high table, and portraits of members and Masters, including bishops, martyrs, poets, and statesmen. We see Marie de Valence and Henry the Sixth, Nicholas Ridley and John Bradford; Archbishop Edmund Grindal, and Bishop Felton, Master in 1617; Matthew Wren and Ralph Brownrig; Edmund Spenser, William Mason (by Reynolds), and Thomas Gray; William Pitt and Roger Long, a clever inventor who, while Master here between 1733 and 1770, designed a metal sphere 18 feet in diameter to illustrate astronomical science, and made a watervelocipede which he used in the garden. There is a bust of Sir George Stokes as well as his portrait, and busts of Pitt and Gray.

The portrait of Sir Robert Hitcham reminds us that his bequest of an estate at Framlingham helped the completion of the 17th century buildings of the second court, where the beauty of mellowed red brick and dormer windows is seen on the north and south sides. Beyond this court, on the other side of an old gateway, is a garden with an avenue of elms and limes and an old mulberry tree daringly called "Spenser's mulberry tree," but to all appearance much too young to be so. A more notable possession is Bishop Ridley's chair in the Combination Room.

GONVILLE AND CAIUS COLLEGE

It has really three founders; Edmund Gonville, a Norfolk rector who died two years after its foundation in 1349; his executor William Bateman, Bishop of Norwich, who changed the site first chosen to the present one near his Trinity Hall; and John Caius, a Norwich physician who refounded the college he had entered in 1529. It was then that the 14th century Gonville Hall became known as Gonville and Caius College. Today it is usually called Caius and pronounced Keys. It was William Harvey's college where he studied medicine before he discovered the fact of the circulation of the blood.

From Trinity Street we enter Tree Court, which occupies roughly the eastern half of the college site. The old buildings have been replaced by a fine modern range designed by Alfred Waterhouse, the walls enriched with gargoyles, oriel windows, and roundel portraits

E
49

of some of the college's famous sons. On the tower, facing the Senate House, are statues of Edmund Gonville holding a church, William Bateman as a bishop, and John Caius holding his Gate of Honour. A statue of Stephen Perse stands in the court: he was a tutor here before he founded his famous grammar school.

Dr Caius added to his architectural ability a leaning towards symbolism, and the new gateway from Trinity Street has taken the place of one of three he designed to represent the course of a student in the University. The first, now in the Master's Garden, was the Gate of Humility; the second, at the entrance to Caius Court, still stands as he built it in 1567, with two figures, one having a palm branch and a wreath and the other a purse and corn of plenty. From Caius Court the student passes through the Gate of Honour to the Senate House over the way, where he receives his degree.

This gate is the most distinctive architectural ornament of the college, though much of the elaborate decoration of pinnacles, sundials, and gilded roses is gone. Over the plastered archway is a middle stage reminding us of the front of a Grecian temple, with architrave and niches between the pillars, and above this is a six-sided structure crowned with a dome.

For his court Dr Caius bought stone from the ruins of Ramsey Abbey church. The chapel and part of the Master's Lodge are between it and the quietly dignified Gonville Court, which has much of its medieval walling. The 15th century hall and library have become houses and chambers; the new hall and the new library were built last century.

The chapel still stands where it stood in 1393, though it was lengthened and had the east end rebuilt in Charles Stuart's day, was refaced in the 18th century, and was given its apse (projecting into Tree Court) in the 19th. Long and narrow, with panelled walls, it has a host of 70 cherubs in the panels of its richly gilded roof (1637). In the marble walls of the apse, below the five windows, are roundels of mosaic showing Eli and Samuel, Jesus in the Temple, Our Lord at Bethany, and other Bible figures; in the mosaic of the dome the sick are coming for healing. The striking thing here is the monument of Dr Caius, who sleeps in the chapel; now on the north wall, it has an ornate pillared canopy above a sarcophagus, coloured and gilded. Here are two kneeling figures of Thomas Legge and

Stephen Perse, and there are brasses of an unknown knight of long ago and Martin Davy, Master at the time of Trafalgar and Waterloo.

Approached from Gonville Court, a two-winged staircase brings us to the hall, where the bearded portrait of Dr Caius presides over the high table. The hall is magnificent with rich screens, panelled walls, hammerbeam roof, portrait gallery, and heraldic windows; but one precious possession it has that must move all who come, for on the right of the portrait of Dr Caius a curtain shrouds a framed blue silken flag with the college arms. It was Dr Wilson's flag, which he took with him to the South Pole. There he was to have left it, but there they found the flag of Amundsen which hangs in another hall in Cambridge (the Scott Polar Institute), and Wilson brought his flag back with him and it was found in the tent where he lay with Scott's arm round him. Like a beacon it shines in his college hall, and a fancy takes us that in its presence these portraits on the walls incline their learned heads. One is Jeremy Taylor, and keeping him company are the father of Nelson, Shadwell the poet laureate, and Sir Thomas Gresham, founder of the Royal Exchange. In another room are Lord Chancellor Thurlow and Charles Doughty of Arabia. The fine buildings on the other side of Trinity Street, curving like a crescent round St Michael's church, are of our own time.

TRINITY HALL

By the side of Clare's magnificence, Trinity Hall seems a humble neighbour, content with a coat-of-arms over an entrance plain to insignificance, opening to one of two small courts by Trinity Hall Lane. On many a milestone on the highways about Cambridge is set the crescent of the shield of its founder, William Bateman. He founded Trinity Hall in 1350 for the study of law, and the buildings rose about a hostel for student-monks from Ely, which eventually became a pigeon-house. The old buildings have been much transformed, but on the south side of the second court medieval windows are still to be seen, one a tiny quatrefoil.

The hall has 18th century woodwork, and portraits of Lord Justice Romer, John Oxenden, Sir Alexander Cockburn (Lord Chief Justice, painted by Watts), Sir John Eardley Wilmot, Sir Nathaniel Lloyd, and Edward Anthony Beck. Among other members of Trinity Hall were Bulwer Lytton, Lord Howard of Effingham, the famous Earl of Chesterfield, and the infamous Bishop Gardiner.

The bright little chapel has traces of medieval work, an 18th century plaster ceiling enriched with shields and huge flowers, a Jacobean altar table, and a huge altarpiece of Simeon with Jesus. The rows of wrought-steel candlesticks on the seats have William Bateman's crescent. There is a brass portrait of Thomas Preston of 1598, dramatist and Master of the college; his hands are at prayer, but part of his head is gone.

Beyond the hall range is a third court, with the lawns and fine trees of the Fellows' Garden. Facing each other on two sides are the Master's Lodge and the library, and curving towards the river are the fine new buildings put up by the growing college. Built into the new is the medieval gateway, taking us now to one of the lovely bridges crossing to the Backs.

The Master's Lodge, with a big gable, is almost new; but the library, a charming little place with creepered brick walls and stepped gables, is almost all Elizabethan. The stone-framed windows have been refaced, and flowering plants and shrubs climb up to reach them. In the long narrow room on the first floor the bookcases stand at right-angles to the walls, with shelves at the top for the readers who stand and book-rests for those who sit.

CORPUS CHRISTI COLLEGE

It does not seem venerable as we come to it from Trumpington Street, but when we pass from its front court into the smaller one on its north side we are in the first closed quadrangle built all at one time in Cambridge, erected when the college was founded in 1352 by two guilds of wealthy townsfolk. For a long time the oldest church in Cambridge, St Benedict's, was the college chapel. The old court has been much changed but has still an atmosphere of early days. Stepped buttresses support the plastered walls, and in the quaint array of windows are dormers in the roofs of mottled tiles, plain and trefoiled lancets, and a new window with a memorial to Kit Marlowe and John Fletcher, the Elizabethan dramatists, who were undergraduates here. In the room above have been found remains of early painted decoration, and curious ledges above the staircase, made perhaps for beds. A new sundial on this north range, made to tell summer and winter time, has the Latin motto *The World and its Desires pass away*. Near the door by which Archbishop Parker entered his rooms is an old pelican in her piety.

Imposing with its battlements and turrets, oriels and bay windows, the modern court has a fine gateway at the head of a flight of steps; over its vaulted archway is a niche, and heads of kings and queens adorn the windows. At the entrance to the new chapel, on the east side of the court, are pinnacled turrets with niches sheltering figures of Sir Nicholas Bacon and Matthew Parker. The chapel walls are enriched with fine stone tracery, a beautiful altarpiece showing Mary and Elizabeth with Jesus and John, an altar cross with lilies and grapes and a pelican, and lovely candlesticks. Among the pictures in the old foreign glass filling four windows we see the Nativity with the shepherds peeping into the stable, the death of the Madonna, and Christ before Pilate. In the top of the windows are figures and shields, at the foot are saints and apostles. Two handsome seats with panelled backs and fluted pillars supporting arched canopies are from the old church.

The hall, lofty and airy, has windows blazoned with heraldry and a splendid gallery of portraits on walls panelled with linenfold. Among them are Matthew Parker, William Colman (by Romney), Dean Lamb, Dr Richard Love (by Mytens), Sir Nicholas Bacon, Archbishop Tenison, Edward Tenison, Dean Spencer (by Van Der Myn), and Sir John Cust (Speaker of the House of Commons) by Reynolds. In the windows lighting the stairway to the hall are tiny scenes in panels of old glass.

The library is famous for the rare gift of Matthew Parker. When he was Archbishop of Canterbury in the early years of Elizabeth's reign he had an unrivalled opportunity of collecting manuscripts scattered about the country after the dissolution of the monasteries, and he gave to his college one of the richest collections now in England. Among its greatest possessions is the earliest manuscript of the Anglo-Saxon Chronicle. He found this manuscript, a thousand years old, open at the page recording the death of Alfred in 892. The holes in the page have a curious origin. This sheet of vellum was made from sheep whose skins were not too clean, and it was the ravages wrought by ticks that made these holes in the parchment, so that we behold here, not only the writing of Saxon scribes but the work of Saxon pests. Another treasure here is the Chronicle of Matthew Paris, delightfully illustrated by his own artistic hand; this was open at a page where he drew on the bottom margin an attack on a Genoese galley by Pisan warriors, whose shafts are hurtling past the Genoese bowman's head. There are many Saxon manuscripts showing their writing and their drawing, a magnificent Roman one of the 5th century with a picture of St Luke in a toga, and a Celtic one with an illustration in enamelled colours. Here are the Canterbury Gospels of the 6th century, sent by Pope Gregory to Augustine, his gift to the men of Kent; a 12th century Bible, finely illuminated, from the Abbey of Bury St Edmunds; and the original of the Forty-two Articles of Religion of the time of Edward the Sixth, before they were reduced to Thirty-nine by Matthew Parker. There are early printed books (two by Caxton), and the Lewis Collection of gems, coins, and Greek and Roman antiquities.

KING'S COLLEGE

One great thing did the most unhappy man among our kings: out of the misery of his times he wrought one of the noblest things in England, King's College Chapel. He was Henry the Sixth, who lived through half of our most famous building century, his pitiful reign beginning in the very year that Joan of Arc shed her lustre over France. The Wars of the Roses forbade that he should see the fulfilment of his dream, but his chapel is as he planned it and today it is the glory of Cambridge, the finest example of English building in the prime of its Golden Age. Milton's words were all unequal to it: Wordsworth could only say:

> *They dreamt not of a perishable home*
> *Who thus could build. Be mine, in hours of fear*
> *Or grovelling thought, to seek a refuge here.*

Henry the Seventh carried on the work, finding the lower walls built and the five eastern bays of the chapel roofed with timber. By 1515 the fabric was complete, with all the glory of its stone vault; by 1531 the great windows were shining in the first splendour of the glass we see today; and a little later much of the handsome woodwork was in its place, resplendent in Tudor arms and badges inside and out, and there is no greater Tudor monument than this noble chapel, arresting outside with its corner turrets soaring to lantern tops with leafy domes, great buttresses rising between the windows and stepping to beautiful parapets with rich pinnacles, and rare doorways adorned with a profusion of heraldry and roses, crowns and niches.

Of truly regal magnificence is the south entrance, with a pendant rose in its vaulted roof.

The founder may have thought to build a college to match it, though that would seem hardly possible, and after five centuries the vision of King's is that of its chapel, and the collegiate buildings are a vestibule to it, though lacking neither dignity nor beauty. Most often we approach from King's Parade, entering the college and the great court through a magnificent gateway with twelve pinnacles and a cupola, designed by William Wilkins last century and flanked by his charming screen-wall with window-tracery. Yet we see the chapel at its best from the edge of the great lawn by the river, or, better still, from the college meadow. The great buttresses are stepped right up and many of them are carved with roses, crowns, and grotesques, ending in finials. Under the parapet in each bay are three great corbels. On each wall nine chantries are neatly packed into the space between the buttresses so that they are hardly noticed, save for their long line of windows, each divided into 20 or 30 compartments with a string of corbels over them, 63 corbels on each side. Altogether there are 180 corbels outside the walls. The west doorway has remarkable carving all round it.

The interior is so spaced that it looks more than its height of 80 feet, its length of 289 feet, and its span of about 40; but its spaciousness is only part of its nobility. It is a marvel of engineering skill as well as of architectural genius, ascribed firstly perhaps to Reginald of Ely, the master mason, followed by John Wolrich. But the vision of this roof, an idea which sprang from an English brain, submerges all speculation in a deep satisfaction that anywhere there should exist a thing so wonderful.

It sets us thinking, of course, of the roofs of Henry the Seventh's Chapel at Westminster and St George's Chapel at Windsor, and we found it in the hands of the restorers as those two roofs have been, so that the delicate beauty of this lace-like stonework will soon be revealed in all its purity after the passing of the centuries. There are 13 fans on each side, and each fan has 12 compartments, divided by cross-pieces into four groups. Each compartment is packed with arches of varying size, 62 arches in each fan, and along the delicate cross-pieces (thin ribbons of stone) run rows of fleurs-de-lys. It is an almost incredible mass of ingenuity worked out with an infinite sense of harmony. Linking the whole scheme together are about two miles of thinly ribbed stone, and within the compartments of the fans are over 5000 arches, trefoils, and little fleurs-de-lys.

This marvellous roof is 80 feet above us as we look at it, and the handles of the fans are in two styles. In the nave the handles begin from the ground, rising in the moulded splay of the bays, nine mouldings for each handle. In each case there is provision for a statuette on a slender pedestal by the side of the handles, with a delightful little canopy for the figure, and the happy idea occurred to the craftsman to let the upper pedestal grow out of the lower canopy, so that as we run our eyes upward the design looks like a great candlestick. In the choir the fan handles begin high up between the two windows, at the transom. There are great stone bosses in each bay at the meeting of the fans, the Tudor rose alternating with the portcullis of the Beauforts.

When we take our eyes from the great roof, so interwoven in curves like repeated melodies, it is to seek the glow of harmonious colour in the windows, described as the "finest series in the world of pictures in glass on a large scale." Wonderfully preserved, they were begun by Barnard Flower, the king's glazier, and the bulk of it is English workmanship and Flemish design. Flower had been brought over from the Low Countries by Henry the Seventh, who stipulated that the windows should represent the "old Lawe and the new," after the model of the windows in his chapel in Westminster Abbey.

The walls and windows of the chapel are set out in a harmonious scheme, the sculptured panels of the lower tier of each bay fitting the size of the two tiers of windows above. The fans of the roof fit into the bays so that the bays are complete designs in themselves; each bay has three tiers, two huge windows above reaching to the roof and below these the front of the chantry sculptured in five great upright panels, with 14 arches and 12 quatrefoils surmounted by the rose and crown of the Tudors.

In the tracery of the 24 side windows are the arms of Henry the Seventh encircled by the Garter, the red rose of Lancaster, and a thorn-bush, recording that Henry found Richard Crookback's crown in a thorn-bush on Bosworth Field. There are Tudor roses, red and white, a white rose in a sun for York, and the initials of Tudor kings and their queens. There are nearly 400 Tudor badges in all. In the

Cambridge   King's College Chapel in all its Glory

The Great Buttresses with the Chantries between them

The Beautiful Screen and the Entrance to the Choir

THE MARVELLOUS CHAPEL OF KING'S COLLEGE

Clare College and King's from the River

King's College and Chapel from King's Parade

THE HEART OF CAMBRIDGE

The Bridge of Sighs, St John's College

The Gates and Bridge of Clare College

central light of each side window are four angels or prophets holding scrolls. Four of these pictures are in every window, two above and two below the transom, and each picture occupies two lights. With one or two exceptions, the pictures of the lower tier illustrate the life of Our Lord and His Mother, and those of the upper tier have scenes to correspond or contrast with the subject below. There are 100 of these great pictures.

One window shows Naaman washing in the Jordan, so typifying the lower scene of Christ's baptism in the river; and Jacob tempting Esau to sell his birthright, above the Temptation of Our Lord. The next window has Elisha raising the Shunamite's son, above a picture of Christ raising Lazarus; and David entering in triumph with the head of Goliath is above Christ's entry into Jerusalem. The plan of the windows is perfect in that of Job tormented by devils while his wife mocks him, and Christ scourged by command of Pilate; Solomon crowned among the daughters of Zion, and Christ crowned with thorns. Elijah being carried up to heaven matches the Ascension, and Moses receiving the tables of the law corresponds with the Descent of the Holy Spirit. Three windows have scenes from the Acts of the Apostles; another has four scenes relating to the Birth of the Madonna—the high priest rejecting the offering of Joachim and Anne, the Angel bidding Joachim return to Jerusalem to meet his wife at the golden gate of the Temple, the meeting at the gate, and the birth of Mary to this childless couple. The next window begins with a curious legendary subject of the presentation of the golden table in the Temple of the Sun, the offering typifying the presentation of the Madonna in the Temple of God; the picture of her actual presentation is below, and to the right are two marriages (Tobias and Sarah, and Joseph and Mary). The window south of the altar with Moses and the brazen serpent (after Rubens) was put in nearly a century ago, and the old glass below it shows Naomi and Ruth and Orpah lamenting, and Christ mourned by Mary and the holy women. The east window has the arms of Henry the Seventh held by a dragon, and six scenes of the Passion. The glass of the west window, showing the Last Judgment, comes from 1879, and is remarkably effective with the sun shining through.

The dark woodwork, panelled and carved, is a striking contrast to the richly-coloured glass. The windows tell the story of the seed of

Abraham and the Son of God; the carving is the emblem of the magnificence of earthly kings, and tells, in arms and badges and monograms, something of their history. The lower part of the stalls in the choir (with figures of men and beasts) and the eight canopies facing east, were the gift of Henry the Eighth. There are 70 stalls in all. The other canopies, and the panelling reaching the new work at the east end, come from 1678. The 17th century wainscoting has heraldry carved in elm-wood.

All this woodwork, though ample and fine, is surpassed in impressiveness by the great screen, a creation of the re-birth of art in the 16th century, declared by a great expert to be the finest piece of woodwork on this side of the Alps. It is the masterpiece of Italian craftsmen brought over by Henry the Eighth, and bears in many panels his arms and initials. Among the emblems are those of Anne Boleyn in whose time the work was done. The gates of the screen, bearing the arms of Charles the First, are 1636; the fine little organ crowning the screen was put here after the Restoration. Its long and varied history began when Elizabeth was queen, and it seems likely that when it was rebuilt by Renatus Harris in 1688 he used portions of the older woodwork. Christopher Tye, the Elizabethan composer, knew it, and Orlando Gibbons played on it. It has two gilded trumpeters with wings.

The eighteen chantry chapels formed by the roofing-in of the space between the buttresses are distributed along the sides. All are vaulted, some have old panelling, fine old doors and ironwork, and old glass—this often fragmentary, but sufficient to be accounted treasure in any place not so rich as this. One has a lovely Tudor door, embroidery of six scenes in Christ's life, and a Genoese tapestry in a frame supported on four little wood figures. The south-west chantry is that of Martin Freeman. Next to it is that of Provost Hacomblen, who gave the brass lectern with the figure of Henry the Sixth. In the glass we see St Christopher, St Ursula, the Angel Gabriel, the Madonna, St Anne, John the Baptist, Henry the Sixth, the Four Latin Doctors, arms and badges and heraldic beasts, and the red dragon and greyhound of Henry the Seventh. Here too is the brass of Provost Hacomblen himself, and the tomb of John Churchill, the great Duke of Marlborough's only son, who died at the college as a student. The next chantry is that of Robert Brassie, Provost in Mary

Tudor's time, whose name is on a traceried window. In the outside window are eight figures in glass believed to be 15th century, though much restored about 80 years ago; among them are Peter and Philip, bishops, a doctor, David, and St James with a scallop shell. Provost Brassie is here in brass.

The first of the chantries on the north side of the ante-chapel is that of Benjamin Whichcote, Provost under the Commonwealth. Its woodwork is 1678, and its glass is of unusual interest, for, besides the old royal quarries of Tudor kings and queens, including Catherine of Aragon's pomegranate, there is some beautiful work by William Bolton who revived glass painting in the 19th century. Some of it is a copy of older glass; a delightful peacock is his own. Next to Whichcote's chantry is the Founder's chantry, furnished in memory of Henry the Sixth and Henry the Seventh. It has a pendant rose boss in its lovely roof, a small coloured figure of Henry the Sixth crowned in a scarlet robe and ermine mantle, a Spanish altar frontal, a processional cross by Bainbridge Reynolds, and a picture of the Madonna and Child for the reredos, painted about 1480 and brought from a convent in Westphalia; it shows the Madonna offering cherries to the Child, and was given to the chapel by Mr C. R. Ashbee, the well-known architect.

Rich stone doorways open to the two eastern chantries, Edward the Confessor's on the north side, and All Souls on the south. The Confessor's has a fine medley of old glass, some old chairs, and a Genoese altar frontal richly embroidered early in the 18th century. All Souls Chapel, now dedicated to the King's men who fell in the Great War, was that of Provost Argentein; his brass portrait of 1508 is on the floor and the names of the Fallen are on the walls. There is a delightful wooden figure of St Nicholas with uplifted hand, and at his feet are the three children he miraculously rescued from the boiling cauldron. In the old glass we see a Jesse Tree, a ship, saints and donors, and a unicorn resting its head in the Madonna's lap, a medieval symbolism. In the chantry joining the Confessor's is the oak pulpit from which Hugh Latimer preached the Reformation in St Edward's church, Cambridge; from it the University sermon is preached in the chapel every year on Lady Day. On the marble altar are beautiful crosses, and the fine bronze candlesticks are over ten feet high.

But this recital of so much that makes King's Chapel famous does not exhaust its treasures, nor can we convey a just idea of its splendour. King's Chapel is King's to the world. To the University it is the unique ornament of Cambridge, and of a college which has striven to preserve it and to make itself and its surroundings worthy of this proud possession. The first design of its founder for a college of which the chapel was to be a complementary part was never carried out, nor was the later design by James Gibbs (the architect of the Senate House in the 18th century) for a four-sided court.

The spreading lawn of the Great Court, with the fountain crowned by Henry Hugh Armstead's bronze statue of Henry the Sixth, is only second in extent to the immense lawn sloping down to the river and the bridge. Facing the chapel are the 19th century buildings, where the ornament follows the Tudor model with the kingly arms and crests. Lofty and spacious, the hall is splendid with its stone screen and the roof with great pendant bosses in colour and gold, walls panelled with linenfold, windows panelled in oak, and portraits of the college's famous men—among them Sir Robert Walpole, Horace Walpole, Henry Bradshaw (by Herkomer), Thomas Ashton (by Sir Joshua Reynolds), and Sir Francis Walsingham, Queen Elizabeth's master spy. Behind the hall and towards the river are newer buildings and courts.

The earliest buildings of King's, known as the Old Court, stood north of the Chapel, and served as the home of the college till 1829, when they were sold to the University, their remains being absorbed into what are known now as the Old Schools. A splendid fragment of the Old Court which has survived the many changes of time is the gateway-tower of Henry the Sixth.

QUEENS' COLLEGE

We may think that this, the college of the great Erasmus, outshines the rest in its modest perfection. Without the splendour of its neighbour King's, or the majesty of the courts of Trinity, or the spaciousness of St John's, it surpasses them all in having kept its picturesque buildings more or less complete.

For the most part of dull red brick, they stand between Queens' Lane and the Cam, the walls of the west range dipping their moss-grown base into the river, which begins to take to itself the incomparable loveliness of the Cambridge Backs. If we cross the curious wooden bridge (built in 1749 and made new last century) there is a lovely vista of the river and its trees, and Queens' itself is a charming picture as of a moated grange above the dark water. Forming a big crescent by the lawns on this west bank is a fine 20th century range with many gables.

Seven years after Henry the Sixth founded King's, his wife Margaret of Anjou lent her patronage to Andrew Doket, the nominal founder of what was at first the college of St Bernard. Elizabeth Woodville, wife of Edward the Fourth, refounded and endowed it, so that it became the college of two queens.

Much that we see today was here before Elizabeth Woodville's time. The first court has the hall on the west side, the library next to the old chapel, and the turreted gateway leading from Queens' Lane, its vaulted roof painted red and green and gold, and enriched with bosses of flowers, a queen, and a bishop. Of the small towers at the corners of the court the south-west is known as Erasmus's Tower, for it is said to have joined the rooms he used when he came to Cambridge as Greek professor. His friend John Fisher, Bishop of Rochester, had been President of the college till 1508, and his patroness, the Lady Margaret, Countess of Richmond, stayed here in 1505.

Through a fine old panelled door with rich tracery we pass from the first court to the second, charming with its cloisters, and the timbered gallery of the President's Lodge. The river wing (in which Wolsey, Catherine of Aragon, and Henry the Eighth were entertained) was built in 1460, and was joined to the rest by the cloisters. The beautiful gallery, with its oriel, and its bay windows resting on oak pillars, is 16th century; the interior was panelled by President Tindall in Elizabeth's day, and some of the 16th century panelling turned out of the hall has been used in the President's study.

The old chapel, remodelled in the 18th century and restored in the 19th, serves now as a lecture room and an addition to the library, which has remains of the older sloping desks beneath the Jacobean bookcases. Old glass in the chapel shows the Annunciation, St Andrew with his cross, and St George and the dragon; and over its entrance is a great sundial so elaborately constructed that Sir Isaac Newton is credited with having designed it. Actually it was painted after his death to replace one that existed before he was born. The signs of the zodiac are round the rim.

The new chapel of 1891 is in Walnut-Tree Court. Designed by Mr G. F. Bodley, it is a lofty building with rich carving in the stalls and in the panelling behind them, under a continuous coved canopy. The reredos has three paintings of the Betrayal, the Resurrection, and the Ascension, under a fine carved and coloured oak canopy. A screen leads us to the ante-chapel, where are three brasses: a headless priest with clasped hands, a tiny portrait of Andrew Doket, and Robert Whalley of 1591, in rich robes and ruff. His family were famous in Notts.

The interior of the hall was much restored in the 18th century. It has a gallery, dark panelling on the walls, a fine fireplace, fire-dogs with the Tudor rose, and windows glazed with coats-of-arms. Elizabeth Woodville presides over the high table. On the right of her portrait is that of Erasmus, and on her left is Sir Thomas Smith, 16th century scholar and author. From the hall a doorway leads to the beautiful Combination Room, roofed with noble beams and looking out on the garden. In the room is another portrait of Elizabeth Woodville.

The range of rooms at the end of the college next to King's was built last century and at right angles to it is a block erected in our own time; its name is Doket Building, a tribute to the founder and first President of the college, whose statue adorns its eastern front.

ST CATHARINE'S COLLEGE

It stands discreetly back from Trumpington Street, with a gate across the court through which we pass into Queen's Lane, once one of the chief thoroughfares of the town. The mellowed red brick of the buildings, with dormers in the roofs and little flights of steps to the doors, and the 18th century iron gates and railings which form the fourth side of the quadrangle, preserve for it a certain homely dignity, though it is rather overshadowed by its magnificent neighbour King's College, of which we might almost say it was a pensioner.

It was founded in 1473 by Dr Robert Wodelarke, third provost of King's; but his college has disappeared, the oldest portion now standing being the 17th century range known as Bull Court. Much of what we see comes from rebuilding in the same century. The chapel in the north range was completed by 1704, and the building corresponding to it on the opposite side of the court was begun half a century later. In the 19th century the hall was given its oriel and other new windows. A charming and gracious apartment with linen-fold and traceried panelling, it has a balustraded old staircase leading to the Combination Room like a Minstrel Gallery above it; and here, as in the hall itself, the walls are hung with portraits. Robert Wode-larke looks down from above the high table; others are Archbishop Sandys, Dr Benjamin Hoadly, Bishop Drury, Bishop Turton, and John Ray the botanist.

There is beautiful panelling on the walls of the ante-chapel, and its richly moulded ceiling has wreaths and bands of fruit and flowers. On the floor is a stone to John Addenbrooke, benefactor of the college and founder of the hospital in Trumpington Street. Restored in 1895, the chapel is a dignified little place with beautiful modern wood-work. The walls have classical panelling, enriched in the sanctuary with pilasters supporting a cornice of leaves and palm. On the benches and stalls are 56 electric candles. The striking reredos has fluted pillars and a pediment with the words, Sursum Corda (Lift up your Hearts); and the fine screen has fluted columns supporting the organ in a richly carved case. In the fine glass in memory of men who fell in the Great War we see a woman reclining in a study, and being welcomed by angels as she enters Heaven.

JESUS COLLEGE

It is secluded from the highway, but from the common by the lower river and the boathouses its red brick buildings, old and new, are plainly seen. Its foundation as a college was in 1496, but the coming of the college for masters and scholars was the end of the Nunnery of St Radegund, which had existed since the 12th century. It was Bishop Alcock who rescued it from decay and adapted the buildings and the beautiful church to the needs of a college, though leaving it in form a monastery, the only one in the University, with a cloister quadrangle entered from an outer court.

The way to it is by a high-walled passage called the Chimney, leading from the pillared gateway with fine iron gates (in Jesus Lane) to Bishop Alcock's gateway-tower, its stepped battlements rising above the old front, which was altered in the 18th century and is dominated by the tower of the nuns' church at the east end. In a beautiful niche on the front of his gateway the bishop stands with his hand upraised, and over the archway are coloured coats-of-arms. The panelled oak roof of the archway, with shields in floral bosses, is modern, but the fine linenfold door is old, opening to a spacious west court where brick buildings with rows of stone windows look on to lawn and cobbles. The north range of the court is 17th century.

Through a narrow opening in the east side of this court we come to the cloister court. The old refectory of the nuns became the college hall; the Prioress's lodging and the guest house became the Master's Lodge and the library; and the old dormitories were made into chambers for the scholars. The entrance to the destroyed chapter house below them was blocked up, its great beauty lost to the world till it was found in 1893. Coming from the close of the 12th century, it has three bays with richly moulded arches on clusters of detached shafts—the middle one the doorway, the others each containing a window. The tracery of one of the windows and some of the capitals are richly carved.

In its conversion to the college chapel the nunnery church lost its south aisle and more than half its nave, and the north aisle was destroyed to make the court bigger. Some new windows were inserted, and the tower was given its top storey; rising from the middle of a cross, it has a fine lantern and rests on four lofty and impressive arches. The north transept, where the earliest work remains, has three round-headed arches blocked in the north wall which once led to the dormitories, and an arch above them which led to the infirmary. High in the east wall is a gallery with round-arched arcading, approached by a spiral stair; and below the gallery are two pointed old arches which were filled with tracery last century to give support to the tower, having once led to an older chapel. There are two windows under a blocked arch in the south transept, and four pillars seen in the outside wall, facing the cloister, tell of the vanished north aisle.

The windows of the long chancel have richly moulded arches on clustered shafts, the east filled with a bright mosaic of colour. At the east end of the trefoiled arcading on the south wall is a charming 12th century piscina with interlacing arches. By the nave doorway is a stoup under a canopy of rich tracery. In the spacious south transept are fragments of old coffin lids, part of a battered figure with a canopy over the head, and a coped stone with a cross and inscription

Queens' College

Emmanuel College
The Chapel and Cloisters

Gonville and Caius
The Gate of Honour

Jesus College Gateway   **Sidney Sussex College**

In the Court of Selwyn College

to one of the nuns. An alabaster wall-monument has the head of Archbishop Cranmer, who was a Fellow here, and a tribute to Samuel Taylor Coleridge (a scholar of Jesus), has lines from the Ancient Mariner.

The windows of nave and transepts have William Morris's rich glass (designed chiefly by Burne-Jones and partly by Ford Madox Brown) showing the Virtues, prophets and saints, and Old Testament figures. One has a company of angels and archangels, saints, and a portrait of John Alcock. Hanging in the nave are sketches by Burne-Jones and a sketch by Morris for the angels painted in the borders of the nave's panelled roof.

Some of Bishop Alcock's beautiful stall-work is still here, adorned with tracery and poppyheads of angels, fleurs-de-lys, a pelican, eagles, seated and standing figures. There are four bench-ends in the nave, and a double Litany desk long lost in a lumber room.

The hall is a stately place with a fine oak roof of stout timbers and arched beams. The beautiful bay window by the high table has glass shining with heraldry, and in the window facing are fragments of old glass including shields and the head of a priest. Fluted pilasters adorn the panelling by the high table, and over it is a great coloured coat-of-arms. Here is the portrait of the bishop, a man with a refined scholarly face and a firm mouth. At one side of him is Henry the Eighth, on the other is Archbishop Cranmer. Other portraits are of Tobias Rustat (by Peter Lely) and Richard Sterne, Master in 1634 and Archbishop of York thirty years later; Laurence Sterne was his great-grandson. On a windowsill is a huge bronze cock which was brought from West Africa by George William Neville and presented to his college as a fit emblem of the founder. Over the screen is a fine little oriel window with a bishop's mitre carved under it.

Pleached limes border one of the greens of the great Chapel Court, of which the fine eastern range of brick and stone is 19th century.

CHRIST'S COLLEGE

Where Petty Cury joins St Andrew's Street and all the business of the town streams by, the grey walls of the college front come to the pavement, with the fine gateway-tower standing as it stood when Lady Margaret Beaufort set her arms on it. They are the same, with a slight difference, as those on the gate of entrance of St John's, the same queer antelopes supporting the arms of England and France.

Through the archway with its linenfold door is the charming quadrangle where creepered walls and dormer windows look on to cobbles and lawn. Much of its early appearance has been lost through repairs. In the range facing the entrance are the hall and the Master's Lodge, the upper floor of the lodge having been used by the founder. Shining with colour and gold below an oriel window here are her arms and her motto, For Remembrance; and here, according to an anecdote of old Thomas Fuller, she is said to have admonished the Dean to correct a scholar gently. A stone fireplace with her badges is still to be seen.

But it is not for its gracious founder that Christ's is best remembered. Beneath her portrait in the hall, showing her in kennel headdress, are those of men who have lent the college everlasting fame, John Milton and Charles Darwin. Here these immortals walked. Even the garden, the most unaltered of all among the colleges, invites attention to its swimming bath as Milton's pool, and claims the old mulberry tree, propped up on a mound, as his. There is a bust of him in the hall.

One of the deep bay windows by the high table has 21 figures, among them Lady Margaret with a plan, John Fisher at whose instigation she established God's House as Christ's College, King Edward the Sixth, Charles Darwin, John Milton, William Paley, Edmund Grindal, Francis Quarles, John Leland, Ralph Cudworth, Sir Walter Mildmay (founder of Emmanuel), and William Bingham. The screen has a traceried gallery, and a border carved with shields, angels, animals, and the initials MB. The passage leading to the hall has linenfold panelling and an oak roof with floral bosses.

In a corner of the main court we come to one of the oldest college chapels in Cambridge, with its original roof, high wainscoting 200 years old, and a portrait of the founder kneeling at a desk. She is one of the kneeling figures in the east window, where a figure of Our Lord Risen, above a fine picture of the college buildings, symbolises its dedication. The old glass showing two crowned figures and a saint was once in God's House, and after being stowed away in a lumber room for a long time was happily recovered. Within the altar rails is the brass portrait of John Sickling, the last Proctor of God's House and the first Master of Christ's. A monument with long epitaphs has the busts of Sir John Finch and Sir Thomas Baines, who founded fellowships and scholarships. On the south side of the chapel is an oak oriel with leaded panes, put here in 1899. Behind it is the stone window through which Lady Margaret looked from her oratory to the chapel; below it is an old doorway with a door of linenfold, seen behind the panelling. The fine brass eagle has the slits in back and tail which was to be found in ancient lecterns. The ante-chapel has four oak pillars supporting the floor of an upper room. Some of the panels open to reveal part of an old doorway, a stoup, and a painted cross in a circle, perhaps a consecration cross. Here is a brass with portraits of a man in armour with his wife, who was lady-in-waiting to Lady Margaret.

With its balustraded parapet and an archway leading to the garden, the Fellows Building is a fine example of 17th century architecture, built just before the Civil War, and is equalled in the beauty of its style only by the old single court of Clare College. Near it is a modern block in similar style.

ST JOHN'S COLLEGE

Its story takes us back to the oldest foundation in Cambridge, for it stands on the site of a small hospital for the sick, founded about 1135 by Henry Frost and managed by Augustinian friars. It was here that Hugh de Balsham tried to establish his college in 1280, but the experiment met with no success, and a few years later the bishop founded Peterhouse for his secular scholars. The hospital carried on till the 16th century, when Margaret Beaufort, mother of our Tudor dynasty, founded a college in its place. As Henry the Eighth seized most of her bequest for himself, the college was not opened till seven years after her death, but St John's is now surpassed only by Trinity in size and wealth.

Its original buildings were destroyed last century to make way for the chapel built by Sir Gilbert Scott, a splendid addition in stone to a delightful court which for the rest is of red brick, keeping much old work in the ranges east and west, and the foundations of the old chapel laid bare in its gracious lawn.

We come to it from St John's Street by the loveliest of all the gateway-towers in Cambridge, Tudor but much restored. The turrets fronting the street have been made afresh and windows framed in new stone; but to replace bricks mouldered beyond repair old cottages were bought and every fragment fit to be used again was numbered. The great stone panel over the archway, gleaming with colour and gold, has the arms of France and England supported by the heraldic antelopes of Beaufort. Beneath the shield is the Tudor rose; to the left and right of it the rose and portcullis are under crowns; the ground is dotted with marguerites and other flowers, and over a band of flowers is a charming cornice of vine. Between the windows above is a statue of St John under a lovely canopy, set here in 1662. The archway has a roof of exquisite fan tracery enriched with two bosses—a red rose and a portcullis among marguerites; and its magnificent old door is carved with linenfold.

South of the gateway in this eastern range was the old library. In the fine old west range of mottled brick, with a statue of Lady Margaret as high up as the battlements, are the kitchen and the buttery, and the beautiful hall. Through a doorway adorned with the rose and portcullis we come to the second court, a truly illustrious example of the brickwork of Elizabethan builders, and the gift of Mary Cavendish, wife of the 7th Earl of Shrewsbury, whose statue is on the turreted gateway in its west range. The north range of this court was originally the Master's gallery; its transformation into the Combination Room, one of the finest of its kind, was one of the alterations by Sir Gilbert Scott.

The first portion of the small third court to be erected was the present Library, an extension towards the river from the Master's gallery. Built in 1624, it has traceried windows giving it something of the appearance of a Gothic chapel; it is well furnished with the old bookcases and desks, and is entered by a richly carved door, guarding among its treasures examples of early printing and valuable manuscripts. The quadrangle was completed in the time of Charles the Second. Through one of the archways of its cloistered west range we come to an exquisite thing, a bridge like a stone screen spanning the river, its window tracery filled with iron grilles, its parapets embattled and pinnacled. Known as the Bridge of Sighs (probably because it has the same delicate beauty as the Venice Bridge of Sighs), it was built last century as an approach to the long narrow court on the other side of the river, its buildings rising impressively on three sides, with many windows in their high embattled walls, and an imposing north entrance with turrets and a tower with a lantern. The fourth side of this New Court is a lofty vaulted cloister, of which the archway leading to the Backs has beautiful fan tracery with a great pendant boss. From this bank of the stream the view of the old buildings of the college and their setting is enchanting; curved gables crown the river front, near by is the old balustraded bridge to which comes John's Lane, and beyond are the gables of Trinity and the turrets of King's College Chapel. On a pier of the cloister in the Library Court are two flood marks of the height to which the river rose in 1762 and 1795.

St John's may well be proud of its hall, its chapel, and the Combination Room. Spacious and stately, the hall has panelling of fine old linenfold with a cornice of leaves and flowers, the screen behind the high table magnificent with richly carved pilasters, coved cornice, and a great coat-of-arms reaching the roof. Much of the hammerbeam roof is old, and in the gallery of fine portraits are many fine folk. Looking down on the hall she never saw, though she planned it, is Margaret Beaufort in white kennel headdress, kneeling at a desk under a striking canopy of rich brocade glowing with dull gold. It is a noble group of men that keeps her company. We see the great John Fisher, whose devotion persuaded Lady Margaret so that all the opposition to the fulfilling of his dream of St John's was overcome; Thomas Wentworth, the tragic Earl of Strafford, who here started that career which ended on Tower Hill; William Wilberforce, who saved the slaves; Roger Ascham, Greek reader at St John's and scholar at the court of Queen Elizabeth; the immortal Ben Jonson and the inimitable Robert Herrick; Lord Palmerston and Viscount Castlereagh; and our noble Wordsworth, who lodged as an undergraduate in dark chambers by the kitchen, as we read in an inscription in one of the windows. With these portraits hang those of Matthew Prior (painted by Rigaud); Richard Bentley, scholar and critic; Sir John Herschel and John Couch Adams, the astronomers (of whom there are also busts); William Cecil, Queen Elizabeth's great Lord Burleigh; Henry Kirke White, Edward Villiers, and Sir Noah Thomas, whose portrait is by Romney.

The fascinating Combination Room has a rich plaster ceiling moulded by Italian craftsmen, and panelled walls on which, on high days and holidays, the silver sconces twinkle with the light of a hundred candles. There are a score of especially fine Chippendale chairs, two fine carved chests, and two beautiful fireplaces, one with inlaid pictorial panels brought to this princely gallery from a Cambridge house. Old glass in the oriel window shows Henrietta Maria, whose marriage contract was signed in this room, and among the portraits of the college's great people is Margaret Beaufort herself. On the stairway to the room is a portrait of Samuel Butler painted by himself, and a collection of his paintings and sketches is in the Green Room by the lobby.

There is architectural splendour in the style of the 14th century in Sir Gilbert Scott's chapel, with its arcaded walls, open parapets, pinnacled buttresses with statues in canopied niches, and the massive tower rising to about 160 feet, saints in niches adorning its handsome belfry. The tower rests on fine arches with clustered pillars, and its roof inside is 95 feet above the floor. In a wall of the ante-chapel is one of the original arches which led to Bishop Fisher's chantry; his head is peeping out of the tracery. Another of the four chantries in the old chapel was that of Hugh Ashton, comptroller of Lady Margaret's household, and his arresting monument is here for us to see. He lies in his robes, a coloured figure at prayer, and under the table on which he lies is a skeleton to remind us that the glory of this world passes away. In the handsome canopy above him, enriched with tracery and a delicate cornice, are ash leaves growing from tuns, and we see this play on his name again on the original iron grille still protecting his tomb. Other figures here are of Charles Townshend of 1817, and William Wilberforce sitting in a chair; this is the plaster model for his memorial in Westminster Abbey. The stalls and bench-ends with saints sitting on pinnacles under the fleur-de-lys poppy-heads, and the beautiful piscina with interlacing arches are from the old church, and are over 700 years old. The fine screen at the west end is modern.

The lecture-rooms at the end of the college front are as old as the chapel, to which they are linked by fine railings. The Master's Lodge, on a site north of the library, is of the same time, and a little later is the range projecting from the north side of the two smaller courts.

MAGDALENE COLLEGE

Beyond the Backs, beyond the bridge where the road linking East Anglia and the Midlands crosses the river, this old foundation, found by Samuel Pepys so much to his liking that he became its benefactor after being one of its scholars, seems at first a little remote from its fellows. But the first impression fades in the sight of its old walls, here dipping in the stream with a river walk, there resting on what is thought to be part of the outworks of the vanished castle.

Seen from the river, the red brick buildings are charming with their many gables, mullioned windows, and clustered chimneys, set in lawn and trees, with an archway in the garden wall. Delightful, too, is the sight of the green lawn of the first court, enclosed by the ivied walls of the hall, the chapel, and chambers. We come to it through the gateway whose rebuilding in the 16th century was helped by the benefaction of Sir Christopher Wray, a judge of Elizabeth's day; and as the fine linenfold door with coloured arms opens on the court we are reminded of the college's monastic origin as a hostel for students in the time of Henry the Sixth.

The hall and the chapel are where they stood when the college was a hostel for the monks. The chapel was altered in the 18th century and restored in the 19th, but it keeps its old roof. The rich screen has an entrance with floral bosses in its panelled roof. The stalls have traceried panels, and in fine niches near the altar are figures of Henry the Sixth with orb and sceptre, Mary Magdalene with her box of spikenard, Etheldreda with a model of her abbey, and Benedict with a staff and a book.

The hall, with a quaint little stepped-spire in the middle of its roof, was built in 1519 by the third Duke of Buckingham. Its richly moulded ceiling and the wainscoting are 18th century, but the bunches of flowers and fruit on the wall behind the high table were carved in Queen Elizabeth's day. Heraldry is in the windows, and among the portraits on the walls we see Sir Christopher Wray in a red gown with a ruff; Thomas Lord Audley in a fur-lined gown; Edward, Duke of Buckingham; Edward Rainbow, Bishop of Carlisle; Samuel Pepys as Lely saw him when a young man, and Lord Braybrooke who presented the famous Diary to the world; Peter Peckard; Henry Howard, Earl of Suffolk, 1745; Charles Kingsley; and Arthur Christopher Benson. The double stairway and the fine gallery leading to the 18th century Combination Room were probably designed by Sir John Vanbrugh.

Beyond the hall is the second court, where pleached limes border the lawn. Here is the beautiful building containing the Pepys Library, a fine example of English Renaissance work by an unknown

17th century architect. The front is of gleaming stone, in striking contrast to the first court; the walls between the open colonnade and the well-spaced library windows are richly carved, and between two gables is a balustraded parapet. The arms of Pepys are above the central window, and his motto also adorns this noble front. He left first to his nephew for life, and then to Magdalene, his library of 3000 volumes and the six volumes of his famous Diary. Here the little shorthand books lay unregarded until by chance somebody looked at them and an undergraduate of St John's spent ten thousand hours in deciphering the mysterious signs and giving the world the immortal Diary. The books now occupy a fireproof room, and the twelve bookcases where he arranged his treasures in his own house are here to keep company with what he gave.

A gate at one end of this east range leads to the gardens, a lovely place with lawns and apple trees and a dog's cemetery. Here a surprise awaits the visitor, for this side of the 17th century library has all the appearance of being a Tudor gentleman's house, built of red brick, with gables and mullioned windows and wings enclosing a small court. In the old walls are trapdoors, not easily seen, though on the occasion of our visit their existence and use were disclosed to us by the activities of two sweeps. The trapdoors give entrance to the old chimneys. One of the sweeps said he had been cleaning them for 45 years, and when he was a boy used to climb in and go along them; the chimney passages were so wide, he said, extending all over the building, that anyone could make a way easily along them.

The Master's Lodge of 1835 is in a garden. The new buildings on the south side of the second court were designed by Sir Aston Webb. More recent still are Benson Court, designed by Sir Edward Lutyens, and Mallory Court behind the other side of Magdalene Street.

TRINITY COLLEGE

Set back between the shadowing trees, the gatehouse (facing Trinity Street) is like a herald proclaiming the greatness of this famous college, which has no equal for size in any English University. Into his magnificent foundation Henry the Eighth absorbed the endowments of King's Hall, Michaelhouse, and a number of hostels, all of which stood on the present site. With the new buildings that began to rise (including the present chapel which Mary Tudor began and Elizabeth finished), the hall and kitchen of Michaelhouse, as well as the gateways and some ranges of King's Hall, continued to serve the needs of the college, and it was not till the time of Thomas Nevile, Master from 1593 to 1615, that the great transformation took place. With Ralph Symons for architect, he planned to bring the mass of buildings into an ordered whole. He kept what was good, he rebuilt and built anew, with the result that Trinity's Great Court, a quadrangle about 334 feet by 258, is the most spacious of any in the world, charming with creepered walls, battlements, dormers, gateways, and the old chapel on one side.

The Great Gateway, which was left standing facing Trinity Street, was built 400 years ago as the main entrance to King's Hall. Over its two archways between the flanking towers stretches a broad band of shields on which are emblazoned the arms of Edward the Third and his six sons. Between this princely row and the handsome parapet carved with quatrefoils are four windows, and a canopied niche in which stands Henry the Eighth, the statue from Elizabethan days. Over the smaller archway is tracery with roses and a crown; the other has fine doors of linenfold and a vaulted roof, and on the side facing the court is a quaint group of statues of a rather unwieldy James the First, his wife Anne of Denmark, and his son Charles Stuart. On the north side of the court is King Edward's Gateway, the earliest of the Cambridge gateway-towers; erected in 1427, it served as the approach to King's Hall till the Great Gate was built, and was moved to its present position from its original site by Nevile, who gave it the statue of the king and much of its ornament of arms and emblems. When Nevile rebuilt the south range of the court he gave it the Queen's Gateway, adorning it with the statue of Elizabeth.

In this noble court, with six lawns about the beautiful 18th century fountain, we are reminded of the men, kingly of intellect, who came and went within it. In the first floor chambers north of the Great Gate Sir Isaac Newton formulated his Laws of Motion and interpreted the action of gravity. Thackeray's rooms were below, opposite Macaulay's.

The chapel and its spacious ante-chapel recall these and other men by their memorials and the glass in the windows. There are statues of Tennyson sitting with his book; Macaulay, another seated figure; Francis Bacon reclining in his chair (a striking figure as we see it from the sanctuary, framed by the arch of the screen); Dr Whewell, who

73

gave two pleasant courts on the other side of Trinity Street, with a fine bronze Mercury seated on a marble rock in the second of them; Dr Isaac Barrow, founder of the 17th century library; and his pupil Sir Isaac Newton (standing deep in thought); it was this statue which seemed to Wordsworth:

> *The marble index of a mind for ever*
> *Voyaging through strange seas of Thought, alone.*

Among the busts and plaques we see John Wordsworth, Richard Sheepshanks, Jacob Spedding, Francis Hooper, Charles Fox Maitland, and Richard Porson (his bust by Chantrey). A 19th century rector, John Beaumont, has a brass portrait showing him in vestments. Among the 120 figures in the windows are kings and queens and a host of great folk, including Latimer, Ridley, Chaucer, Tyndale, Wycliffe, Erasmus, Bacon, George Herbert, and Newton with his apple. The glass was part of the chapel's decoration last century. The rich 18th century woodwork includes the canopied panelling, the great altar-canopy (its fluted pillars shining with gold), and the massive organ screen.

Nevile gave the hall (in the west range) the proportions of that in Middle Temple, London. It has a hammerbeam roof, a richly carved screen, windows bright with heraldry, and many portraits telling again the college history. Henry the Eighth presides over the high table, and on one side of him is a fine copy of Antonio More's unsmiling portrait of Mary Tudor, a rose in her hand, while on the other is the charming William Frederick, Duke of Gloucester, painted as a boy by Sir Joshua Reynolds. Others are Sir Isaac Newton, Francis Bacon, Earl of Essex, John Dryden, and Charles Montagu, Earl of Halifax; Byron, Tennyson, Sir Charles Stanford, Sir J. J. Thomson, and Stanley Baldwin.

The old hall of Michaelhouse became the buttery, with the Combination Room above, and this part of the range was rebuilt in 1774. The Master's Lodge, flanked by a turret, still stands on the other side of the hall, its oriel window having replaced an earlier one last century. The old library in the north range reached King Edward's Gateway, through which we pass to the bowling green, a delightful place shut in on the eastern side by the remains of the medieval quadrangle of King's Hall.

The passage through the screens opens into the Cloister Court, built by Nevile out of his own pocket. It is still pleasantly Jacobean, though much altered, and its fine eastern terrace with steps and balustrading was probably of Wren's designing. Above the northern cloister Byron lodged; the south cloister gives on to the New Court, built last century; and the fourth side of the quadrangle is closed by the library, the noble building designed by Wren. He raised it above the cloister after the fashion of the library of St Mark's in Venice; he put in the bookcases we see, made by a Cambridge carpenter and enriched with Grinling Gibbons's carving in limewood of fruit and flowers. Wren designed the ceiling.

On Wren's pedestals at the ends of the bookcases the white busts of Trinity's great men gleam in rows extending the length of the room. Many are by Roubiliac, and the vista is closed by a statue of Byron which has an unusual history. Thorwaldsen sculptured it in the expectation that Westminster Abbey or St Paul's would receive it; but the Abbey declined to accept Lord Byron, and after the statue had lain 12 years at the Custom House the poet's old college gave it honoured lodging. There is the cast of Sir Isaac Newton's face taken shortly after his death, and a telescope associated with his name.

Great possessions of many kinds are in this illustrious library. Among the manuscripts by monkish scribes centuries before the college was founded are 10th century Gospels, wonderfully illuminated with much gold; St Jerome's Commentary on the Psalms (12th century); exquisitely illuminated work of the 13th and 14th centuries; and, for comparison, examples of the fine printing of the Kelmscott Press. Among the manuscripts in the handwriting of Cambridge men is a book in Milton's hand, containing his Lycidas and Comus and the first dramatised version of Paradise Lost. Here also in manuscript are Thackeray's Esmond, Tennyson's In Memoriam, and Macaulay's Diary. Most curious of all is a 15th century Roll of Carols, the first known harmonised musical manuscript. The notation is hard to make out, and the setting appears to be for two voices, tenor and treble. There are 13 of these carols, and the Roll displays the Agincourt Hymn beginning:

Our King went forth to Normandie
With grace and might of chivalrie
There God for him wrought marvellouslie.

Pepys saw it and copied it, and Burney published it.

From New Court, where Arthur Hallam lived, a gate leads to Bishop's Hostel, a small block built in 1670 on an older site. The ranges on two sides of it are 19th century. Through the gates of the fine iron screenwork below the library we come to the river, where an 18th century bridge crosses to the Backs.

EMMANUEL COLLEGE

Every good American accepts the invitation of the gateway in its classical front to enter the older quadrangle, for through it John Harvard passed as an Emmanuel man. At the tercentenary of the college in 1884 Harvard men placed a memorial window to him in the chapel. But the expectation that his room can be found is an illusion. Nobody knows exactly where he lodged; yet certainly he sat in the chapel, dined in the hall, and let his eyes rest on the ancient wall of the monastery of the preaching friars which was here when Queen Elizabeth's Chancellor, Sir Walter Mildmay, took over their 13th century monastic buildings and established in their stead this college. The story is told that when Mildmay came to Court Queen Elizabeth charged him with setting up a Puritan foundation, and Sir Walter answered: "No, madam; but I have set an acorn which, when it becomes an oak, God alone knows what will be the fruit thereof."

The old wall is one of the few reminders of this origin, and the delightful garden of which it is the boundary has the old fishpond, now a lake where swans and cygnets float among the lilies. The noble gardens are the most abiding impression of Mildmay's foundation, which has been considerably extended by other benefactors.

The buildings are a mingling of styles, perhaps the most persuasive being the cloistered block designed by Wren. Its striking west front, facing the entrance, embraces the gallery of the Master's Lodge above the cloister, and the west end of the chapel roof, which has a clock tower with a cupola breaking into a pediment. The chapel itself pushes into a garden, which has a mulberry tree, a tremendous beech, and a swimming bath for the Fellows, whose garden this is.

The chapel has a floor of black and white marble, and Cornelius Austin's woodwork in the fluted and gilded background of the altar and the rich wall-panelling. In the magnificent plaster ceiling is a lovely oval wreath of flowers, and from it hangs a splendid candelabra in 18th century glass. In the fine gallery of portraits filling the windows we see John Harvard (with a ship in the background), Laurence Chaderton, who was chosen by the founder to be first Master of the college, Thomas Cranmer with his Book of Common Prayer, John Fisher, Anselm, and Augustine; with churches or colleges for their background are John Colet, Tyndale with his New Testament, Benjamin Whichcote, Peter Sterry, John Smith, and William Law.

The hall on the north side of the first court has a richly moulded ceiling, and a classical screen with fine doors of ironwork. The panelled wall behind the high table has gilded pilasters, and here hangs the portrait of the founder in a fur-lined gown, with ruffs at the neck and wrists, and rings on his fingers. Other portraits here are of Sir William Calvert 1761, John Balderston 1719, James Gardiner 1705, Peter Giles 1935, F. J. Anthony Hort 1892, William Richardson 1775, Anthony Askew 1774, and Thomas Young 1829. A second hall near by was originally the founder's chapel, and the lower part of its walling belongs to the monastic buildings Mildmay found here. Some of the modern panelling opens to show the old masonry. We enter through a massive oak screen which was hidden for centuries behind plaster and brickwork. Here are painted portraits of John Bickton of 1675, Sir Walter Mildmay of 1589, Thomas Holbeach of 1680, and Archbishop Sancroft in his robes, sitting at a gilded table on which is a paper with the words, To the King. Sir Anthony Mildmay of 1617 and Charles Fane of 1691 are also here. This old chapel served for a time as the library; now a modern library stands by the Close, with a low brick building of the 17th century for company.

SIDNEY SUSSEX COLLEGE

Founded by a bequest of Lady Frances Sidney, aunt of Sir Philip and widow of the Earl of Sussex, it stands on the site of a suppressed house of Franciscan Friars. Its two small courts are in Sidney Street in the busy heart of the town, their buildings embattled and gabled, and the gateway like a tower with oriel windows and archways leading to both courts. The Master's garden behind the courts has lawns and trees and flowers; the garden close by has a splendid chestnut tree with branches making a circle 80 yards round, above a white and gold carpet of snowdrops and aconites. North of the Hall Court is a court of brick and stone built in 1891 from designs by Mr J. L. Pearson, charming with its richly carved bay windows, curved gables, and arcaded cloister.

The first buildings set up were those of the Hall Court at the end of the 16th century. A few years later the refectory of the Franciscans, which had survived the general destruction, was fitted up as a chapel and a room was built over it for a library. The south range of the Chapel Court was added about 1628.

In the middle of the 18th century the hall (about 60 feet long) was given its rich ceiling, its wall-panelling, and the screen, which has fluted columns supporting the gallery. Over the high table is a fine portrait of the founder in a rich fur-trimmed gown with a ruff, a tiny dog jumping up at her feet. Other portraits here are of Bishop James Montagu, the first Master, wearing a cap; Sir William Montagu, a judge, in fashionable dress with much lace and embroidery; Lord Montagu in a red and white robe. Linking a man greater than these with the college is the curtained portrait of Oliver Cromwell, who came as a fellow commoner in the year Shakespeare died, and went down the following year on his own father's death.

The portrait is a magnificent presentation of the man as history tells of him, and of what we believe him to have been. The big forehead, the sagacious brow, the observant eyes, the rugged features, the stern mouth and slightly underhung jaw—all are in this portrait, which has a curious history. In 1766 Dr William Elliston, Master of the College, received a letter informing him that "an Englishman, an assertor of Liberty, Citizen of the World, is desirous of having the honour to present an original portrait in crayons of the head of O. Cromwell, Protector, drawn by Cooper, to Sidney Sussex College, in Cambridge." The writer requested that on the arrival of the picture "the favour of a line might be written to Pierce Delver, at Mr Shove's, Bookbinder, in Maiden Lane, Covent Garden, London." The portrait arrived, and the letter of acknowledgment was written, but the donor did not make himself known; and it was not until 1780 that the identity of Pierce Delver with Thomas Holles was discovered.

This portrait has sometimes been attributed to Peter Lely and not to Samuel Cooper, partly because of the anecdote that Cromwell sat to Lely and while sitting said, "Mr Lely, I desire you would use all your skill to paint my picture truly like me, and not to flatter me at all; but remark all these roughnesses, pimples, warts, and everything you see, otherwise I never will pay a farthing for it." But we do not recognise the style as that of Lely. It is much more like Samuel

Cooper, to whom Cromwell certainly did sit; and this superb piece of portraiture has a curious resemblance in strength to that of Charles the Second, painted when he was an elderly man, now hanging in the Fitzwilliam Museum.

The chapel, with a big bell in the stepped gable facing the street, was rebuilt in the 18th century, and in our own time has been transformed into a dignified and stately place more than double its old length. Its floor, of different levels, is paved with coloured marbles; and the woodwork with which it is adorned makes it perhaps the richest in any Cambridge college. The panelling covering the walls to the coved ceiling has a cornice carved with flowers and cherubs. There are carved benches and stalls; two beautiful stalls with domed canopies are on the screen at the west end, which has a lovely coloured figure of St George in armour. The oak recesses with seats on the north side have arches carved with flowers, cherubs, and birds. On the south side, leading to a dainty little lady chapel with a white vaulted ceiling, is a fine oak arcade with a richly panelled gallery where scenes of Bible story are carved in roundels. Behind the high altar is Francesco Pittoni's lovely painting of the Flight into Egypt, with cherubs above Joseph and Mary and the Holy Child. In a recess is an oak figure of St Francis as a monk, birds about him.

DOWNING COLLEGE

The dignified buildings of its irregular quadrangle look on to one of the most spacious of green courts, shaded by trees. It is the college of the Sir George Downing of the family after whom Downing Street is named; he died in 1749, leaving estates for the founding of the college after the death of his heirs. The charter was obtained in 1800, and the three ranges of buildings are 19th century. One pillared portico leads to the Master's Lodge and another to the hall, where are portraits of the founder and Masters. Behind the hall are the Combination Room and the kitchen; the north side, designed by Sir Herbert Baker, is being completed with a new chapel and library.

SELWYN COLLEGE

Founded by public subscription in memory of George Augustus Selwyn, the famous Bishop of New Zealand (and later of Lichfield), its fine buildings of brick and stone are about a big sunken court, most of them built before the close of the century from designs by

Sir Arthur Blomfield. The chapel of 1895 has a handsome west front, enriched with niches in the gable and flanked by turrets with traceried lanterns. There is beautiful stone carving in the canopied sedilia and in the screen to the vestry, the cornice above the screen's window tracery supporting another screen to the room above. Other rich wood-carving is in the rows of benches, the lovely canopied stalls, and the splendid screen at the west end. In the southern range (chiefly 20th century) are the Combination Room and the fine hall, which has a two-winged flight of steps to its gabled entrance, and buttresses climbing to the slender pinnacles rising above the stone parapet of pierced carving. The 18th century woodwork behind the dais of the hall was once in the church of St Mary at Rotterdam.

RIDLEY HALL

Standing on the west bank of the river, Ridley Hall was founded in 1879 as an Anglican hostel for University graduates to study theology. Its buildings are of brick and stone, with battlements and gables and a gateway-tower. The simple chapel has a bell turret with a lantern, and among the figures in its windows are Ridley, Cranmer, Tyndale, Wycliffe, Luther, Hooker, and George Herbert.

NEWNHAM COLLEGE

Newnham's halls, with their spacious gardens and lawns and shaded walks, are farther from the river than Ridley Hall. They had their beginning in 1871 in a house for women students under Anne Clough, daughter of a Liverpool cotton merchant and sister of Arthur Hugh Clough. She was a pioneer in the cause of education for women and became a great inspiring force in Cambridge. Clough Hall has a charming front to the lawns, with delightful domes over projecting window bays, and an elegant cupola.

GIRTON COLLEGE

Housed in a fine block by Alfred Waterhouse, it is a 19th century foundation which has grown from a movement begun in a house at Hitchin, moved to Girton in 1872, a gallant pioneer for women students. The college grounds cover nearly 50 acres, and under one of its lawns have been found Roman and Saxon graves. Portraits of founders and Mistresses of the college hang in the hall, and the library has some interesting possessions. One is a portfolio of water-colour drawings by Kate Greenaway, given to Girton by John

St John's College Gateway

The New Court from the Lawns

The Gateway and the Chapel Tower

ST JOHN'S COLLEGE

Ruskin; and another is the gold medal given to Caroline Herschel by the London Astronomical Society. The college is equipped for about 200 students.

It was a Girton girl, Ethel Rhoda McNeile, who is remembered for ever in the annals of heroes for giving up the last seat in the last boat of a sinking ship. She was on the Egypt when it went down off Ushant in 1922. The women and children were lined up, the Marconi operator had given his life-jacket away, the ship was heeling so that people could hardly stand on deck, and there were three more seats in the last boat. The Girton girl was Number 3 and Number 4 was a mother who was weeping to think of her children at home. Miss McNeile put her arm round her and changed places, the mother was pushed into the boat, which was cut adrift just in time for those aboard it to see the Egypt turn turtle and disappear.

BELONGING essentially to the University, yet apart from any college, is a group of institutions (laboratories, libraries, institutes, museums, gardens and research stations) housed in noble buildings which we may visit quickly to complete our tour of Cambridge. We begin with the most important of them all, the renowned Fitzwilliam Museum, following with the Library in its magnificent new home, the Polar Institute with its memory of Scott and the rest.

THE FITZWILLIAM MUSEUM

The Fitzwilliam Museum is a temple of gifts from the University's sons, founded in the year after Waterloo by the will of Viscount Fitzwilliam of Trinity Hall, who bequeathed to Cambridge his marvellous collection of books and illuminated manuscripts, pictures and drawings, with £100,000 to build a house for them. The work began in the year the Victorian Era began, 1837; it was finished in the year of revolutions, 1848. Its treasures have been added to again and again, and the growing collections have made the Fitzwilliam a centre of art and archaeology unsurpassed in England. To its original collection have been added the pictures given by Daniel Mesman in 1834, John Ruskin's gift of Turner's water-colours, and Disney's collection of ancient marbles. In our own century the museum has been extended by the building of the Marlay Galleries to accommodate the rich collections of paintings, furniture, and other objects of art bequeathed by Charles Brinsley Marlay of Trinity College. The fine Courtauld Galleries, the Print Room given by Mr John Charrington of Trinity College, and the galleries built with a bequest from Mr J. S. Henderson, are all 20th century.

The noble front of this 19th century building has a score of Corinthian columns and a pediment with symbolical figures. By the main doorway are copies of Donatello's St George and King David. The loggia has a magnificent ceiling with panels of rich moulding from which flowers hang like bosses, and a cornice with children and animals among foliage. The entrance hall has a statue of Prince Albert, and a fine double stairway mounts to the upper vestibule which has four great pillars supporting the domed roof, rich with colour and gold. The walls here are adorned with marble figures in niches, and round the walls are cases of English and Continental porcelain and a rare display of ancient glass.

The ground floor of the older part of the museum has the Greek, Roman, and Egyptian antiquities, and the library and the five upper galleries are devoted mostly to paintings by English artists, with some of the French, Dutch, Flemish, and German schools. We remember a striking portrait by J. L. David of a Guardsman at the execution of Marie Antoinette, looking as if he knew that they had done a thing the world would wonder at. Among those represented in Room One are Hogarth, Millais, Watts, Morland, Gainsborough (a fine group of six), Reynolds, Romney, Rossetti, and William Blake. Here too are Alfred Stevens' beautiful painting of A Woman Reading, The Last of England by Ford Madox Brown, and a fine head of Charles the Second by an unknown artist. Room Two has portraits of famous men and women, with self-portraits by Wilson Steer, Rossetti, George Clausen, William Orpen, and William Strang. With these is Manzuoli's great painting of the Salutation, 1575. Room Three has a fine portrait of the founder, Raeburn's portrait of a Scottish Gentleman, and landscapes by Turner and Morland. Hogarth is again represented, and one of two paintings by Vinckeboons is of Old Richmond, full of humour as well as interest. Room Four has works by Continental artists. Modern painters represented in Room Five include William Nicholson, William Orpen, Walter Sickert, and Augustus John. The water-colours of Girtin, Turner, Cozens, and De Wint are in these old galleries.

From this mingling of painters we pass into the brightly lighted Marlay and Courtauld extensions, where the Italian School, beginning with the primitives, merges into the Dutch, Flemish, and Spanish schools. Among the more notable of the Italian paintings are one by Simone Martini whose frescoes in Siena are famous, a superb altarpiece by Crivelli of Venice, an Annunciation by Domenico Veneziano, and some subject pictures by early Florentines, one on a beautiful marriage chest, gleaming with gold. There are works by Tintoretto, Titian, Veronese, the Canaletto School, Salvator Rosa, and Guardi. In the Octagon Gallery are Rembrandt's portrait of himself; Rubens's Faith, Hope, and Charity; Ravesteyn's fine portrait of a Woman; and Vandyck's Archbishop Laud. There are landscapes by Hobbema and Ruisdael, and a Dutch village scene by the younger Breughel. One of the Spanish pictures is Murillo's John the Baptist among the Scribes and Pharisees. In a small room leading from the Octagon Gallery are drawings by Old Masters, including Rubens and Rembrandt, and small oil paintings by Rubens and Gerard Dou.

As we wander through these picture galleries there are other beautiful things to see. Cases of pottery and porcelain, well chosen to accompany the pictures, include one of 17th and 18th century Delft and one of fine Italian majolica. Among the rich tapestries is one of a boar hunt, made in Tournai in the 15th century. In the rare collection of miniatures are several by Cooper, and in the most interesting collection of watches is one striking the hours and one set in a ring. There are autographs of famous members of the University and letters from famous folk—Dickens, Charlotte Brontë, George Eliot, Browning, Byron, Robert Louis Stevenson, Horace Walpole, Thomas Gray, Macaulay, Tennyson, Dryden, Newton, and Bacon; and there is a letter of Erasmus. The originals of Keats's Ode to the Nightingale, and Rupert Brooke's poem on Grantchester are here for us to see. In Room One is Handel's bookcase with 67 books of transcripts. In the Titian Room is a painted and decorated old Venetian harpsichord which belonged to Eleanora Duse, and in the Spanish Room is a panel of sculpture with two rows of eight mourners from a Spanish nobleman's tomb, a strange little procession of white figures. Some of the exquisite illuminations treasured in the museum are seen in the Psalter and Hours of Isabelle of France, sister of St

Louis, the Metz Pontifical of 1316, an English Book of Hours of 1460, and a Breviary Missal. Of our day are the bronze busts by Jacob Epstein of Helena and Albert Einstein.

At the foot of the stairs leading to the ground floor of the new galleries is the Persian and Turkish pottery, and here also are small rooms with armour and metalwork, the hearse cloth of Henry the Seventh, altar plate of pewter and silver from churches round about, lovely enamels, and exquisite ivory caskets. The fascinating collection of pottery in the Glaisher Room is notably strong in the court of the Staffordshire potters, as well as in Dutch and Spanish enamelled ware. In the room beyond are Chinese and Japanese wares from early times to the 18th century. In the Lower Marlay Gallery is housed most of the priceless Marlay gifts of silver, bronzes, pictures, engravings, and Rembrandt etchings. The cases of illuminated manuscripts have great beauty and variety.

At the entrance to the Greek and Roman Galleries are the Greek coins, well displayed, as are the collections of bronzes, and the objects excavated in Crete, Melos, and Sparta. Chief among the sculpture is the colossal mutilated figure from Eleusia. She was formerly believed to be a statue of Demeter herself, but it is now established that she was one of two caryatids in the arch of a temple to the goddess. The statue represents one of the basket-bearing maidens who at festivals carried the Holy Basket with offerings to Demeter. A melancholy interest attaches to this basket-bearer of Demeter's rites. Eleusis was the Holy of Holies of Greece. Here were celebrated the mysteries which were the culminating point of Greek religious aspiration, searching after the unknown God. When the site had long been desecrated and the temples destroyed, there remained of the fallen fragments this colossal figure, venerated by the peasants of the district as the divine protector of their fields and crops. Permission was obtained to remove the statue in spite of the bitter opposition of the people, who prophesied that no ship would bear the sacred relic from their shores, and though the ship was actually wrecked off Beachy Head, the statue was recovered.

To the right of the statue is a very beautiful sepulchral urn of Pentelic marble, of the fourth century BC. On it in low relief a father bowed with grief is holding out his hand in farewell to his son. The boy is standing by his horse, about to start on his long last journey; a servant behind him holds his hound in a leash. Near by is a small marble altar from Delos, with bulls' heads and garlands. Another altar of special interest from Kanawat in Syria, below a window to the right in the Egyptian Room, has a relief of a god supposed to be Baal, his head surrounded by rays; on the opposite side is a head of Ashtaroth over a crescent moon.

A charming seated statuette of a youthful satyr playing the flute is almost complete. It is an engaging little figure. Among a row of busts on a high shelf between the windows is a fine head of Serapis, an Egyptian god whose worship was introduced into Greece about 300 BC. An interesting dark marble statue of the same god, seated, has the three-headed dog Cerberus, the guardian of Hades, beside his throne. The head of Serapis is missing.

The museum has four fine tombs. One of very fine Roman workmanship was found in Crete and is attributed to the 1st or 2nd century AD; another, in almost perfect preservation, represents in spirited detail Achilles disguised as a maiden among the daughters of Lycomedes. At the entrance to the Egyptian Room is the curious and interesting Brough Stone, remarkable for the length of its Greek inscription commemorating the death of a boy called Hermes.

In the smaller room the treasure of the collection is the rare and beautiful marble statuette of a Cretan goddess, with the characteristic low-cut bodice and bell-shaped skirt. She is wonderfully modelled, and has remains of colour after more than 3500 years. A fine Cretan goblet is in the case, and there are also good specimens of pottery of the prehistoric period, with the familiar concentric circles.

Etruscan art is represented in pottery and bronzes. Near the Cretan goddess are cases with a number of small votive offerings from a sanctuary of Artemis in Sparta, and there are early bronzes and Greek and Roman vases showing the development of that lovely art from the earliest times through the black-figure and red-figure periods.

The last room of all on the ground floor, contemporaneous in its assemblage with that of Greek antiquities, is that of Ancient Egypt. Its greatest prizes are the coffin of Nesi-pa-ur-shef, a priest at Thebes, one of the finest examples of such things in Europe, and the sleeping granite figure of Rameses the Third on the lid of his sarcophagus. With these relics of Egypt are flat sculptured figures of an Assyrian king and kingly priest from the palace of Nimrud. These and the alabaster panels from the same palace are of great power in design, worthy additions to the splendid possessions of a palace of art built 3000 years later. Perfectly lovely is this great palace, indoors and out; we sat looking out from a window on to a daffodil lawn, reflecting that all these centuries Man and Nature have been building up such beauty.

Facing the museum is Fitzwilliam House, dating from 1727, and reconstructed to become the headquarters of unattached students.

THE LIBRARY

Massive simplicity is the dominant note of the University's new library, built in our time from designs by Sir Giles Scott at the cost of half a million pounds, half of which was paid by the Rockefeller Foundation. Its most charming approach is from Queen's Road, passing through the buildings of Clare College; but it is more impressive if we begin the walk at Clare's lovely bridge over the Cam, coming to Queen's Road along the avenue of lofty trees with its handsome iron gateways. The sun brings out the warmth of the fine red brick, relieved by the stone of the cornice, plinth, and doorway, the walls rising in simple dignity in a setting of green lawns. The massive tower is a landmark 160 feet high, rising above the façade 420 feet long. Parallel with this is the west range with the great reading room, 190 feet long, and the two are joined by three ranges running east to west and forming two square courts.

A striking feature of the Library is the series of high narrow windows, alternating with strips of walling. Stone figures symbolising the Four Winds are high up on the tower. On the fine bronze screen of the entrance, reached by a flight of steps, are plaques symbolising Knowledge and Inspiration and over the lantern is a dainty figure representing Scholarship. The hall, lofty and spacious, has walls with a dado of mottled stone, and a fine panelled ceiling touched with colour, from which hang glass candelabra. Stairways mount to the long corridor, where doors of bronze open to the catalogue room in the central block. At the south end is the room with manuscripts and rare books, and at the north end is the historical library of Lord Acton, its 60,000 volumes given to the University in 1902 by Lord Morley. Near by is the map room, with the music room below. The twelve floors of the tower are filled with periodicals.

The seven floors of the Library hold over 20 miles of books and have room for as many again.

Among the treasures to be seen in glass cases are: a manuscript of the Gospels presented to the University in 1581; the first book printed in English, the Recuyell of the Histories of Troy; Bede's Historia Ecclesiastica, written about 730; the Book of Cerne, 9th century; the Book of Deer, 10th century, with charters in Gaelic added in the 12th; Chaucer's translation of Boethius, presented by John Croucher early in the 15th century; Chaucer's Annelida and Arcyte, printed by Caxton about 1476; and a corrected proof-sheet of Milton's Lycidas, 1638. The museum library has also a small piece of fabric of thrilling interest, for it is declared to be a fragment of the shroud of Edward the Confessor.

THE POLAR INSTITUTE

The Scott Polar Research Institute is a neat little building of brick and stone in Lensfield Road; it is, of course, in memory of the Captain of Captains, Robert Falcon Scott. In a niche over the entrance is a fine bronze bust of him by his widow. She was the sculptor of the little bronze figure in the little garden, a man with outstretched arms, in memory of Scott and the four companions who perished with him in 1912. The Institute was established to carry on their work by encouraging research into matters concerning Polar regions. In the two domes of the bright hall are charming picture-maps of the Arctic and Antarctic, showing many of the famous ships which have sailed to the Polar seas; round them are the names of their explorers. The Institute has a museum, a library, and a map room, and among the things to see are fishing canoes and sledges with all kinds of equipment for Polar exploration. There is a bronze portrait plaque of Dr Wilson, who was found in the tent with Scott's arm round him, and many of his fine drawings and water colours are here, with the Bible and the copy of In Memoriam which he took to the Pole. With these is Scott's last letter to Mrs. Wilson, and a picture of a very gallant gentleman walking out to die, Captain Oates. Here, too, is the flag Amundsen left at the Pole, the flag which broke their hearts and (who knows?) may have cost them their lives.

UNIVERSITY INSTITUTIONS

Standing back from Trumpington Road are the buildings of Cheshunt College, where ministers are trained. It was founded by the Countess of Huntingdon in 1768, removed to Cheshunt in Hertfordshire in 1792, and brought to Cambridge early this century. Designed by Mr Morley Horder, these impressive buildings look on to a green court, and are attractive with gables, dormers, and pantiles. Over the north doorway is the head of George Whitefield, who was chaplain to the countess.

Wesley House is another modern building in which students are trained for the Wesleyan ministry, while at the corner of the road leading to Madingley is the Westminster College for ministers of the Presbyterian Church of England. Not far away, up Mount Pleasant, is St Edmund House, founded in 1896 for training Roman Catholic students.

Facing Cheshunt College is an entrance to one of the town's open spaces, the Botanic Garden covering 20 acres, belonging to the University but open to all. It is like a little park with its fine trees and its ornamental sheet of water. The belt of trees surrounding the garden is arranged botanically, all telling us their story from the magnolia at one end to the oak at the other—English trees and foreign trees, stately and humble, common and rare, as well as choice shrubs. There are fine conifers, birches, alders, planes, limes, and hornbeam with willows and poplars and a collection of bamboos. Among the conifers on each side of the main walk from Trumpington Road is a wonderful Cedar of Lebanon with branches making a circle over 90 yards round, reaching across the walk to another spreading tree. Here, too, is the curious Pinus Pinaster, the Maritime or Cluster Pine, its trunk with serrations inches deep, and only branching at the top; it grows in the pine woods at Bournemouth. There are hardy Alpine plants, and herbaceous plants set out in families for our instruction and delight. The rock garden is full of colour in spring with plants from the Alps, the Pyrenees, and the Himalayas; ferns and moisture-loving plants grow in the Water Garden.

The fine range of Plant Houses has been rebuilt in Burma teak through the generosity of Mr W. J. Courtauld. A corridor nearly 100 yards long connects the houses and the laboratory, and in it are the climbing plants. We found the lovely rose-coloured Chinese Camelia in bloom, and the strange Strelitzia Reginae of South Africa, with great leaves and a flower looking like the crested head of a bird, blue, orange, and red. In the temperate house are plants

Corpus Christi College

Peterhouse

Clare College

The Chapel of Trinity Hall   The Hall, Gonville and Caius

Hall of St John's College   Hall of King's College

THE SPLENDOUR OF CAMBRIDGE COLLEGES

Trinity College

Corpus Christi

TWO FAMOUS CAMBRIDGE LIBRARIES

The University Library

The Great Court of Trinity College

of climates such as in Australia's and the Cape's, including specimens of the eucalyptus, the date palm, the blue gum, and New Zealand flax. There is a cool fern house, and in a house with tropical heat is the Musa Paradisiaca of tropical Asia, its straight stem bearing leaves bigger than a man. Contrasting with this is the paper-reed papyrus in the aquarium, which still grows in the Upper Nile and Abyssinia, though extinct in Lower Egypt. Its companions in the aquarium are the sacred bean, the sugar cane, rice, cotton, as well as water plants. The flowering plants make the conservatory here like a gorgeous piece of living chintz and a box of rich perfume. There is the orchid house with its fascinating display, including the vanilla orchid, the only one of commercial value. In front of the rest is the Alpine house with an array of flowering plants whose blooms are so exquisitely dainty as to seem hardly real.

The beautiful iron gates at the Trumpington Road entrance to the Botanic Garden were brought here 30 years ago from the site it occupied from 1760 till the middle of last century. Then it stood on the north side of Pembroke Street and Downing Street, bounded by Free School Lane and Corn Exchange Street, where are now the University's two great group of laboratories, lecture rooms, and museums.

As long ago as 1784 lecture rooms were built on a corner of the old garden for the Professor of Botany and the Jacksonian Professor of Natural Philosophy, and were used by them till 1863. In that year the central block designed by Salvin was begun for the accommodation of Zoology, Botany, Mineralogy, and Mechanism. The Cavendish Laboratory of Experimental Physics, with an attractive gabled front, was given by the Duke of Devonshire, and has portraits of the founder, of Clerk-Maxwell its first professor, Sir Joseph Thomson, Sir Henry Cavendish, Lord Kelvin, Lord Rayleigh, and Sir George Stokes. It has also some historic pieces of apparatus, including Maxwell's model of Saturn's Rings, a revolving coil used by Lord Rayleigh, and a piece of Babbage's calculating machine. The Physiological Laboratory is now devoted to Zoology and Anatomy, the range for Human Anatomy (facing Corn Exchange Street) having been built in 1890. The Anatomical Museum has 6000 crania, including 1500 Egyptian skulls, and has a magnificent collection of Saxon skeletons. The Chemical Laboratory of 1887 (facing Pembroke Street) has been enlarged in our time thanks to a munificent gift of

£200,000 by the British oil companies. The Humphrey Museum and buildings for the Medical School were opened in 1904. The Arts School and the Examination School are of our own century, and in 1934 were opened the Mond Laboratory and the Zoology Laboratory.

The imposing ranges on the Downing Site are set about spacious green courts, entered under a triple archway with fine gates, in a front of brick and stone with curved gables and turrets, bay windows, and dormers. Behind the five striking windows of Sir Thomas Jackson's splendid front is housed the Marshall Library of Economics. East of the entrance, and turning into Downing Place, is a building with a domed tower, approached by a double flight of steps at the front of which are bears and bison sculptured in stone. It is the Sedgwick Museum of Geology, a memorial to Adam Sedgwick, Woodward Professor of Geology. The building was designed by Sir Thomas Jackson. It has a bronze statue of Dr Sedgwick by Onslow Ford and a crayon portrait of him by Lowes Dickinson. Dr Woodward's collections are still here in the cabinets in which they arrived 200 years ago. The Museum of Archaeology and Ethnology was begun in 1910, the architect being Sir Thomas Jackson. The nucleus of the collections was that of the Cambridge Antiquarian Society, given, with its library, to the University in 1883, when it was housed in what is now the Museum of Classical Archaeology in Little St Mary's Lane, a small museum with a fine collection of casts of ancient sculpture from the earliest times, and such things as brass rubbings, Tudor fireplaces, canoes, and sculptures from the long-buried cities of Guatemala. The Botany School facing it is a building 200 feet long, with a flat roof for experimental work. The School has plants brought by Darwin from his voyages, and a collection of fossil and Arctic plants. It tests 30,000 samples of seed every year and has a farm of 700 acres outside the town. South of it is the School of Agriculture, a fine block with projecting bays and a copper dome. Among the other departments on the Downing Site are those of Pathology, Mineralogy, Physiology, Psychology, and Geography.

The buildings known now as the Old Schools are in the midst of a noble group—the Senate House, Great St Mary's church, King's Chapel, Clare College, Trinity Hall, and Caius College. The name Old Schools is no misnomer, for the East or Pebble Court is indeed

Trumpington
Sir Roger de Trumpington, 1289

Ely
Bishop Thomas Goodrich, 1554

TWO OF CAMBRIDGESHIRE'S FINEST BRASSES.

the site of the University's medieval lecture rooms as well as of its original Senate House; and much of the old architecture has survived.

The East Quadrangle was built during 1347 and 1474. Its north range, completed about 1400, had the Senate House (called the Regent House) and the chapel on the first floor, and the Divinity School, in which Erasmus must have taught, on the ground floor. The School was absorbed in the Library in 1856, and in 1879 was built the Selwyn Divinity School opposite St John's College. The Regent House is still here, seen through an iron grille on the stairway to be a fine room with a lovely plaster ceiling (about 1600) resting on old beams with carved spandrels. Most of the furnishing is modern, but the splendid table, long and narrow and richly carved, is Jacobean. Five old shields are in a window looking down on Pebble Court, where, carved in the spandrels of an old stone doorway, St George and St Michael are seen fighting dragons. The east room (now a reception room) comes from the 18th century; the south room (now a council room) has its 15th century roof.

The West Quadrangle was originally the Old Court of King's College, and when it was bought by the University in 1829 the intention was to build a vast quadrangle which would cover the whole site, and so mean the destruction of the Old Schools. Designs for it were made by Mr C. R. Cockerell, but only the north range was built, housing now on the ground floor the Seeley Historical Library and above it the Law School and Squire Law Library from the Downing site. The new entrance was opened in 1905; in the hall are busts of Charles Simeon, a founder of the Church Missionary Society, and Frederick Denison Maurice, who helped to found Queen's College in London and inaugurated the Working Men's College there.

The West Court is almost all modern. What remained of the Old Court of King's was left till Sir Gilbert Scott rebuilt the south side and Mr J. L. Pearson the west side. Mr Pearson's restoration included the addition of another storey to the gateway-tower which had stood since Henry the Sixth's day. This great tribute to 15th century building is restored on its eastern side, but facing Trinity Hall Lane it is in all its old glory with panelled turrets, lovely windows richly hooded, and statues under handsome canopies, Henry the Sixth having pride of place. The spandrels of the archway are carved with roses, and the old panelled doors (with a wicket) are traceried.

The Senate House was built in the early 18th century. A noble structure of Portland stone, over 100 feet long, it has pilasters supporting a frieze and cornice, surmounted by a balustraded parapet and decorated pediments. The panelling, the galleries, and the richly panelled plaster ceiling are original; the floor is black and white marble. At the east end are statues of Charles, Duke of Somerset (by Rysbrack) and William Pitt by Nollekens.

Extending between Silver Street and Mill Lane, the University Press has a Trumpington Street frontage of warm sandstone, resembling a church with its fine tower, splendid entrance, and lovely oriel. It is part of the eastern range designed by Edward Blore and built with the subscription raised in memory of William Pitt, whose college (Pembroke) is over the way.

TWO FAMOUS SCHOOLS

Not far from the Scott Institute is the Perse School for boys, founded in 1615 by Stephen Perse. The Perse School for girls was established in 1881. A few hundred yards away, facing Hobson's Conduit, is The Leys, founded by the Wesleyans in 1875, standing on the corner site between Trumpington Road and the road leading across the river by Coe's Fen and Sheep's Green to Newnham. Leys School's fine group of red brick buildings is set off by lawns. The imposing gateway, the library, and the hall were designed by Sir Aston Webb. The chapel, standing detached, has windows shining with rich glass of scenes in Our Lord's life, the walls are enriched with carving; round the nave is a band of inscriptions to old boys who fell in the Great War, framed in dainty mosaic. There is rich wood carving in the hammerbeam roof, on some of the misereres of the stalls at the west end, and the bench-ends with flowers and trees, a ship at sea, an owl, a lion, a peacock, a stag, a fish, and an eagle. Under the vine border of the pulpit are carved panels illustrating the Psalmist's Song of Praise; they show an eagle with the rising sun, an owl flying under a tree as the sun sets, a ship at sea driven by a stormy wind, two peacocks, dragons, and fishes, rabbits under an oak and squirrels above.

The Unwanted Queens

CARLTON. It lies in open country on the Suffolk border, with a small church from the 14th and 15th centuries and two bells that have been ringing since before the Reformation. The leaning walls are golden inside below a white ceiling and they shelter a simple 15th century chancel screen, a font from the same time, and a Jacobean pulpit. One great old beam with a kingpost supports the nave roof; it is probably as old as the ancient glass in the chancel. On an illuminated parchment are the names of nine men, and of them it is said that "They were a wall unto us both by night and day."

Here lies a man who found fame by curious ways, for he was sent out by the king and some of his manoeuvrings were for the divorce of Catherine of Aragon and some for the arrest of William Tyndale. He was Sir Thomas Elyot, scholar, diplomat, and author, who died and was buried here in 1546. While abroad on his diplomatic plottings Sir Thomas complained bitterly that he had no replies from his letters home, and that he received an allowance which only half covered his spendings. When he was ambassador to Charles the Fifth it was from the emperor himself at Naples that he learned the bitter news of the execution of his friend Sir Thomas More. He was also an intimate friend of Roger Ascham. He published many learned books, original works, translations, and anthologies, one of them On the Knowledge which Maketh a Wise Man, a dialogue between Plato and Aristippus. Having helped the king to dispose of his unwanted Catherine, he was one of the men who took part in the reception of the king's unwanted Anne of Cleves.

CASTLE CAMPS. In this pointed corner of the county, surrounded on three sides by Essex, Aubrey de Vere, first Earl of Oxford, built his castle as a defence against all comers. It was held by the de Veres for nearly 400 years after their fighting ancestor died in 1194, and its last remnants fell in the 18th century. Now only the great moat with overhanging trees is left as a reminder of its story, with a farmhouse on the site. The church stands by the moat in glorious isolation, in a lovely bower of trees which crown the hilltop. The best thing about it is the picture it makes as we approach. What it has of old work is chiefly 15th century, with a tower rebuilt after falling last century, and many modern windows. Only the base of the old oak chancel screen is here. The baluster altar rails are 17th century, and there are arms among fragments of old glass.

CAMBRIDGESHIRE

Seeing the Young Pretender

CAXTON. The Roman road goes through it on the way from London to York, and the inn with a show of Jacobean woodwork was known to all as a stopping-place for coaches while the horses were changed. Once it let its windows to Cambridge undergraduates, who wanted to see the Young Pretender go by, but they were disappointed, for Prince Charlie never got beyond Derby. The place has dwindled since those days, for with the last coach went much of Caxton's prosperity.

But it is still a fine place to see the world go by, and for those who would sit and see it there is a wayside seat in memory of Emma Hendley, whose family have done much for the village. Long before the Romans ruled their straight military roads across the maps of England, here was a little road and a fortified place beside it called The Moats. At the cross roads a mile or so away still stands the old gibbet, grim reminder of the days when three men were hung for stealing sheep and were buried here.

The church, with cobbled walls, is in a quiet retreat and has been much restored, but its low tower, and the arcade of four lofty arches with mouldings reaching to the floor, are all 15th century. A step down takes us two centuries farther back into a chancel with a double piscina and the simplest of sedilia. The font is 500 years old. A modern artist has given the simple chancel screen six painted saints.

The Choirboy Who Won the VC

CHATTERIS. Lying on a busy road in the fenlands, it has a very old story, for here bones of extinct animals have been found, a bronze sword has been brought to light in a dugout canoe, and the plough has turned up an urn with a thousand Roman coins. An Elizabethan manor house hiding behind a wall stands on the site of a vanished convent founded by the wife of Earl Athelstan the Saxon. The Vermuyden Drain near the town recalls the draining of the fens by the great Dutch engineer in Cromwell's century, and Honey Farm keeps green the memory of Huna, the faithful chaplain of St Etheldreda, who lived here as a hermit after her death.

The medieval church has been refashioned by the generosity of a sexton's son who made a fortune in America and spent much of it on the church his father had cared for. It is spacious, with the tower and its lead spire, the lofty arcades and the font, all from the 14th century. Between two of the arches is a sculpture of an old man sitting cross-legged, and there are figures of two bishops among the heads looking down. One is a bishop of our own day, and looking across the nave at him is the vicar who restored this church in the first quarter of our century. He was Henry Bagshaw; the fine oak screen is his memorial.

The beautiful pulpit with St Edmund and St George is in memory of his son, who fell in Flanders. The heroes of the village are remembered by a cross with a lantern head in a wayside garden, and also in the east window of the church, which shows Our Lord with a great company of saints and apostles, prophets and martyrs, and the armed knights of the Allies carrying their flags.

Among the 158 men of Chatteris who died for peace was one who has a window to his memory, George William Clare. He was a choirboy here, and won the VC by carrying wounded men to the dressing station during heavy bombing. When the garrison of a detached post had all fallen he crossed a space of 150 yards swept by heavy fire, dressed all the cases, and manned the post single-handed. He carried one man to cover through intense fire. Learning that the enemy was using gas, and that the wind was blowing it towards the trenches and shell-holes, he personally warned every post of the danger, being all the time under shell and rifle fire. He died a very gallant gentleman, killed by a shell, and it is good to know that the street from which he went out to the war is named after him.

The Young Captain

CHERRY HINTON. The factory chimneys give place to orchards and elms as we draw near this cherry village with a church of chalk, strengthened outside with cobble and stone. It has a low tower, and a 15th century porch shelters a fine 13th century doorway, in which a medieval door with new tracery opens on a spacious interior where nearly everything is 700 years old—the stately arcades, the perfect chancel, the bowl of the font, the altar stone in the south aisle, and the rare coffin lid carved in relief with the head and shoulders of someone at prayer between two roses. The double shafts of the tower arch are even older though the arch itself is 15th century. So are the five benches with leafy poppyheads, and the oak chancel screen, much patched and with a new cornice.

Loveliest of all is the simple beauty of the chancel, a flawless gem from the 13th century, full of light, with side walls gracefully arcaded from stringcourse to roof, the arches framing elegant lancets in pairs. There is a charming three-stepped sedilia, an exquisite piscina, and a fine little doorway for the priest. Except for the east window and a doorway altered in Tudor times, still with its ancient door, this chancel is as the builders left it 700 years ago.

There is a tablet in memory of Walter Serocold, who fell in action off Corsica in 1794, when the floating battery he commanded was burnt by redhot grapeshot. Admiral Hood wrote that the king had not a better young captain in his service.

Near by are the remains of an earthwork known as War Ditches, the site of a massacre of men, women, and children in prehistoric days, built over in later centuries by the Romans and the Britons.

A Chapel of Ely

CHETTISHAM. The oldest thing the village has is a grotesque head carved by a Norman sculptor; it is built into the vestry wall of the church which comes from the first days of our English builders 750 years ago. With the head are three small capitals, probably from about the same time, one with scallop carving, and one with stars, the other a quaint little man meditating by a tree, his head on his hand and his legs crossed.

Ely, with its great cathedral, is but two miles away, and this small shrine was a chapel of St Mary at Ely, seeming to cling to the skirts of its powerful neighbour. It has a shingled turret and a series of pointed lancets in which are beautiful Madonnas, the archangel Michael in a blue cloak with gold wings, and a fine Good Shepherd with a red and white cloak in memory of a vicar who lived in every decade of the 19th century and in the first decade of ours. There are ancient tiebeams in the roof, and the font is 15th century.

An Italian Throne

CHEVELEY. The trees of the Duke of Rutland's old park, a ducal domain no more, spread over into the roadway and gardens of this wooded outpost of the county, near the Suffolk border. By the road outside the church, in memory of the men who did not come back, stands a soldier with bowed head in a niche below a cross. The Jacobean rectory has great iron gates of the 18th century.

The fine aisleless church, in the shape of a cross, has a 600-year-old tower beginning square and ending with eight sides, a turret rising from the ground, with a winding stairway to the belfry and a summit once used for beacon fires. The fine arches with clustered pillars on which the tower rests are the glory of the church indoors, recalling the days when there were four guilds here, each guild keeping a light burning on these piers. Three of the four brackets for the lights are here, one carved with a face and one a grotesque little fellow with his legs doubled under him.

The church belongs to our three great building centuries, and still has the oak screen set in its chancel arch 600 years ago. The choir-stalls are modern with fine carvings of dogs, fishes, birds, bats, dragons, and a wolf. There are two Jacobean chairs, and a richly inlaid one of cypress wood, the seat opening to form a chest; it is thought to be the throne of an Italian Doge, and to come from the 14th century. A little glass in a transept window is older still. The painted font is 15th century, most unusual in its blaze of colour, a new dress in medieval style.

Under an arch on the chancel wall is one of the Folkes family, in a red cloak, reading a book. He died in 1642. There is a memorial to James Hand who was rector for 49 years till 1830, and an old alms-box has on it these lines:

> *If aught thou hast to give or lend,*
> *This beautiful old church befriend,*
> *If poor but still in spirit willing,*
> *Out with thy purse and give a shilling.*

Charles Stuart Keeps Cheerful

CHIPPENHAM. Charming with red roofs, spacious ways, and lovely trees, it lies near a patch of undrained fen where the true fen plants still grow. Near the church are quaint cottages with long gardens, and an equally quaint brick school of 1714.

It was here, at the home of Admiral Russell in the park, that our first King George was entertained by the admiral, who at La Hogue in 1692 won the first great success of the British Fleet since the destruction of the Spanish Armada; and it was in an older house here that Charles Stuart was kept for a while after the raid on Holmby House, the king being very pleasant and cheerful, we are told, taking his recreation daily at tennis and delighting much in the company of Colonel Joyce.

The church is as charming as the village, and wears the dignity of age unspoiled. At the sides of the 15th century porch are heads so huge that they almost touch our shoulders as we enter, and if we prefer to go in through the 500-year-old tower we open an ancient door in a doorway carved with roses. Seen from under the tower arch, the interior makes a most attractive picture, the avenue of battered 14th century arches ending with the fine arch of the chancel. The arcades are in seven bays, the pillars round and clustered and eight-sided, delightful in their oddness. The oldest masonry is in the chancel wall, where there is a big Norman arch, and a small Norman doorway with a carved medieval door. There are old benches with poppyheads, and a beautiful 14th century screen with its canopy gone, leaving the traceried bays like a delicate arcade. Over the entrance are angels, and among the little carvings are lions and grotesque faces.

A finely preserved monument to an Elizabethan family shows Sir Thomas Revet kneeling in armour opposite his two wives, and four children kneeling below. Another of the 17th century is of wood painted to look like marble, and has the figure of a woman at a prayer desk. It covers an old wall-painting of St Michael weighing a soul, and the figure of Mary can be seen dimly at one side. Among other remains of painting are crude masonry patterns and a patchy St Christopher.

Near the porch lies Sir Thomas Erskine May, who was Clerk of the House of Commons and became Lord Farnborough just before he died in 1886. A learned lawyer and parliamentarian, he was also the author of a standard work on the Constitutional History of England. A sculptured bust of him by Bruce Joy is in the House of Commons.

The Buried Playground

COMBERTON. Two items of underground news we came upon here: a buried Roman house and a playground under a playground. It was a wealthy Roman who built the house at Fox's Bridge by the Bourn Brook, for it had a heated bath and must have been occupied for generations. Roman coins of 300 years were dug up in its foundations. A relic of a later time was the curious maze, one of the odd features of our countryside in medieval days, which was at least 400 years old when it was covered over by the school playground.

The old thatched cottages by the Tit Brook remain to make a pleasant picture, and away on the little hill by the fields an old church looks over the plain to the towers and spires of Cambridge. Its warm cobble walls stand out against its plastered 14th century tower, where the monk and the devil look from beside the west window. Four medieval folk look down inside the tower, two by the richly moulded arch. The many 15th century benches catch the eye with their traceried ends, and among their few worn poppyheads is one carved with lions and another with two men fighting. The medieval roof of the north aisle has carved beams, three old stalls and a new one have angels on them, and the rood stairs still lead to the top of the 15th century screen. The 700-year-old font has a Jacobean cover. A 13th century arch and a 14th century priest's doorway open into the chancel, where are two lovely medieval windows with leaf tracery, one with fragments of old glass and at its side the smiling face of a lady of 600 years ago.

Home of the Cottons

CONINGTON. Here is one of the homes of the Cottons, to whom the nation owes one of the great libraries in the British Museum, saved from the wreck of the monasteries by Henry the Eighth, and cherished by a man who was happy in the friendship of Francis Bacon and Ben Jonson. The Cottons are remembered in the neat little church, with a gabled lychgate set at the little square by a pond, and two of their marble monuments are by sculptors no less famous than Edward Marshall and Grinling Gibbons. Marshall, who was Master Mason to Charles the Second, sculptured the head of John Cotton's wife Alice with her curling locks; we have seen her twice on our journeyings, for her figure is also at Eyworth in Bedfordshire, on the tomb of her first husband, Sir Edmund Anderson.

Grinling Gibbons carved the head of a boy in a rich frame of flowers, with palm leaves below, and cherubs supporting the family arms in memory of Robert Cotton, a boy of 14 of whom we are told that "he had marks of sprightly courage." Here also are remembered three Cotton children who died a few years after the

Restoration, none living for a week, and two sisters in their teens who died in two days of fever.

The church is a landmark in this flat countryside, the spire rising above the trees on its 14th century tower; in it are three bells older than the Reformation. The old chancel was made new last century, and the nave 200 years ago, with the Cotton vault running along its outside wall. There is a little old glass, and two ancient chests.

A Bible Maker

COTON. Like a shepherd with his flock this church looks down from a hill on the road which goes from Cambridge into Hunts. The high stone by the stream may be the shaft of an old cross. Here still are relics of the days of Norman England when the church was built, for in its walls are two charming windows by Norman masons with deep splays, roll mouldings in the arches, and shafts inside and out. There is a fine built-up Norman arch, and the great square font they used. In the Norman windows are fragments of ancient glass in black and gold.

For the rest this compact little church with its tower, its short spire, and two porches, is all from the 15th century, the north porch with its stout timbered roof, the south with its stone seats. The south arcade is 14th century. The great east and west arches have both been here 500 years, but the odd-shaped chancel was made new last century, keeping the links with the Normans. There is a low window in one wall blocked with a stone wheel carved with a rose in the middle and a sword across the spokes.

The oak screen has much of the work of a medieval carpenter, with Jacobean gates, but is spoiled by the organ over it. The stalls are also Jacobean with later carving, and a Jacobean carpenter's work is in a table, the pulpit, the reading desk, and the old nave benches.

Here lies a learned man who translated the Apocrypha for the Authorised Version of the Bible, Dr Andrew Downes. His tablet has winged angels, a head, skull, and cross bones, and a spade and a pick. A brass plate tells us that Richard Hobson sang in the choir for half-a-century.

The Line that led to White House

COTTENHAM. We should come when its great orchards are in bloom, for it is a lovely sight. Its pleasantest corner is where the village ends, where the 15th century church is crowned by a tower seen for miles. Round the walls of the church runs a gallery of ancient gargoyles, which may keep off evil spirits, as their medieval carvers believed, but do not frighten sparrows, which we found nesting in their very mouths. Indoors eight heads look out from between the 14th century arches, crowned with 15th century clerestories. The chancel has richly moulded stone seats, and an east window with tracery like water-lily leaves. An old chest has five locks with keys kept by five men, and there are oak benches made by a village craftsman last century. He has carved on them flowers, plants, and ferns growing in this countryside. None of the pews are the same and they are carved with thistle, clover, figs, berries, ivy, reeds, and arum lilies.

On the chancel wall is a record of the great storm which destroyed the steeple in 1617, it being rebuilt by Katherine Pepys. This was once a place full of that immortal name; Pepys of the Diary tells us that in Queen Elizabeth's day there were 26 families in Cottenham named Pepys. Here was born that Thomas Tenison who was enthroned at Canterbury and was one of the Seven Bishops who sounded the death knell of the Stuarts in 1688. A brave man, he remained at his post through the Plague, and lived to preach the funeral service of Nell Gwynne and to crown the last of the Stuarts and the first of the Georges.

In the churchyard sleeps Florence Cox, Commandant of the Red Cross Hospital here in the war, and by her sleeps her husband after 40 years work as a doctor, friend of the friendless, as his inscription says. Her name is inscribed with those of the 59 men who fell in the war, the memorial to them having a striking figure in marching kit; it is floodlit by night and its noble words are these:

> *Their lot the glorious price to pay,*
> *Ours to receive, with grateful pride*
> *That freedom lives with us today*
> *Because they died.*

But what will seem to most people the best story of this village is that in September 1604 a baby was christened here, doubtless at this very font, whose name was John Colledge. He grew to manhood and, like many liberty-loving men of those days, crossed the Atlantic, where his family took root and after nearly 300 years produced a

President of the United States. In this corner of our countryside began the line which led to the White House.

COVENEY. Most of its houses line up on one side of the road for a view of Ely Cathedral majestically dark against the sky. Coveney's little old church shares with the chapel in the Tower of London the rare distinction of being dedicated to St Peter in Chains, as we see him portrayed in oak in the peace memorial lychgate. The 15th century gave a new top to the unusual tower, which stands on three 13th century arches, two forming a passage we can walk through, the third opening into the aisleless church; or we may enter by a medieval door which a porch with a new brick arch has been sheltering for 600 years. From the oddest jumble of windows of all shapes and at all levels the light falls on woodwork of various countries and ages. There is a pulpit with painted panels made in Denmark in 1706, a big reredos of 15th century German work with curious painted carvings of the Passion, and a coloured figure from Oberammergau on top of the green chancel screen of our own day, the work of English craftsmen whose forerunners made the benches 500 years ago with fantastic poppyheads showing men and animals and birds and one a flying lizard. There is a plain font 600 years old, and two double piscinas, one cut in a window.

The Beautiful Door

CROXTON. Thatched cottages and a timbered house almost invade the park, where a church hiding in the elms and a Georgian house have a delightful setting by the lake.

On the churchyard lawn is the medieval cross, shortened but still with its canopied head on which are fading away with time and weather figures of Christ on the Cross, Michael weighing a soul, Anthony with his pig, and a pilgrim with a staff. Old Stones make up the 20th century north porch, which is an astonishing patchwork of Norman pillars, medieval tracery, part of a stone coffin, and most of a 14th century doorway, all helping to shelter the treasure of this place—an ancient studded door with a battlemented border round its arch, and fixed to its panels a beautiful relief of the scene at Bethlehem, with the ox and the ass standing behind Jesus and his mother, all so perfect that its centuries might be only years.

The church is mostly 15th century, with a font as old as itself and a piscina 200 years older. At each corner of the nave roof stands a white-robed angel with golden hair, odd painted figures, two with their wings missing. The benches where the village folk sat in Tudor days are strong still and their tracery little worn, and more old woodwork screens the side walls of the chancel. From among fragments of old glass look out angels and men, and among the pictures in the modern east window is Ely Cathedral.

The brass portrait of Edward Leeds on his canopied tomb shows this Elizabethan benefactor of Emmanuel College in his doctor's robes, a man of peace whose tomb has been turned into a little armoury, for on it we found a steel cap and breastplate of Cromwell's time with two helmets of later wars, one German, the other French.

Downing of Downing Street

CROYDON. We pass by the woods of Croydon Wilds, a rare place for birds and butterflies, and where the roads meet below the church we find a cross with its noble words:

> Sons of this place, let this of you be said,
> That you who live are worthy of your dead.
> These gave their lives that you who live may reap
> A richer harvest ere you fall asleep.

Over all this we look from the church embowered on the hill, so patiently brought back to its old charm after long neglect. Its sloping walls, the tower, and the leaning arcades are 14th century, but the chancel is new. In the south transept is a niche which has long been hidden by a fireplace in the squire's pew. The massive font comes from early Norman days, the arcaded pulpit is Jacobean, and one of the two women whose heads are carved on the south arcade wears a quaint three-cornered headdress which was the height of fashion 600 years ago.

We read that six centuries ago Croydon's first vicar died of the Black Death, and last century Edmund Lally was vicar here for 58 years.

Though they have no memorial, three Sir George Downings, father, son, and grandson, are buried in this church. The first was Charles the Second's ambassador to the Hague, an extraordinary man who died in 1684, leaving his name to London's most famous street. The last gave his name to Downing College, Cambridge, which he founded before he died in 1749.

Ely   **Western Tower of the Cathedral**

Seen from the South

The Eastern Walls

ELY'S MAGNIFICENT CATHEDRAL

Prior Crauden's Chapel and Lodge

The Cathedral Towers
FAMOUS SIGHTS OF ELY

Ely   **Cromwell's House**

Ely   **The Porta**

CAMBRIDGESHIRE

It is a sad thing to remember that our famous Downing Street should take its name from a man not worthy of its fame. Sir George Downing, born in 1623, had for his father a sturdy Puritan lawyer, and his mother was a sister of John Winthrop, the famous Governor of Massachusetts.

The family emigrated to America, where George was first a pupil and then a teacher at the new Harvard University. Returning to England in 1645, he joined the Commonwealth forces as chaplain to Colonel Okey, and was promoted by Cromwell to be head of the Army Intelligence Department. His success in this capacity and as a member of Commonwealth Parliaments, during which time he urged Cromwell's acceptance of the Crown, led to his employment as ambassador, first to France, and next to Holland. His post at the Hague enabled him secretly to ingratiate himself with the exiled Charles, to whom he betrayed secret despatches from home. At the Restoration his perfidy was rewarded by the bestowal of other offices of profit.

His zeal whetted by gain, Downing exerted his skill in luring from Germany into Holland three exiled Commonwealth men, among whom was Colonel Okey, to whom he owed all his early success. Having laid his trap, he and his servants effected the arrest and transport to England of all three, where they were executed. In his comment on the event Pepys writes down his old friend as a perfidious rogue, adding that "all the world takes notice of him for a most ungrateful villain."

In the dishonourable scheme which enabled Charles to earn a secret pension from Louis the Fourteenth by making war with France on Holland, Downing had a nefarious share, deliberately enraging Dutch opinion and making armed conflict inevitable.

Accumulating great wealth, he took a lease of land in what is now Downing Street, and built houses there, two of them being Number 10 and Number 11 today. His ignoble service to Charles is said to have brought him secret gifts amounting to £80,000, but nothing satisfied his avarice, nothing made him generous, and his mother left it on record that while he was rich and acquiring property he kept her on a starvation pittance. It was his grandson who founded Downing College at Cambridge, thereby redeeming his grandfather's evil fame to such an extent as he could.

A Plain Word for Queen Elizabeth

DODDINGTON. It has known great days, for here was the palace of the bishops of Ely, and it was once the biggest parish in the county, with 40,000 acres and the wealthiest rectory in the kingdom. In those days one of its rectors was Christopher Tye, a famous musician in four reigns. He wrote masses when Henry the Eighth was king, composed Protestant hymns under Edward the Sixth, was music master under Mary Tudor, and was probably organist to Queen Elizabeth. He is said to have been rebuked by Elizabeth for playing out of tune, and to have told her majesty that her ears were out of tune. He has been called the Father of the Anthem, and he wrote a tune that is known to every English boy and girl, While Shepherds Watched their Flocks by Night. We may be sure that Christopher Tye would have been delighted with the story we heard from the rector. For years he had longed for a new organ, but his people were too small a flock to buy one, and Mr Ridge, the hopeful parson, inserted an appealing advertisement in the personal column of The Times with a result equal to all expectations, for the appeal touched the generous heart of somebody unknown who presented Doddington church with a brand new organ.

Doddington is great no more, but a quiet place set in the fens like an island in the sea, the fens being now all green with patchwork fields. It has a black timber windmill a century old, and its church, just off the busy road, has a few things to show us of medieval days. The tower and spire and the lofty arcades are five or six centuries old; the porch, with its pinnacles and battlements, is 15th century, the chancel arch is 13th, and in it is a 15th century oak screen. The modern roof rests on corbel heads of men and women and is adorned with angels. One of the windows is by William Morris, a Calvary, with the Madonna and three saints at the foot of the Cross; it was brought here from London in memory of a rector who had come from the East End for his health's sake, and it was dedicated by the hero of Kut, Sir Charles Townshend. It was his last public act. Another window is to a churchwarden for 66 years, and there is a tablet to Algernon Peyton who was rector last century for 57 years.

The Reluctant Guest

DRY DRAYTON. It lies among pretty byways and in peaceful meadows, between two busy roads. On one side of it runs the

Roman road to Cambridge, and on the other side stands Childerley Hall, hidden in the trees.

Here it was that the Spanish Ambassador was sent to escape the plague in Queen Elizabeth's reign, and to this hall there came a more reluctant guest in 1647, for Charles Stuart was brought here to be interviewed by Fairfax and Cromwell. The house has been rebuilt and is now on a farm, but the room in which Charles slept is still preserved, with the old barn 100 yards long.

The long grey church has crazy stone walls, medieval windows, and a squat tower of the 15th century, when the chancel arch was built and the font was made. We come in by a 14th century doorway to find angels and human folk looking down from the arcades they have adorned for six centuries. There are brass portraits of Thomas Hutton at prayer with his wife, he in knightly armour with a quaint little face, carefully dressed hair, rings on his fingers, his head on a helmet; she in a pretty pointed headdress and a gown with lace-trimmed cuffs. They are 16th century. In the east window the glass is in memory of Samuel Smith, Dean of Christ Church, Oxford, and rector here last century. It has a portrait of him in his robes kneeling at an altar, and a sculpture with seven coloured medals in the south aisle is to one of his sons who was at the Relief of Lucknow.

DULLINGHAM. Once a Roman farmer lived here, and after he had gone the Saxons cleared more of the forest, where now are fine meadows and trees, none much finer than the sycamore at the churchyard gate. The massive tower and the fine porch are both 15th century. The roof timbers of the porch shelter an ancient door, and as we enter we are watched by three women in wimples and two gargoyled men. Much is old among the great beams and kingposts above the clustered medieval pillars. There is a Jacobean font with worn painted shields, an Elizabethan table, a 13th century piscina, and a sculpture by Westmacott of General Jeaffreson.

The Old Church Dying

DUXFORD. Its crowning beauty is dying of old age; it is the great church of St John's, enthroned above the village street like a ship at high tide but weary with the centuries, its days of worship over. Its tower rises proudly enough with its battlements silhouetted against the sky. There is an attractive 15th century window and a priest's doorway with a rough little door and the big lock that has turned for the priests of so many generations; but the crumbling walls have been condemned. It is pathetic to see the old tower, which begins with Norman work and ends with 14th century work, crowned with a crippled spire, bent not with age but by the pulling up of a flagstaff for Queen Victoria's Diamond Jubilee.

This small neighbour of Cambridge will miss St John's, but happily it has St Peter's safe and sound after 500 years, also with a Norman tower mounted by a small lead spire, and with a row of grotesque animal heads outside and a wide low arch inside. High up at the clerestory are eight old stone corbels looking down on the nave, lions with open mouths among them. There are two deeply splayed tower windows, an ancient piscina, 15th century arcades, a crude 13th century font of immense strength, a Jacobean pulpit, an ancient door on the south, and at the east window of the north aisle two niches borne up by winged angels at prayer.

From that excellent observation post, the railway, the traveller to Cambridge has long looked out for these two old towers, and the day will come when St John's will disappear; but St Peter's will remain to let the traveller know that he nears the towers and turrets and domes of the university city without a rival in the country (or perhaps in the world).

E AST HATLEY. Its few farms and cottages and the little old church made new are in the meadows sheltered by the woodlands of Hatley Park. There is an altar tomb in the church to Mistress Constance Castell whose family owned the park in Shakespeare's day, and the brass portrait of a lady a hundred years older, wearing a fur-lined gown and the kennel headdress fashionable before Queen Elizabeth was born.

Cromwell on the Table

E LM. Its glory is not in its elms, for we found not one in this trim village of trees and orchards; we remember it for the stately tower which has stood like a fortress for 700 years, except that its top is new, crowned by a small spire. The tower is 70 feet high with beautiful arcading, a west doorway with rich mouldings and three shafts on each side, and turrets climbing with every stage. Its architecture is characteristic of the best type in the county, and may be compared with some of the gateway towers of Cambridge Colleges. We found red snapdragons growing in its crannies.

And not less impressive is the tower inside, for the beauty of its wide arch and the lovely lancets round the walls. In front of the west lancets tall clustered columns form a triforium from the turret stairway to a tiny cell in another turret, below which is another little chamber on the ground floor. High above the tower arch is a primitive little window with a gable top through which the light may have fallen in Saxon days. It is now blocked up.

It is from this fine tower that we see the beauty of these medieval arcades, the 20 medieval clerestory windows, and the impressive roof of double hammerbeams. The clerestory windows have shafts and rich hoods; the roof is adorned with angels, and in the spandrels are dragons and flowers, a pelican with its young, and two rowing ships on the sea.

We come into this impressive place, so little changed since the 13th century, by its original doorways, both richly moulded, one of them with seven shafts on each side, making a beautiful arch.

The traveller who finds himself a mile or so away at Friday Bridge may be fortunate enough to see a storied relic of Oliver Cromwell preserved at Needham Hall. It is an oak table from the old house of that name which stood here, and it is said that Cromwell slept on the table, so that he should be no better lodged than his soldiers.

Mox Nox

ELSWORTH. It stands on a rock which is known to all geologists, a hard limestone full of the fossils of the sea. It has two old houses of Elizabethan days, the Guild House with its timber porch and the manor with its orange walls and gables, giving a touch of colour to the village green. A stream spanned by rough timber bridges winds among the cottages, and in flood time rises so near to one of them that it is called Noah's Ark.

The fine church has still something of the dignity its builders gave it 600 years ago. The pinnacled tower is low but its high arch opens into a lofty nave in which ancient wood figures of eleven apostles hold up the roof. The chancel has a piscina and three stone seats which are among the best in the county, the seats having trefoiled arches and the piscina two tiny shelves. The lovely 15th century stalls have foliage poppyheads and backs of rich linenfold, and they are curious for having little lockers under the book-rests, some still with their old doors, hinges, and locks. There are two Jacobean chairs and some old benches, ancient altar rails and an old chest, and a pulpit which was new 500 years ago. In the sanctuary is an 18th century brass almsdish on which two men are shown carrying a bunch of grapes.

The rare distinction of the church is its register, dating from 1528 and one of the three earliest known, the others being at Carburton and Perlethorpe in Notts. The date from which registers were kept by order of Thomas Cromwell was 1538, so that these three are ten years older than the oldest official record.

A fine wheel cross adorns the chancel gable, and on the sunny wall is a dial with the warning Mox Nox, *Soon the night will come.*

Oliver's Sister Jane

ELTISLEY. The charm of the village is its rare green like a velvet lawn, round which cluster the church, the thatched cottages, and (when the cricketers come out of their fine thatched pavilion) nearly all the village folk. There is shade for the onlookers under the chestnuts at three corners, and a row of limes in memory of six men who were missing when cricket began again after the war. There are two fine timbered houses, one the old rectory, and the other the birthplace of Major-General Disbrowe, who married Oliver Cromwell's sister Jane in the church next door in 1636. We called on our way home from here to see two descendants of Jane Cromwell still living in a village of Huntingdonshire.

It is a small stone church, mostly 13th century, with a 14th century spire topping the tower, and a brick chancel which fortunately keeps the old arch. The pillars of the arcades with their leafy capitals are 700 years old, and there are two stone figures from the Middle Ages on a canopied tomb in the chapel. The knight has his hand on his sword but his feet are gone and his lady is headless. The plain old font has a pointed Jacobean cover carved with thistles.

The church's unique dedication links John the Baptist with the Saxon saint Pandiana, daughter of an Irish king who fled from her lovers to Eltisley's nunnery. The nunnery was removed to Huntingdonshire in the Conqueror's day, leaving here only the outline of its moat among the pools, and in the 14th century the saint's body was carried from beside the spring still called St Pandiana's Well and buried in the church dedicated to her. St Wendreda, another obscure Saxon saint, whom we come upon again at March, is also said to have been buried in this church.

The Crowning Glory of the Fens

ELY. It is far from the world's ignoble strife, a quiet country town with not 10,000 people in it, an isle of refuge in the Fens in ages past, and today a magnet drawing to itself all who love beautiful things. To walk about this little city and to come upon its cathedral splendour is to be stirred with a new sense of the spiritual and intellectual enrichment of our English heritage.

It stands on almost the highest part of Fenland, the northern capital of Cambridgeshire, bounded on the south by the River Ouse. In the days when its willowy marshes made the Isle of Ely a place of refuge against invaders, it was here that the Saxons made their last stand against the Conqueror. Every English boy knows Charles Kingsley's romance of Hereward the Wake, the thrilling story of the last resistance to the Normans who were to transform our country and set it on the way to greatness. In 1069 and again the next year the siege of the Isle was resisted, and the long struggle ended only in 1071 with the Abbot's promise of obedience if the Normans would spare the city and the church.

Today the marshes have become green pastures, orchards, and cornfields, and where nothing but reeds and sedge held back the sea in olden days long banks are raised as barriers against the floods. In the midst of it all, like a jewel above the plain, rise the unique cathedral towers of medieval England, crowning a shrine which takes us back more than 1200 years, to the 7th century when Etheldreda founded a monastery here. She had married a rich noble who gave her the Isle of Ely as a marriage settlement. It is said that it is called Ely from the number of eels caught in the Fens, and certainly for many years tithes were paid in eels at Ely. Widowed and orphaned a few years after her marriage, Etheldreda devoted herself to good works, and left the management of her estate to her steward Ovin. It is one of the thrills that come to us as we walk down Ely's marvellous nave to see the broken shaft of a cross which is believed to have been set up to Etheldreda's steward, for on the base is inscribed in Latin: Grant, O God, to Ovin Thy Light and rest. The cross was used for a time at Haddenham as a mounting-block.

After a few years of widowhood Etheldreda was persuaded to marry Egfrid, who became king in 670, but after a few years she was moved to obtain his consent to leave his court to live a holy life, and in 673 she founded a monastery for monks and nuns, endowing it with all the riches of the Isle of Ely, so investing the bishopric with the peculiar power it possessed in later days. When her time came she was buried as she desired, in the graveyard of the church she had built. Somewhere in this dust she lies, and it is a strange thing to reflect upon that, though we know it not, her name comes to our lips a thousand times. One form of it was Awdrey, and an annual fair granted 800 years ago was known as St Awdrey's Fair, its sale of showy laces and gay toys giving rise to one of our familiar words, tawdry. It would do us no harm if, when we talk of tawdry things, we let our mind run back to that Awdrey who began the story of Ely and its glory.

It is recorded that Ely repulsed the first attack of the Danes, but in 870 they returned, stripped the monastery of its riches, and set fire to it. It was set up again for monks only, and the last Saxon abbot (Thurstan) was appointed by Harold. The Norman abbots recovered the old rights, and it was one of these, Simeon, who began the foundation of the cathedral as we know it at the end of the 11th century. The building went on after him, and in 1107 the Norman church was complete with transept, choir, central tower, and the east end of the nave.

In the heyday of their time the bishops of Ely had their town house at Ely Place in Holborn, which comes into Shakespeare, who makes the Duke of Gloucester ask my lord of Ely for some strawberries from his garden. The strawberries are gone, but Etheldreda's chapel remains, a stone's throw from the never-ceasing traffic of Holborn, the only pre-Reformation church in London which has been restored to Rome. From the curious little house in the middle of the road a man emerges every night to shut the iron gates of Ely Place, sounding curfew at ten, assuring the people in their beds at midnight that all is well, and opening the gates at five in the morning.

Rising like a mighty cross in the bosom of the Fens, the magnificent pile of Ely Cathedral is a superb sight for miles. It can be seen from the tower of Peterborough 35 miles away. It rises like a beacon from the plain, dominating the little town where the past still lives.

Ely   Bishop Alcock's Chapel

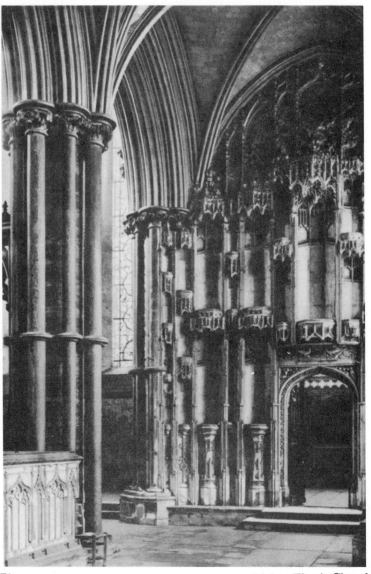

Ely
Bishop West's Chapel

The floor of the cathedral covers an area of 46,000 square feet, with a length from east to west of 537 feet, transepts 190 feet apart, a nave 208 feet long and half as high, and turrets on the western tower climbing to 215 feet above the street. In plan it is simple, in aspect and detail it is magnificent. The Norman nave has 12 bays with triforium and clerestory, and side aisles with vaulted roofs. The western tower was set up between two transepts, one of which has fallen, while the other remains. The west porch, known as the Galilee, was finished about Magna Carta time, the Norman transepts embrace some of Abbot Simeon's building; the eastern half consists of the 13th century presbytery of six bays and the 14th century choir of three bays, with their continuous aisles ending in superb chapels of the 15th and 16th centuries. Centred in it all is the glorious 14th century Octagon, and detached from the north side of the choir is the 14th century lady chapel.

It has changed, like all our ancient buildings, from century to century, the triforium being raised, flying buttresses rebuilt, Norman windows replaced and medieval windows inserted in the great transepts, a curious one under the south gable being short and wide and having seven lights. The falling of a corner in the north transept in 1699 was Christopher Wren's opportunity for laying his unmistakable touch on the cathedral where his Uncle Matthew was bishop nearly 30 years.

We come into the cathedral by the beautiful Galilee porch, 45 feet long and two storeys high, remarkable for its perfection of style from so early a time as 1200. Its north and south walls outside have four tiers of diminishing arcading, and on each side of the great entrance are four tiers of double niches. The interior is richer still, its vaulted roof springing from walls with double arcading and stone seats. Of the two doorways, like two great windows, all that can be said is that the inner one is even more magnificent than the other, with rows of dainty carving resting on shafts with curling foliage, though its original tracery has been replaced by an oval window.

The porch brings us into the tower, a marvellous construction of tier upon tier of windows outside and in, the light shining on a representation of the Creation painted on the ceiling; it shows the right hand symbolising the Creator, Our Lord holding a globe, the dove, sun, moon, and stars, and angels bearing scrolls. Crowning the older part of the tower is an embattled octagon 500 years old, supported by flying buttresses from the turrets.

It was probably the pressure of this great tower that brought about the collapse of the northern arm of the western transept. It was a tragedy indeed that it should go, for the southern arm which still stands is one of the most spectacular pieces of Norman work in England. The great tower inside has nearly 100 Norman arches, but this western transept, known as St Catharine's Chapel, has nearly twice as many and is a wondrous sight. It has two great arches of three orders, with three rows of carving on each. The walls of the transept rise in stages, one stage with two tiers of arcading, the next stage with great arches enclosing smaller ones; the upper stage with low arches and carved capitals. In the apse of the little chapel, to which one of the two huge arches leads are two windows deeply set and carved all round, a delight to see. The chapel was rebuilt on its old foundations last century, and has a simple vaulted roof with a window over the altar of Our Lord on the Cross, crowned and in a robe of red and gold.

It is impossible not to be impressed by the hundreds of arches, single and interlacing, which make these walls such a marvellous spectacle. They are on single and clustered shafts, and crowd the great walls everywhere. Outside is the same rich mass of craftsmanship with elaborate stringcourses, rows of heads and humans and grotesques, and two fine octagonal towers 120 feet high, each with a ring of open lancets at the top. Inside and out we are held spellbound by this wonderful corner of Ely.

We come back to the tower, the floor of which is a maze designed by Sir Gilbert Scott, and here we stand enchanted by the majestic Norman nave. It is simplicity itself, the simplicity that nothing can surpass. Beyond it we see the screen, the choir, the presbytery, the long vista ending in the east windows hundreds of feet away, shining like jewels, and above us is the richly painted roof; but it is this marvellous avenue of Norman arches that holds the eye. It was begun 850 years ago and finished after about two generations, and it shares with Peterborough Cathedral the fame of being the finest nave of its time. So massive are the piers of the main arcades that as we look along the nave the aisles are shut out, and as the space narrows in the distance the great piers (24 of them) rise like sheer walls of stone with golden tints, ribbed with the glorious arcading of their three storeys. Touched by the rainbow light from the windows, the great floor of the nave is at times like strips of patterned carpet, and crowning it all is the ceiling of rich but delicate colouring—red, blue, green, and gold.

These 24 great piers have clustered mouldings round them, square and round, and everywhere the distinctive feature is the simplicity and purity of style. The massive lower arches rise to the triforium, where the arches become double, supporting the clerestory with three arches in each bay, so that in each bay of the nave the arches rise for 80 feet, in tiers of one, two, three, 144 arches in the 24 bays, those at the base on massive piers, the smaller ones on tall and slender shafts which carry the eye to the painted roof, with a picture for each bay painted on wood. The western half of the roof is the work of Mr Henry S. L'Estrange, the rest is the work of Mr Gambier Parry, who carried on the work when Mr L'Estrange died in 1861. The twelve subjects, beginning at the west end, are the Creation, the Fall, the Sacrifice of Noah, the Sacrifice of Isaac, Jacob's Dream, Jesse, David, the Annunciation, the Nativity, the Adoration of the Shepherds and Magi, Our Lord in Glory: there are patriarchs and prophets who told of the promised Messiah, and a border of medallions in which are heads representing the ancestors of Our Lord according to St Luke's Gospel. The aisles of the nave have roofs of simple vaulting and walls enriched with Norman arcading.

We pass from the nave into the Norman transepts. The chief remains of Abbot Simeon's 11th century work is in the lower portion of the transept walls, which have the simple grandeur of the nave in the arcading of their three storeys. Both have end galleries resting on round arches, both have east and west aisles, both have medieval roofs gaily coloured in the old style, with a captivating collection of painted angels looking down, 48 of them. The west aisle of the south transept is walled off as a vestry; the eastern aisle is the library. In the middle of the floor of this transept are old tiles laid in cart-wheel fashion. The east aisle of the north transept is divided into chapels. St Edmund's chapel, with its wall-painting showing the bowmen shooting the king, has a restored 14th century screen with delicate tracery in the bays; and St George's, entered by a modern screen with three crowns in a border of vine, is a memorial to the men of Cambridgeshire who fell in the Great War, over 5000 names being written on the panelled walls. Here hangs a flag of the Cambridge Regiment which was carried at Alma, Inkerman, and Sebastopol. Except for the later windows in the ground storey, the east wall of this north transept is the best example of the ancient church extant, the triforium and clerestory being here in their original condition. The furnishings of the memorial chapel are by Sir Guy Dawber.

Sharing with the Galilee porch in the 13th century additions to the cathedral is the presbytery of six bays, added to the choir. At its consecration in 1252 there were present Henry the Third, Prince Edward, and many prelates and nobles. Except for the alterations to its windows it stands today as they saw it, arresting in the beauty of the chaste enrichment of its three storeys. There are clusters of marble shafts with capitals of lovely foliage; the trefoiled arches of the triforium and the spandrels of the arcading are tipped with leaves; and magnificent foliage corbels bear up the marble vaulting shafts.

The three bays of the choir have the richness of carving and elaboration of detail expected from their time, both in the three tiers of traceried arcading and the vaulting of the roof, with about 80 golden bosses. The east window has effective glass in its lancets (Ely has very little glass). The choir is only part of the magnificent building undertaken at Ely in the first half of the 14th century, which included also the incomparable Octagon, the lady chapel and Prior Crauden's Chapel (detached from the rest). The grandeur this work attained was made possible by the zeal of the Three Friends, friends of each other and of their cathedral, whose efforts for nearly 20 years brought into being what has been described as "the noblest series of works of the 14th century, or perhaps of any period of medieval building, in England." The three were John de Hotham, Edward the Third's chaplain and Bishop of Ely; John de Crauden, prior from 1321 to 1341; and Alan de Walsingham, sacrist in Crauden's day and prior after him. It was a disaster which gave them their greatest chance, and well they used it.

The catastrophe which became the opportunity of the Three Friends was the falling of the square central tower of the Normans, destroying as it fell the bays of the Norman choir and the nearest bays of the great transepts and the nave, so that the transepts have now only three bays each instead of four, and the nave 12 instead of 13.

The great transformation that followed the fall of the tower was the creation of Ely's crowning glory, the Octagon. No other cathedral has anything like it inside or out. When the rubbish was cleared away the idea came to Walsingham to utilise the whole of the space that had been opened up (three times the space of the original crossing) for what is generally accepted as the finest lantern in the world. It is like a poem in wood and stone, a stone octagon with a timber lantern covered outside with lead. The concrete foundations had been laid and the eight stone piers had been set up when the truth dawned upon Walsingham's mind that the space to be roofed was too vast for a stone vault. The span is 74 feet. He decided, therefore, to build a timber lantern. He built it, the only Gothic dome in the world, and in this case necessity was not only the mother of invention but of beauty too. The construction of this wonderful thing is a marvel of engineering. As we see it today, rising above the great mass of the cathedral, it is Alan de Walsingham's intention brought to its fulfilment, for in the 20 years he was building he did not complete his design for the enrichment of the stonework. Its beautiful wreath of turrets and pinnacles, rising above a lacy parapet and joined to the lantern by flying buttresses, is part of the restoration in memory of Dean Peacock, who inspired the restoration of the cathedral last century; we see him in the painted ceiling of the nave, where the face of Isaiah is his.

Outside the Octagon rests on the crossing like a beautiful two-tiered crown; inside it is as one conception, the lantern seemingly poised on the timber vaulting, which spreads like a wreath of glorious palms above great stone arches and windows, and shines with colour and gold. It is a unique experience to sit in this massive place, in this forest of majestic columns, with probably 1000 Norman arches all about us, and to look up into this dome of light and colour, the light from 32 windows, the colour from 32 painted panels, all resting on eight great fans as if to hold this exquisite thing from floating into the sky.

It is said that all England was explored for the eight oaks that were to form the eight corners of the Octagon, and that they were found at last at Chicksands in Bedfordshire. They must have been growing in Alfred's England, for they had to be 63 feet long and free from any fault as the vital part of this vast structure. A big system of timber-work is hidden from our sight, but these oak trunks we see in all their pride and glory. The rich painting of all this timber work is chiefly the work of Mr Gambier Parry, who finished the roof of the nave. On the traceried panels below the eight windows of the lantern are minstrel angels and angels with Passion symbols; the ceiling is like an eight-pointed star, and has the original oak bosses showing our Lord with his hand in blessing. The very top of the lantern, once a bell chamber, is seen only outside.

The eight sides of the lantern are equal in width, and none are parallel with those of the stone octagon below, which has four long sides with great arches opening to the four arms of the cross (nave, choir, and transepts) and four short sides with smaller arches opening to the aisles. Over the small arches are modern sculptures of the apostles seated under canopies, and the hoods of these arches are adorned with heads, two of them grotesque but the other six said to represent Edward the Third and his Queen Philippa, Prior Crauden and Bishop Hotham, Walsingham, and perhaps his master mason. Fascinating are the great corbels supporting canopied niches on the slender vaulting shafts, for in their rich carving we read the chief events in Etheldreda's story—her marriage to Egfrid, her taking the veil, the flood which forced Egfrid back from his pursuit of her, her staff taking root and bearing leaves while she slept, her installation as abbess of Ely, her death and burial, her liberation of a captive from prison, and her translation. The remains of Etheldreda and two other abbesses were removed into the Norman choir in 1106, and later into the presbytery, where the position of Etheldreda's shrine at that time is marked by a boss in the roof showing the Coronation of the Madonna; another boss here shows Etheldreda wearing a crown and holding a staff and a book, and in a third we see her with two keys and a model of her church.

We come now to the chapels of this great place. We have looked at St Catharine's at the west end, at St Edmund's and St George's, and there remain the lady chapel and the two elegant eastern chapels of Bishop West and Bishop Alcock.

The lady chapel is detached and is reached by a passage from the north-west transept. It is a wondrous place; a great lantern of light, a marvellous mass of carving, 100 feet long and 60 feet high, the width giving it what is said to be the widest single span of any English church, 46 feet. It must seem almost a miracle of building, for even with this great span the walls are half glass, yet they carry a stone vaulting. There are five four-light windows with beautiful tracery in each side wall, and east and west windows of seven and eight lights. The shallow vault, springing from the tops of canopies between the windows, has hundreds of coloured bosses and painted roses, among the bosses being flowers and tracery, a Crucifixion, Adam and Eve, Mary and Elizabeth, the Ascension, and the crowning of the Madonna.

The canopies are an amazing spectacle, running right round the walls with stone seats under them, an almost incredible array of tabernacle work with canopied niches and statuary, delicately enriched with tracery, cusps, and diaper work, making the interior like a casket of exquisite sculpture. It is a tragedy that so much has been battered by stupid men in ages past. The architect Pugin is said to have wept as he looked upon its mutilation, and to have said that it would cost £100,000 to restore it to its original glory, even if men could be found to do the work. We found the men doing it, and those who come in a little while will find this chapel a dream of beauty once again. The carving in the spandrels above the projecting canopies must once have looked something like the famous spandrels in the chapter house at Wells; they tell the story of the Madonna according to scripture and legend. For many generations the lady chapel was a parish church, but it is now back with the cathedral and one of its chief glories. In the wall of the north choir aisle is a battered but charming medieval doorway, which led to the passage linking the cathedral with the chapel.

Worthy of their place among the richest chapels in the land are the two at the end of the eastern aisles, each built by a bishop to be his own last resting-place. On the north is that of Bishop Alcock, founder of Jesus College, Cambridge, and builder of the Palace at Ely. Built in 1488, the chapel is remarkable for being of chalk, the hard local chalk called clunch; it is one of the most richly carved and best preserved chalk buildings in England. It is entered by two doorways, and has in its windows old glass showing the bishop's device of a cock on a globe. It is an astonishing sight with its mass of niches and canopies and pinnacles, wreathing the walls like the tops of a forest of pines, crowned by a roof of fan-vaulting with a great pendant. The bishop's battered figure lies on a handsome tomb, enriched with cocks in a border of vine, and bands of quatre-foils and passion flowers. The figure and most of the tomb are in the curious little chantry in the north side, entered by a charming doorway. We should note the mermaid at the end of the doorway moulding on the south.

Bishop West's, the companion chapel in the south aisle, is a lovely example of 16th century work. There is classical scrollwork over the doorway, and in the vault, with its rich panels, are two pendant bosses of angels holding shields. Here the sculpture is of the utmost delicacy, and the 25 canopies on the front, so dainty that they look like frills of lace as we approach, are only the foretaste of the loveliness within, where are over 100 canopies with roofs all differently carved. The iron gates through which we enter are as old as the chapel, wrought at the top into roses and leaves. Above the bishop's tomb were placed in the 18th century the relics of seven early benefactors, which had been moved several times since being buried in the Saxon church. They were Ednoth, Elfgar, Alfwyn, Osmond, and Athelstan, all of the 11th century, and Brihtnoth of 991, earldorman of the East-Saxons, who fell in battle against the Danes. A man of great wealth Brihtnoth gave the monastery certain manors in return for hospitality given to him and his soldiers, with the promise of still more if the abbot would see that, if he were killed in battle, his body should be buried at Ely. The Danes took away his head but the monks recovered his body and laid it in the church. Others sleeping in this chapel are Bishop Sparke and Bishop Keene (18th century), and Bishop Woodford of 1885, a rich brass cross marking his grave. On his fine canopied tomb in the north aisle of the nave is his figure in cope and mitre; he has his pastoral staff, and angels at his head; on the front of the tomb are angels holding shields, and on the wall under the canopy is a sculpture of the Crucifixion. On the north wall of Bishop West's chapel lies the headless figure of Cardinal Luxembourg, made Bishop of Ely by Henry the Sixth; the canopy work above him is almost perfect. The cardinal had been archbishop of Rouen before he came to Ely and must have known Joan of Arc; he may have seen her burned in the marketplace.

Among the memorials between the two eastern chapels are the tomb of Canon Hodge Mill of 1853, a fine copper figure with students

Ely   **The Octagon**

Ely   The Choir

Ely   **The Nave**

Ely   The Prior's Doorway

at his feet; a battered headless figure; a Norman gravestone with
the Archangel Michael holding in his robe a figure with a pastoral
staff beside it; and an interesting mosaic over the grave of Bishop
Allen of 1845, whose tomb in the south aisle of the choir has his
figure reclining in robes. The mosaic is interesting because it is
made of material left over from the building of Napoleon's tomb in
Paris. On a tomb under the arch north of the altar lies the fine but
battered figure of Bishop Northwold, builder of the presbytery,
who died in 1254. Angels with censers are at his head, and on the
sides of the canopy are figures of Etheldreda, a crowned abbess,
a nun, a king, an abbot, and a monk. At his feet are a lion and a
dragon, and a relief of the martyrdom of St Edmund. By the tomb is
what seems to be the end of a great stone seat, the arm-rest carved
into an animal holding a man's head; it represents the wolf which is
said to have guarded the head of the king after his shooting and
beheading by the Danes.

In one of the next three bays of the presbytery we come upon the
14th century base of Etheldreda's silver shrine, some of which is said
to have been used to pay the fine imposed on a bishop for supporting
King Stephen against Queen Maud. In the next of these three bays
is the mitred figure of Bishop Kilkenny, traveller and statesman,
who died in Spain in 1256 while on embassy for Henry the Third,
his heart only being buried here; and in the third bay is the splendid
tomb of Bishop Redman of 1505, who lies, a mitred figure, under a
lovely canopy with a vaulted roof. By the tomb is the beautiful
stone stairway to the organ. Under the four arches of the south
side of the presbytery are four other tombs. That of Bishop William
of Louth, builder of the 13th century Ely Chapel in Holborn, has a
splendid canopy with gable and pinnacles. Bishop Barnet's tomb of
1373 has a plain top and sides with quatrefoils. The two wives of
John Tiptoft, Earl of Worcester, lie under a rich canopy with a
traceried roof; the earl was beheaded in 1470 and he does not stain
the cathedral with his presence. As Constable of England he was
guilty of great cruelties, and was known as the Butcher of England;
for his learning (gathered abroad) he was called the Pilgrim Scholar.
Bishop Hotham's tomb has lost the figure which once lay on it; a
gravestone in the middle of his choir marks his resting-place, and
by it is that of Prior Crauden.

Three monuments along the south wall of the presbytery aisle are the tomb of the Bishop Heton of 1609, his marble figure with a skull cap and a rich cope with disciples in the border; the mitred figure of Bishop Peter Gunning of 1684, reclining in elaborate robes; and Canon Selwyn's marble figure in a wall recess. He died in 1875. One or two fine brass portraits in the floor of this aisle show Dean Tyndall of 1614, in skull cap and academic gown; the other is Bishop Goodrich, a zealous reformer who lies in his robes and mitre, his staff in one hand and in the other a book from which hangs the Great Seal, for he was Henry the Eighth's Lord Chancellor.

In the south aisle of the choir is a monument with weeping cherubs to Bishop Moore, a great scholar whose library was bought by George the First for Cambridge; a monument with the bust of Bishop Butts of 1748; Robert Steward of 1570, reclining in armour under a canopy; Sir Mark Steward of 1603; a bulky coloured figure in armour, holding a gauntlet on his chest; a modern tablet to Robert Steward de Welles of 1557, last prior and first dean; an inscription to William Lynne, whose widow married Robert Cromwell and became mother of Oliver; and a bronze portrait plaque of Harvey Goodwin of 1891, Bishop of Carlisle. Another plaque has the portraits of Michael Glazebrook and his wife; he was canon here for 20 years and they died within a fortnight of each other in 1926.

Entering the north aisle from behind the altar we pass over the stone of Bishop Gray of 1478, his brass gone. In the aisle is a wall-monument to Bishop Mawson of 1770, a benefactor of the cathedral and of the countryside. Here, too, in the floor is the brass portrait of George Basevi, showing him under a canopy and holding a plan; he was an architect, and was visiting the cathedral during restoration in 1845 when he fell from the scaffolding in the western tower and was killed. In his canopied memorial of 1636 Dean Henry Caesar kneels at a desk. Two vergers who served the cathedral for 60 and 58 years of last century have inscriptions.

Here among so much of his work sleeps Alan de Walsingham, who is thought to have died in 1364. He lies probably under the great flat stone just west of his wonderful Octagon. The brass which has gone from the stone showed a mitred figure with a staff. This Flower of Craftsmen, as he is called in the existing record of his epitaph, is said to have designed the wonderful stalls which stand mostly as in his day, except for the modern Belgian carvings under the lovely old canopies. These modern scenes show, on the north side, the Life of Our Lord from the Annunciation to the Ascension; and on the south side Old Testament scenes, among them the creation of Eve and scenes in the Garden of Eden, Moses with the serpent and striking the rock, the spies returning with the bunches of grapes, the Ark, and Jonah cast up by the whale. All but five of the stalls on each side are modern, but their misereres are worthy of taking their place among the superb company which have been here for six hundred years.

The old ones are 59 in number, an astonishing collection considered to be the finest of their time, every one beautifully carved in three sections with figures and scenes in high relief, sometimes with exquisite foliage as well. We see a bear in a tree, a demon with two women, men holding up the seats, Adam and Eve cast out of the Garden, a king and a queen resting, men playing dice, two women quarrelling, a huntsman with a dog and a hare; a huntsman with horn and hounds, a deer, and a horse between them; an old man and wife, grinding corn in a handmill; Samson fighting a lion. A splendid one shows two men holding a horse's head and tail while a third attends to its foot. Another has Salome dancing at Herod's birthday feast, the beheading of John the Baptist, and the bringing of his head on a charger. At one side of a huntsman thrown from his stumbling horse are the hounds and deer, at the other side is a praying figure in a chapel. A modern stall on the south side has an old miserere showing the two bowmen, and St Giles with the hind they have shot.

Sir Gilbert Scott's oak screen is rich with tracery and has saints in niches. The seats of the bishop and the dean on its eastern side are guarded by saints on pedestals and their canopies with figures of saints rise like tall spires. Scott also designed the alabaster reredos, set in a stone screen with traceried arcading. In the wealth of sculpture in the reredos are twisted pillars glinting with polished stones, statuettes crowning the pinnacles, and canopied scenes of the Last Days in Jerusalem. A splendid old oak chest is covered with studded iron bands. There are dainty iron screens to the choir aisles, one enriched with wheat and poppies and vine. Hanging in a case is a handsome velvet cope, richly embroidered with lilies and a border of saints, which may be 15th century. An exquisitely embroidered banner shows Etheldreda with her staff and a book. A window in the north choir aisle has a fine medley of old glass, with heads and figures here and there. A recent loan to the cathedral is the splendid tapestry hanging on a wall of the tower; it shows the Annunciation and the Nativity, and was being made in Rouen at the time the small Octagon was being set on the top of the west tower.

Captivating as is the interior of this great place, we walk outside it, in and out of all its ancient ways, with growing wonder. We are not surprised to find ourselves in a small passage with ten Norman arches on the front of the houses, or looking at the walls of the grammar school with the stamp of the Saxon on them, or climbing up the little stone stairway into Prior Crauden's chapel, with medieval tiles set in its floor. It is wonder everywhere at Ely, and indoors and out is an equal delight. The western facade has more Norman arches creeping up it than we can count, and the eastern facade has few rivals as an example of this time. Especially fine is the grouping of the lancets in tiers of four, five, and three, the storeys divided by stringcourses and adorned with quatrefoils. On each side of the gabled end are buttresses with niches; the buttresses of the aisles, and the dainty arcaded turret, have leafy tops like spires. The lady chapel comes into the lovely north-west view of the Octagon, its west wall adorned with a lacy parapet and a fine array of canopied niches round the great west window. Over the east window are more niches, and the niched buttresses have leafy pinnacles climbing above the roof. It is the work of Walsingham that we are looking at, begun in 1321 and completed by John of Wisbech in 1349.

We may leave the cathedral by what is known as the Monk's Doorway in the south aisle, and we find ourselves in a corner of the cloister. The doorway itself (now the south entrance of the cathedral) has a trefoiled inner arch, and in its rich display of ornament are dragons, flowers, kneeling monks and trailing leaves. By the doorway hangs a fragment of oak window tracery and an oak door frame from Prior Crauden's study. In this south wall of the cathedral is another doorway by which in olden days the monks came in; it is called the Prior's Doorway, and has an amazing mass of carving in high relief. Its Norman arch has four depths of carving, the four orders resting on one round shaft, one twisted shaft, and two square pillars richly carved. The inner pillars have trailing leaves and are shaped at the top into faces, the outer ones are carved with rings in which are curious devices and figures, including the signs of the zodiac, a man drinking, two figures drinking from one cup, a woman mixing wine and oil, an ape fanning himself and another juggling, and two people in a boat rowing against one another. In the tympanum of this fine doorway Christ sits with one hand raised in blessing and the other holding a book, and round the tympanum is a roll of intricate spiral carving of foliage which continues below the capitals, running into the shafts on each side.

We find ourselves now in the midst of a captivating group of buildings which are for the most part monastic, and have been restored for the clergy and the grammar school. Their jumble of old roofs with mossy tiles are a charming foreground for a view of the cathedral from the park. In some of the walls of the school buildings is the long and short work of the Saxons, and there are traces of six Saxon windows.

A gem of six centuries ago among all these ancient buildings is the little chapel of Prior Crauden, 30 feet long and half as wide. It is a gabled building of two storeys, so beautifully restored that we can hardly believe it was once used as a dwelling. The lower storey which has suffered the indignity of being a coal cellar, has been restored for the use of the school; it has a low stone vaulted roof, and a tiny east window with St Michael in its glass. A newel stairway climbs outside to the lovely chapel, lighted by big windows with tracery it would be hard to surpass: it is certainly the finest in Ely There are two tall windows in each side wall. In the tracery of the west window is a big shamrock leaf, and the east window has a quatrefoil in a frame of trefoils. The figures in the lower part of the east window are said to have come from Cologne Cathedral. The modern oak vault springs from clusters of shafts with fine foliage capitals. There are stone seats round the walls, which are richly arcaded and have lovely canopies reaching the roof. In the fine sculpture are hoods of vine trail, tiny faces peeping from buttresses and pinnacles, and little men crouching. A very rare treasure is the floor of this place, for it is made up of medieval tiles, and in the old tiling on the platform of the altar is a crude mosaic with big lions and small lions, stags, and flowers, and a remarkable panel of the Fall of Man—the serpent coiled round the trunk of a tree, its human face coming from the branches and whispering to Eve, who is offering the apple to Adam. It is 14th century.

The chapel serves now as the chapel of the grammar school, which is of rare interest because it goes back in its beginning to the monastic school in which Edward the Confessor received his early education. It was refounded by Henry the Eighth in 1543, and occupies the fine range of buildings on the east side of the street called the Gallery. Of uncertain origin, this delightful range has in it Norman walling, medieval windows, and later gables, and ends on the south at the Ely Porta, which the school shares now with the verger. This fine gatehouse stands almost as when it was the principal entrance to the abbey, sturdy and strong and stately with its three storeys, square corner turrets, postern, and the great archway through which we pass from the Gallery to the Park. Through the gateway is the medieval barn now used by the school as workshops and gymnasium; it has a splendid roof of original timbers, and is 68 feet long and 24 wide. By the barn is an artificial mound covered with trees and shrubs, known as Cherry Hill but said to be the site of an ancient keep built for the defence of the monastery. New buildings for the Kings' School (it is particular about its apostrophe because it has two kings in its pedigree) were built last century on the other side of the Gallery (not, alas, in harmony with the old ones). Looking across a small green to the Ely Porta is Ely Theological College, its chapel adorned outside with statues of Bishop Woodford (who founded it in 1876) and St Etheldreda.

Grouped with Prior Crauden's Chapel are the Prior's Lodge, the Deanery (which has absorbed the 13th century Guest House and has remains of the refectory and the Norman kitchen in its grounds), and the Fair Hall, which was used for entertainment and is now the house of the headmaster. The chapter house is gone, but east of the cloister site are interesting remains of the infirmary buildings, now for the most part absorbed into houses for the clergy. The hall and the chapel, over 50 yards long, are a roofless space, divided by an archway. The arcades of the hall with arches of zigzag and pillars with carved capitals, are seen in the walling on each side. The fine north arcade of the chapel is still to be seen, with the arch which led to the chancel. West of the infirmary is part of the wall of its cloister, showing the pointed arcading of a little later time. It is known as the Dark Cloister.

On the north side of the cathedral is an entrance to the close from High Street, known as the Sacrist's Gate. Over the entrance is the muniment room; the eastern portion is for the choristers. Another entrance from High Street is the archway of an old house, which has a shield with three crowns on an oak beam. This is Steepil Gate.

Looking across the Gallery to the cathedral is the Bishop's Palace, a dignified place of diapered brick and stone. Bishop Goodrich added a gallery to John Alcock's hall and its two wings, built in the closing years of the 15th century, and Bishop Keene made improvements in the 18th century. Bishop Alcock's work is adorned with his device, angels holding shields, and a fine triple niche. In the palace is a curious painting known as the Tabula Eliensis, with pictures and names of 40 knights the Conqueror quartered on the abbey. Their names and shields, and figures of monks, are with them. With the fine trees in the high-walled garden is a magnificent plane planted three centuries ago, said to be the biggest plane tree in England.

The palace comes into one of the lovely pictures of Ely and its cathedral, seen as we stand in St Mary's Street, where the smooth lawns of Palace Green are the setting for a captivating group of buildings. Beyond the Green is the cathedral's noble west front with its soaring tower, Galilee porch, and turreted transept, and by the roadside is a timbered house which is now the vicarage, and is of historic interest because Oliver Cromwell lived here from 1636 to 1647. He was Governor of Ely, and is said to have ordered the discontinuance of the cathedral services so that the soldiers should not be incited to desecrate the building. Nearer the cathedral is another timbered house, and between them stands St Mary's church, with its spire rising above the long low roof; it is reached by a dainty avenue of almond trees across the sward. Below the vicarage are the almshouses, with gables and a tower, standing round three sides of lawn and garden.

St Mary's church, begun in 1198, has a 14th century tower and spire, and windows of all three medieval centuries, filling the interior with light, some of them shining with rich glass. The long nave arcades of seven bays have pointed 13th century arches, and tall pillars with scalloped capitals marking the passing of the Norman style. A fine doorway of this time, sheltered by the north porch, has an arch with elaborate carving of zigzag under a hood, and clustered shafts with capitals of graceful foliage. The blocked south doorway has lost its shafts after 750 years, but keeps its arch of zigzag and its leafy capitals. The old priest's seat in the chancel has a trefoiled arch and there is a fine little double piscina in the south chapel, which is entered by a low medieval arcade. The triple lancet of its east window has the Crucifixion and Our Lord in Glory, St Edmund and his martyrdom, and St Etheldreda with a fine picture of the cathedral. The east window of the chancel has glass showing the Nativity and the Shepherds. Another window has Our Lord Risen, with blue-winged angels; and one in memory of the men who fell in the Great War has figures of St George, the Archangel Michael, and Earldor-man Brihtnoth as a warrior. St George is fighting the dragon with the princess looking on. Below Brihtnoth is a fine picture of the boat bringing his body to Ely, rowed by nuns, candles burning by his bier. A big broken font is in the churchyard, and on a buttress of the tower is a tablet reminding us of the Ely riots, with the names of five men executed in June 1816 "for divers robberies."

Perhaps we should think much more of St Mary's if it were not in the shadow of Ely Cathedral; it would be a superb building indeed which could endure such rivalry. A rare town it would be, also, which could compare with this, a gem in England's coronet.

The Old Fiddle

FEN DITTON. It is famous, for its thatched cottages and its church are on a charming slope by the river, and at Ditton Corner in June all is alive with fluttering skirts and eager eyes, for it is the Grand Stand from which to view the races on the Cam in Cambridge Eights Week.

It lies at one end of the Fleam Dyke, the great earthwork built by prehistoric Britons for defence and long used as a highway. We come into the church by a doorway 500 years old, sheltered by the old timbers of the porch in which we found a swallow building her nest—yea, the swallow hath found a house. There are old timbers in the roofs, with massive beams and kingposts sheltering the nave. We are in the presence here of our three great building centuries, for the four massive arches of the tower are 13th century, the chancel

The Rich Interior

The Marvellous Carving of the Canopies

THE LADY CHAPEL OF ELY

The Painted Roof of the Nave

Angels in Transept Roof

One of the Corbels of the Lantern

Kilkenny Monument

Carving on one of the Choir Stalls

THE RICH DETAIL OF ELY CATHEDRAL

is just 14th, and the light and lofty arcades are 15th. There are 15th century clerestory windows, and a font with winged angels from the same age. On a windowsill we found fragments of old stone carved with angels with gold wings, and hanging on a wall we found a quaint possession, the fiddle of old Jack Harvey, who used to play it here till he died at 71. Like Watts's harp in his famous picture of Hope, it has only one string left. There is also a brass tablet to Sir William Ridgeway, a familiar figure here for 45 years; his tablet is engraved with a camel loaded with two chests, and a squirrel sitting on a stump eating nuts. Under a spreading chestnut tree in the churchyard is a pathetic wooden cross from Flanders.

The Dutch Engineer

FEN DRAYTON. Here every traveller comes to see a thatched house at the corner of the village with the Dutch inscription meaning "Nothing without Labour." It is said to have been the home of a man whose life was one long tribute to this fine motto, Sir Cornelius Vermuyden. He was the Dutch engineer brought over by Charles the First to reclaim the fens, but the fenmen opposed his schemes and fought his Flemish labourers. For years they quarrelled and it came about that Oliver Cromwell, then MP for Cambridge, led the opposition. But when the Civil War was over the project was revived, the Dutchman was recalled, and 40,000 acres of waste land were reclaimed. The work has stood and was maintained and improved by John Rennie, who built the Waterloo Bridge that London has pulled down.

Far older than those days is the church, with a low tower of the 14th century, and older also is the inn, which is believed to have kept the church company through all its years. Attractive outside with its rosy walls and its roofs of thatch and tiles, it has inside one of the treasures of the county, a magnificent oak ceiling, a mass of richly moulded beams, four of immense size quartering the ceiling and meeting in a carved boss.

In the windows of the church is a jumble of old glass, a font 600 years old, heads of men and lions holding up the roof, and one of the rare 19th century brasses, on which George Shaw, a vicar, kneels with his wife. A modern window shows a woman in blue nursing a sick child. It is in memory of a girl nurse, Katherine Shaw.

Henry Cromwell's Daughter

FORDHAM. Here the River Snail turns the wheel of the water-mill on its leisured way through the fens, creeping like snail unwillingly to sea. The glory of the village is its church, which was old when our first Stuart king came to it. There is a King's Path by the river, its name explained by a record in the parish register of the day when James the First "did hunt the hare with his own hands in the fields at Fordham, and did take his meal in the fields at a bush near the King's Park."

The tower which saw the dawn of what we call our 15th century building is a landmark in this spacious countryside. It crowns a church with an impressive and lofty interior with soaring arcades of the 13th and 14th centuries, and with some Norman stones in its walls. The fine priest's doorway is 700 years old, and a group of miserere stalls carved with lions and angels on their elbows is 14th century. Old bench-ends have carved poppyheads of sunflowers, an angel blowing a trumpet, men with fiddles and flutes, and faces peeping out from leaves; and old stone corbels of queens, a king, and ordinary folk hold up the roof. There is modern painting on the chancel walls showing saints, prophets, and martyrs, and a window of David playing his harp, in memory of James Withers, who wrote poems about this countryside and was laid in this churchyard in 1892.

On two Tudor brasses are William Chesewright of 1521 with his wife in a draped headdress and a girdled gown, and there is a 15th century font. But we may think it is the porch which is the best of all Fordham's possessions, for it has something about it quite unfamiliar. A 13th century doorway brings us into it, and we find it like a crypt with a simple and beautiful stone vaulted roof of six bays, the ribs springing from two central pillars. Above this roof is a gabled chapel which for 600 years has been dedicated to St Mary; it is lit by lovely windows with beautiful tracery and is reached by an outside stairway. On one side of the chapel are modern arches opening into the church. In the porch below is a window with a medley of 14th century glass with pinnacles and leaves, and among them a small roundel in black and yellow with an archbishop thought to be Thomas Becket holding two fingers in the act of blessing.

It was in this village that Elizabeth Cromwell, the daughter of the

Protector's best son Henry, found her husband, an army officer named William Russell, who lived far beyond his means, keeping a coach and six, and covered himself with debt before he died. His widow, struggling to keep up appearances, took her children (or as many as she could of her 13) to London, where she died of smallpox through keeping the hair of two of the children who had died from it. Her daughter married a man who spent a fortune (Robert D'Aye of Soham) and came to the workhouse, Cromwells begging for bread.

Pepys Sleeps

FOWLMERE. Both fowl and mere went from it when the marsh was drained as part of Rennie's scheme, but the small ring of earthworks called Round Moats has survived from untold centuries, strong defences which prehistoric men made stronger by turning the water from a neighbouring brook into the moat.

Here is Chequers Inn, with 1675 written on the plastered walls which sheltered Pepys for a night on his way to Cambridge; and near the Round Moats is a fine flint church of 600 years ago with a lofty central tower and a needle spire. The four tower arches and the nave arcade have clustered columns, and the chancel and transepts have each a pair of rich niches. The font is also from the 14th century, and the oldest double piscina marks the change-over from Norman to English styles. A sword and two helmets are left hanging in the chancel from long ago. The 15th century provided the crude and battered chancel screen, the clerestory, the west doorway, and the splendid porch where traceried windows light a handsome carved doorway guarded by angels. Over the door which has opened and shut to generations of village folk is the cross of an ancient coffin stone. Typical of the 18th century is the draped woman with her child mourning over William Mitchell's plaque. From 1561 to that day in 1925 when Alexander Yorke fell dead in the church as he prayed, Fowlmere had but 11 rectors, John Crackanthorpe outspanning them all by his 53 years of service.

Medieval Timbers

FOXTON. It has many thatched cottages and an old flint church which had a tower added to it 500 years ago, when the nave arcades were two centuries old. From the 13th century also come the crude oval font and a beautiful east window made up of three tall lancets with deep splays, shafts carrying moulded arches, and carved hoods. There are two medieval oak screens, the one in the chancel arch having a half-timbered wall above it. The fine roofs have 15th century beams and bosses carved with flowers, animals, and people, and there are 15th century benches in the clerestoried nave. Both aisles have fine east windows 600 years old, and in one are fragments of the original glass.

Curfew—the Knell of Parting Day

FULBOURN. It has rambling leafy lanes, pleasant houses, cottages with long gardens, a farm with thatched barns, an old red manor house with a statue of William the Third in its park, a windmill working for 200 years, and a medieval church with curfew still sounding, calling to the workers among the summer flowers which turn this reclaimed fen into a bright patchwork.

For centuries two churches stood here in the same churchyard, serving two parishes, the chancel of one only three yards from the steeple of the other, but two centuries ago the tower of All Saints fell down. The remaining church has a rare dedication to St Vigor, the 6th century bishop of Bayeux which only one other church in England remembers, the little Somerset shrine at Stratton-on-the-Fosse.

As a building the church is not remarkable, but it has a fine collection of brasses. A tiny spire raises a bellcot on the top of the 13th century tower. The porch has an upper room. The chancel has a curious piscina, and a king and a bishop among its old roof bosses. Under the tower arch is a scrolled coffin lid which may be Saxon, as is the cross stone found in the nave floor here which we have seen in Cambridge Museum. The oak pulpit incorporates a lot of 14th century work, pinnacles and arches, tiny heads, and surely the earliest of our bluebells among the birds and animals in the spandrels. Some 15th century benches have fleur-de-lys poppyheads, and the solid tower screen has some old tracery.

Two chalk figures of Edward Wood of 1633 and his tiny-faced wife lie on a high tomb, he with a lion at his feet, she with a broken dog, and below them two sons and a daughter. Less pleasant is the cadaverous stone figure of John Careway, which has lain for 500 years in its winding sheet under an arch in the chancel. He was the parish priest, and four other priests have their portraits in brass. A 15th century one in miniature now kneels on a board in the aisle with his brother and his mother, while another lies on the floor, possibly Roger Grymm of 1520. A dainty 15th century lady kneels in prayer in the south aisle, and the two other priests are on the chancel floor, a small one in vestments with his hands crossed downwards being Geoffrey Bysschop of 1477, who came from the fallen church and is remembered for having given 63 acres to the villagers to help them to pay Ely's farthing tax on chimneys. The splendid lifesize figure under a canopy, in richly embroidered vestments, is William de Fulbourn, chaplain to Edward the Third.

The Great Fire

GAMLINGAY. Its row of snug red almshouses was built in the year of the Great Plague, and the old folk who first lived in them would remember seeing the great fire which destroyed most of Gamlingay in 1600, leaving so little of the prosperous town that its market was transferred to Bedfordshire. But the fire spared the fine little cross-shaped church and in it we came upon three of the great pole hooks which possibly did good service at the time, dragging the thatch off the roofs. Its walls of cobbles and richly tinted stone rise from a garden of lawns and flowerbeds, and from the tower rises a spire like a needle.

The church is mostly of the 14th and 15th centuries, and we can sit on coffin lid seats 700 years old to admire the vaulted porch, with roof bosses of three angels. The tall arcades have traces of medieval painting and a tiny peephole through a pillar. The tower arch is small but stalwart, and across the chancel arch is an oak screen with fine tracery from the last years of the 14th century. Next century came the stalls, with arm-rests of animals and birds, angels and a bishop, and misereres with a demon and odd little men. Some of the pews are 500 years old; the font may be 700. Full of life and colour is the modern glass in the east window, showing Christ surrounded by a great company of kings and queens, saints and angels. Some bits of old glass are in a south transept window.

Gamlingay is a cheerful place, its misfortunes quite forgotten, with many a pleasant walk made out of the marshy land drained by Sir William Purchase, who left this village to become Lord Mayor of London but never forgot it. Where three ways meet is a cross with the names of 65 men Gamlingay will not forget.

A Pioneer

GIRTON. Its pioneer College has carved its name throughout the world. It is little like the place that Tennyson imagined:

With prudes for proctors, dowagers for deans,
And sweet girl graduates with their golden hair.

It has far surpassed the expectation of the poet, and a host of brilliant women have passed through its halls. It was a Girton girl well known in this village who gave up the last seat in the last boat on the Egypt when that ship went down in 1922. She was Ethel Rhoda McNeile. The college is a long red brick range of hall and chapel and quarters for students. What was once a rather endearing hamlet is being drawn into Cambridge, but the view across the valley to the woods of Madingley has been saved from the destroyer.

In the medieval church of cobble stone and plaster are the brass portraits of two 15th century rectors in their robes, William Malster who became Canon of York, and William Steyn who became Canon of Lincoln. The low 15th century tower with older windows stands on a wide arch to the nave, and on two narrow ones to the aisles. Three oak doors have been opening and shutting for centuries, one by which we enter and one into the tower, and all this time the heads of a king and a monk have kept watch by the priest's doorway outside. Across the wide chancel arch is what is left of a 15th century oak screen made by the builders of the roof. The 14th century font is under the tower. A neat little Jacobean chest has diamond panels and is carved with ferns. There are a few fragments of old glass, and in the churchyard some ancient coffin stones.

Rupert Brooke's Village

GRANTCHESTER. It is Chaucer's village, and Tennyson's and Rupert Brooke's, but it is with the thought of Rupert Brooke that most of us come, for he loved it better than any place on earth. We may come to this Poets' Corner by the way beside the water meadows of the Upper Cam from Cambridge, or along the road from Trumpington, and then between the hedges comes a corner where

Dan Chaucer hears his river still
Chatter beneath a phantom mill.

The mill is a phantom now in another sense than when Rupert Brooke wrote these happy lines, for its brick and shingled walls have been burned down and it is nothing much; but we may still say with the youngest of the three poets

Oh there the chestnuts, summer through
Beside the river make for you
A tunnel of deep gloom, and sleep
Deeply above, and green and deep
The stream mysterious glides beneath.

The bridge remains as of old,

And laughs the immortal river stil
Under the mill, under the mill.

Long before Rupert Brooke came here Tennyson stood by these same waters working out the romance of the Miller's Daughter:

I loved the brimming wave that swam
Through quiet meadows round the mill
The sleepy pool above the dam
The pool beneath it never still.

So that, though the mill has vanished, it remains immortal with all those other beauties Grantchester still offers us. Through the trees we see from the bridge a wistaria-covered house where the Miller's Daughter lived, and not far from the church is the old house where Rupert Brooke revelled in honey with his tea; it was the vicarage before his day, and is a lovely peep as we come to it down the little path from the bridge. Here and in the orchard Rupert Brooke spent the happiest days of his life; even in Florence he was thirsting for the Old Vicarage with the wonderful garden, the apple blossom and the sunsets, and when he was far away in some other land he thought of this place and wrote these lines:

God, I will pack, and take a train,
And get me to England once again!
For England's the one land, I know,
Where men with Splendid Hearts may go;
And Cambridgeshire, of all England,
The Shire for Men who Understand;
And of that district I prefer
The lovely hamlet Grantchester.

Other places are what they may be

> *But Grantchester! ah, Grantchester!*
> *There's peace and holy quiet there.*
> *Ah God! to see the branches stir*
> *Across the moon at Grantchester!*
> *Say, do the elm-clumps greatly stand*
> *Still guardians of that holy land?*
> *Stands the church clock at ten to three?*
> *And is there honey still for tea?*

The village has a far more ancient tale than English poetry, for on the lowly hill on which its old houses and its old church stand have been found the bones of the mammoth and the woolly rhinoceros, and evidence has been found of Roman, Saxon, and medieval settlements. By the church an ancient elm with a stout trunk and a lusty green crown keeps company with a pretty black and white thatched house; next door to it is an inn with a hanging sign of a green man blowing his horn.

The medieval church has a small window which may be Saxon, and part of a Norman doorway, and built with them into the walls are Roman tiles and pieces of a Roman quern. The massive round bowl of the font is Norman.

It is a Tudor porch with a timbered gable which leads us inside, where candles still light the dim hours, burning in upright candelabra standing like little trees among the benches. There is a Jacobean pulpit and fragments of old glass in the windows, but it is the lovely 14th century chancel that Grantchester's people delight in; it is an exquisite possession. The walls on each side above the stringcourse have a series of windows and fine niches in brick making an arcade of niches linking up the windows with their flowing tracery. The decoration runs round the east wall where the lovely window has tracery like a great butterfly among leaves. The arch into the chancel is 15th century. A low medieval tomb carved with flowers and shields has lost its brasses. A brass inscription tells of Robert Nimmo, a naval chaplain who was drowned on his homeward voyage in 1880. In the churchyard lies the first principal of Newnham College, Anne Jemina Clough. Here also is the peace memorial with Rupert Brooke's name and 16 others, the "men with splendid hearts." This countryside that he and they loved is to be kept beautiful for ever, for with the help of the Pilgrim Trust the

Outer West Doorway

Inner West Doorway

Choir Arches

Cloister Doorway

THE SPLENDOUR OF ELY CATHEDRAL

Great Abington **Cottages in the Village**

Cambridge **Church of St Mary Magdalene**

On a Cambridgeshire Farm

Rupert Brooke's Pool on the River Granta

A Row of Cottages

The Old Church

GRANTCHESTER, RUPERT BROOKE'S VILLAGE

Cambridgeshire Preservation Society is saving the approach to Grantchester from spoilers for all time. We must hope that it will always be as he loved to see it, walking home down Trumpington Street on his way from King's College.

Rupert Brooke of England

RUPERT BROOKE perhaps more poignantly than anyone else brought home to lovers of poetry the appalling waste of war when he died on an island in the Eastern Mediterranean.

He was not killed in battle, but, having refused a place on Sir Ian Hamilton's staff (preferring to stay with his platoon) he fell ill from blood-poisoning in the trenches, followed by sunstroke, and, being moved into hospital on the Greek island of Scyros, died there on April 23, 1915, Shakespeare's day and St George's day. By his will he left the profits of his writings to be divided between three brother poets, saying that if he could set them free to write the poems they wanted his death would be a gain and not a loss. The drama of his early death was heightened by his having written immediately before the immortal lines beginning:

> *If I should die, think only this of me:*
> *That there's some corner of a foreign field*
> *That is for ever England. There shall be*
> *In that rich field a richer dust concealed;*
> *A dust whom England bore, shaped, made aware,*
> *Gave, once, her flowers to love, her ways to roam . . .*

It was a time when all hearts were heavy with the thought of countless thousands laid in foreign graves, and Rupert Brooke spoke for them all.

He was born at Rugby, where his father was a house-master. He played cricket and football for the school, wrote much poetry, and won prizes by poems on the Pyramids and the Bastille. At King's College, Cambridge, he became president of the University Fabian Society, and was deeply interested in literature, drama, and social progress. A Marlowe Society was founded by him, and he acted in a performance of Marlowe's Dr Faustus. The three things in the world for him, he said, were "to read poetry, write poetry, and best of all to live poetry."

After leaving Cambridge he lived at the Old Vicarage at Grantchester, a place that will always be associated with his name through a poem on it written when he was visiting Berlin in the spring, and longing for English sights and sounds:

> *I only know that you may lie*
> *Day long and watch the Cambridge sky,*
> *And, flower-lulled in sleepy grass,*
> *Hear the cool lapse of hours pass,*
> *Until the centuries blend and blur*
> *In Grantchester, in Grantchester.*

One term he served as a house-master at Rugby after the sudden death of his father. In 1911 he published a volume of poems and later wrote a one-act play called Lithuania which promised more ambitious successes.

His good looks and personal charm made him admired wherever he went, and aroused keen interest in him as a poet. Henry James expressed a general feeling that he was "a creature on whom the gods had smiled their brightest."

In the year before the Great War he made a leisurely journey through the United States and Canada and the Pacific Islands to New Zealand, returning the same way. His companions during part of this year of travel were fellow-poets—Lascelles Abercombie, John Drinkwater, and Wilfrid Gibson.

When the war burst upon the world in August 1914 he obtained a commission in the Royal Naval Division and took part in the expedition to Antwerp. After training in Dorset the Division was sent to Gallipoli and there the end came in a lovely bay sheltered by mountains and fragrant with the scent of sage and thyme. He lies in a lonely place where the path to the grave took the bearers two hours, though but a mile. He lies in a foreign field for ever England, his spirit with those who "died with half their music in them." Had he lived his music might have been a glorious orchestration.

By the Granta

GREAT ABINGTON. It is not great, but small. The Granta meanders past its thatched cottages on its way to become the Cam, and near by runs an overgrown Roman road and something older still, the Brent Ditch which the Bronze Age men dug for over a mile as a defence in the gap between forest and marsh.

The ancient church door in the 15th century porch opens on an interior of simple charm, with curious walls of flint and stone pierced by lancets, the most striking being a group of three framed by the arch of the 13th century tower. Completing the picture is a simple Norman font with a Jacobean cover. More rich Jacobean woodwork makes up the reading desk. The clustered pillars of the arcade are 14th century; the battered aumbry and the double piscina are a century older. Two odd features are a peephole cut through a pillar and a window splay, and the rood stairs with a small window at the top to light the now vanished loft. At the top of the 15th century east window are fragments of old glass with a tiny figure under a canopy, and near it a 17th century lawyer, Sir William Halton reclines in his armour, his feet on a cross-legged lion, his hand on a mighty sword with a steel blade.

G REAT CHISHALL. Its old windmill greets its new church tower across half a mile of trees and houses; very picturesque is the mill with its spinning sails, its timbers stout and strong after 200 years, its cap painted green, its wheels still grinding corn. The new tower looks down on a grey flint church of five centuries with a light interior in which a high arcade and a low one contrast pleasantly with cream plastered walls. The little chancel arch has an archway at one side and traces of painting over it. There are fragments of old glass in the windows, ancient beams in the modern roof, and an old font. A stone column rises above a flower garden in the churchyard with 26 names and these lines:

> *True love by Life, true love by Death is tried;*
> *Live thou for England; we for England died.*

The Old Chronicler

G REAT EVERSDEN. Here lived John Eversden in the very long ago. He was chronicler of the Benedictine abbey of Bury St Edmunds when he died, and he attended the Parliament of 1307 as proctor for his abbot. The College of Heralds in London has a list of names in his own handwriting, compiled by him in the year 1270. His village today lies between dark woods and the Roman road, set in orchards and golden meadows and the church which rose a hundred years after John Eversden was gone is sheltered by fine chestnuts in a trim churchyard. A primitive place without an aisle, but with a tower and a short lead spire, its quaint timbered porch has 1636 on the gable and roof beams that all but touch our heads. There are black old timbers in the roofs indoors, Jacobean panels in the chancel, a Jacobean pulpit with borders of flowers and stalls with faces on the arms, and under the seats are carvings of flowers and shields, a rose, and a lion's head.

Cambridgeshire Delight

GREAT SHELFORD. It gathers round a triangle of roads on the way from Cambridge to London, and, like the violet by the mossy stone, it keeps much of its beauty half hidden from the eye. One of its byways, close to a low gabled house with a plaster front, leads us to an old mill and cottages like a picture by Samuel Prout.

It is all very charming round the church, the churchyard like a wayside garden, the porch embowered in greenery and an ancient window framed with hanging blooms of wistaria. The church has been much as we see it since Thomas Patesle rebuilt it in 1307; we see him in brass in his vicar's robes on the chancel floor.

We come in by a two-storeyed porch with a splendid pelican in its fine vaulted roof, the doorway having an old niche with a modern Madonna. The tall arcades in the spacious interior have medieval clerestories over them and heads between the arches, and eight fine oak angels look down from the hammerbeams of the roof. There is a beautiful 15th century screen in the chancel arch, and the canopied Jacobean pulpit is the best we have seen in this countryside. There is another 15th century screen with dainty tracery in the north aisle, enclosing an altar in memory of a soldier killed on the Indian frontier; above the altar is a painting of two saints and a Roman soldier by the cross. The chancel stalls are finely carved with wild roses, the sedilia with grapes and acorns, and the reredos has a gleaming white sculpture of the Crucifixion with saints and angels under rich canopies. There are a few fragments of old glass, fragments of Norman carving set in a wall, and above the chancel arch a medieval painting of Doom, fading away.

On the peace memorial, among 45 names under an oak canopy, are those of two women, Gladys Jones and Ada Sillitoe.

Carpets of Gold

GREAT WILBRAHAM. Summer carpets its meadows with gold where the fens creep up to within seven miles of Cambridge. Ancient Britons left a trackway near Shardelow's Well, and close by the Romans left a trace and the Saxons buried their dead. Never for a thousand years has this countryside been without inhabitants.

The church rises above the treetops, cross-shaped, yet with a quaintly embattled tower at the west end; there are not many churches with four central arches carrying no tower. The south doorway and the arch built into a wall of the south transept are both lovely with carving 700 years old or more. By the arch is a dainty little piscina, and there is a font carved with stars and zigzags, waves and flowers, at the time when Norman art was giving way to English. The four central arches are impressive, their simple chequer pattern touched with red paint 700 years ago. The east window has three lancets framed with graceful pillared arches, and there is a narrow Norman window with a picture of Our Lord as a boy. The peace memorial is a fine painting of St George in an oak-panelled recess.

The Curious Screen

GUILDEN MORDEN. Far away as we come to it we see the massive church tower with its crown of pinnacles and its needle spire, all 15th century except for its arch, which is 14th. The rest of the church, with its stately porch and its ten clerestory windows, is generally 15th century, but the 14th is here again in the arcades, traced from its beginning in the clustered pillars to the end in the octagonal ones. A seat for a priest has been fashioned out of a windowsill in the chancel, on which eight angels look down from the hammerbeam roof. The bowl of the font is Norman, and the oldest possession of the church, but the best possessions are the two oak screens, both 600 years old. The one in the tower has delicate tracery, but the chancel screen is something unique; we do not remember anything like it, for it has two compartments like small chapels one on each side of the middle opening. The screen has needed a little patching, but it remains a fascinating piece of medieval craftsmanship, gay with green and red and white and gold. About 500 years ago an artist came along and painted two saints in its panels, Edmund in an ermine gown, and Erkenwold with his mitre and crozier as Bishop of London.

Ovin the Saxon

HADDENHAM. Here where Holy Trinity's fine tower marks the highest and most southern village in the Isle of Ely, Ovin the Saxon founded a church in 673, the same year when Queen Etheldreda, to whom he was steward, founded Ely Cathedral. When his queen no longer needed him, Ovin turned to St Chad's monastery at Lichfield, and Haddenham was left with his cross inscribed "Give, O God, to Ovin Thy light and rest." For centuries it remained here, the goal of pilgrims, but now, battered and worn, it has found sanctuary at Ely, and there we have seen the old steward's cross in his queen's cathedral.

Ovin made Haddenham holy ground, and Hereward the Wake took refuge close by, where Aldreth's cottages cluster near a windmill. Here came the Conqueror against him, to build the strategic Causeway which carried the Norman soldiers to the conquest of the Isle after a three-year struggle, a half-mythical story told in Kingsley's Hereward the Wake.

Ovin's church fell down and the medieval church which took its place at the end of the 13th century has been largely made new, the massive tower rebuilt stone by stone, with its row of little arches supporting the flower-carved parapet, its three rose windows in circles of trailing ballflowers, and a new bishop keeping watch on each side of the grand west doorway where a squirrel nibbles a nut and birds peck among the leafy capitals.

It seems strange to find clear glass without leads lighting the long church, where a medieval kingpost roof covers the nave and a 15th century arch opens into a chancel 200 years older. It has a window-sill sedilia, and a dainty peephole gives a view of the altar from the vestry. The 15th century chancel screen was patched and brought back after spending a generation in a builder's yard, and the plain font bowl in the south porch was dug up from the churchyard. The fine font used today was made 500 years ago, with angels and Tudor roses round the bowl and caricatures of lions round the base. Two griffins support the carved arches of an Elizabethan altar table in the lady chapel, and a brass of 1454 shows John Godfrey in a little cap and a belted gown, still praying for himself and his wife, whose portrait has disappeared.

The Towers of Cambridge

HARLTON. It has one of the best views in this flat plain of the Cam, with the tower of the Chapel of St John's College, the pinnacles of King's College Chapel, and all the other Cambridge colleges scattered in the town or sunning themselves by the river. The church comes from the days when the 14th century style was passing. A low embattled tower crowns the plastered walls, and the porch brings us through a fine doorway into an impressive interior with graceful arches east and west, all richly moulded and with a quaint gallery of faces between them.

Two grim little faces look down from the chancel arch into a chancel with two treasures. One is a sturdy old stone screen with cinquefoil arches, beyond which we see the delicate beauty of the east window, a niche at each side with canopies like spires. Below the window is the second treasure, a rare stone reredos with 13 dainty niches, modern saints in 12 of them. There are only two seats in the choir, one with a medieval stall worked into it, and the stone seat for the priest is formed from a windowsill. On the wall are stone brackets like bunches of ribbon. The old door is still in the rood stair doorway, hanging on delicate hinges. There is a shield of old glass and a Jacobean pulpit.

On an elaborate tomb reaching nearly to the roof, its canopy borne by two figures, is the Fryer family, Dr Thomas Fryer, bearded and grey, with a skull cap and a black gown and ruff, his wife with a gold chain, a ruff, and a hooped skirt, and their son Henry in red and gold armour. Henry died in the days of Charles Stuart, and his wife is in a black and white dress in the fashion of the time, holding a book and a handkerchief and leaning thoughtfully on a cushion.

Old Times by the Stream

HARSTON. Through its long wide street the traffic passes endlessly, for it is on the main road to Cambridge used by undergraduates in a hurry. Behind the trees and gardens or tucked away in pleasant corners are some delightful things.

The Upper Cam passes by the churchyard and the mill, and saunters with many a willow-fringed pool through Burnt Bridges. We found here a party of Boy Scouts camping by the stream, the blue smoke curling up from their fire, and we wondered if they guessed that thousands of years ago a traveller may have come upon the same scene with Beaker Folk for scouts, for here was one of the most ancient trackways in the eastern counties.

Long after these mysterious invaders the Romans had a settlement here, and in two Harston houses are remarkable collections of their pottery, and glass dug up from the fields. Dug up from the same fields in the war were coprolites, fossil evidence of ancient beasts that roamed the valley before man found it. There is a beautiful Tudor manor house by the church, perhaps on the site of a manor house of Saxon days; and at the cross roads is the 17th century Harston House, also most comely with its red brick windows. The water mill is not so old as either, but it stands where the water wheels of an older mill were turning in the 13th century.

Very charming is the corner where the church stands by the river, with the vicar's garden next door. It has stood 500 years as we see it, but the quaint stone figures supporting the roof of the nave are perhaps Norman. Some are sitting on their haunches, one has a pitcher, and one has what looks like a horn in its mouth. There are fragments of old glass, and the font and the pulpit are medieval, the pulpit one of about 100 medieval ones in wood still left in England.

A Hundred Towers in Sight

HASLINGFIELD. Like a mountain in this flat land is the little Chapel Hill, from which we have a superb panorama of the whole valley of the Cam and almost half the county. On the horizon a gleam of sunlight reveals Ely Cathedral a score of miles away, and the towers and spires of Cambridge, and of no less than 80 village churches, peep between the trees. Many of these churches were made from the white clunch quarries of this hill, known for centuries as White Hill, but now named after the famous shrine which crowned its summit, and we fancy that the prehistoric track through Burnt Mill Bridges on the Cam below was the way the medieval pilgrims came to this shrine of Our Lady of White Hill. Between the pilgrims and the prehistoric roadmakers came the Saxons, whose cemetery was near by.

But the villagers need go no farther than their own hill of Haslingfield for a view, never more delightful than when the limes about the church tower put on their spring finery. This 15th century tower is the glory of the church, and well it may claim to be the finest village tower in the county, with its magnificent windows, its turrets rising round the wooden spire, its band of quatrefoils like a piece of embroidery, and gargoyles peering from under its parapet.

Most of the rest of the church is 14th century, including a big porch and a little porch, arcades rising with clustered pillars in a spacious interior, and exquisite windows. Those to the south have tracery like butterfly wings, and many have fragments of medieval glass. The glass in one window is interesting, not for its beauty but for its story of Bishop Mackenzie, Haslingfield's vicar, who died in 1862 as a missionary in Africa. We see him preaching to the natives while chained slaves tramp through the jungle, and we see his grave, which Livingstone himself marked with a wooden cross. The oldest part of the church is the chancel, with Norman stones in its walls and a carved arch on clustered pillars made when Norman ideas were passing. The 600-year-old font has a painted Jacobean cover. The pulpit and many of the bench-ends are 15th century, and quaint corbels of men and animals support the old open timber roofs with pierced spandrels.

A curate (William Clark) who was here for 54 years of last century, has his memorial, and there are several to the Wendy family, who entertained Queen Elizabeth at their moated manor house when she was on her way to Cambridge. She arrived a few years after the death of her old physician Thomas Wendy, whom we see here in alabaster kneeling with his wife, he in armour and she in a farthingale and a hooped skirt; below them is their son, also in armour, with his bonny wife in a fashionable trimmed cloak and a bonnet on her curly head. Sir Thomas Wendy of the next generation appears as a white marble figure standing in a niche with a crested helmet, gauntlets, and a sword hanging above him, and by the side of Francis Wendy's wall-tablet kneels the wife who survived him for 42 years, out of the Civil War into the reign of Dutch William and Mary.

HATLEY ST GEORGE. Its great house stands in a fine park looking on to the road; so it has stood 200 years, with a little church close by to keep it company, looking not much older though it all began 600 years ago. It is a simple aisleless place with a 17th century tower, a hammerbeam roof held up by angels, and painted shields of the St George family from medieval days, 28 in all. A brass portrait on the wall has been here 500 years, showing Sir Baldwin St George, who lived at the old manor house and is here in armour with his feet on a lion.

Thomas Becket's Oldest Portrait

HAUXTON. Away from the road it lies, shepherded by a simple church with a medieval tower rising boldly from the meadows of the Cam. Here herons come to fish, here coaches used to change their horses, here the Romans would cross the river.

The church is a famous little shrine, for there are few in the county keeping so much of their Norman work. Everything is odd and charming within its white walls, windows of four centuries and at all levels, arches and niches squeezed in quaintly here and there, two Norman windows in the chancel and two in the nave, two Norman doorways and two mass dials. Noblest of all in this rich Norman legacy is the splendid chancel arch, massive for so small a place and with two pillars at each side, and cable mouldings in the arch.

In the days when this arch was barely a centenarian a recess was made on each side of it, and on the wall of one of these is Hauxton's rare treasure, one of the very earliest paintings of Thomas Becket. It is 13th century and shows him in his mitre, with the cross in one hand and the other raised in blessing. It is in almost perfect state, and a remarkable survival of the saint whose pictures Henry the Eighth strove to drive out of every church. It is older than the portrait at Maidstone, and was saved by being hidden for centuries in the wall, Hauxton having the good sense to build up the niche to save it from the destruction of Thomas Cromwell and his king.

The medieval transepts have gone and we see their filled-in arches, but the font has been here 700 years. There are many 500-year-old benches, and the roof has delicately arched beams made by Tudor carpenters. We noticed that two vicars here covered a span of 103 years of service, through the French Revolution till after the Jubilee of Queen Victoria. They were Thomas Finch who came in 1788 and was followed in 1837 by George Williams.

The Spreading Chestnut Tree

HEYDON. High in the chalk hills stand its thatched cottages, with a pond for the ducks, and a medieval church hiding behind the trees, one tree a chestnut stretching 18 yards from the gate, nearly to the church door.

A key a foot long opens for us the ancient door of this 15th century church, which still has its old font, and has a patchwork of old glass in one of the windows. The glass in the modern chancel makes a fine gallery of colour, one dramatic scene showing Peter walking away as the cock crows. The east wall is decorative with alabaster arcading and gold mosaic, roses in the spandrels, and vines trailing under the arches. A memorial to one of their daughters recalls the Soame family who lived here 300 years ago, and whose right it was to hold the towel at the king's coronation. The lord of this manor attended with his towel at the coronation of George the Fourth.

There are traces of a defensive dyke which extended three miles to Fowlmere, and a trackway from that misty time still leads to Royston. It is called the Green Road, and was trodden by men before the Romans came to England and dropped their coins and pottery here.

The Home of Matthew Paris

HILDERSHAM. It lies in its wooded dell where the River Bourne slackens its pace on the way to the Cam. Outside it a windmill stands forlorn and sail-less, but an avenue of beeches, or a roadway bordered by firs, brings us to a village of much charm. Its church has for a companion the stump of an old elm four yards round, with its branches trimmed like a cup, and indoors coloured windows in the cobbled walls turn daytime into twilight, while candles in the candelabra light up the dark hours. The tower, with its gargoyles, is 13th century, and is climbed by a gnarled old ladder of 23 rungs made from rough-hewn blocks. It opens to the nave with two small archways, and looks along it to a chancel as old as itself, its walls covered with modern paintings from floor to roof. Hanging in the tower is an old flute played in the choir of long ago.

It is believed that Matthew Paris lived here, and it is a proud association if it is true, for he was the best Latin chronicler of the 13th century, and some of our oldest English paintings are his work. He is thought to have belonged to the family whose brass portraits are here, Robert Paris of 1379 and his wife, and two Henrys of the 15th century. Robert wears a tunic and mantle and has a dagger at his side, his wife has an embroidered gown, both kneeling at a cross engraved with God the Father holding a Crucifix. Henry Paris of 1466 is under a canopy, with short hair and wearing armour, and a Henry of 1472 is in armour with his feet on a lion, and his wife charmingly and simply dressed.

Contrasting with these charming brasses is one of the most gruesome we have seen, a skeleton in a shroud about a yard long, 400 years old. Much more attractive are two oak figures of the 13th century, carved from solid blocks. One is a splendid knight and the other a dainty lady, the knight six feet long in armour, drawing his sword, with his crossed feet on a lion, the lady at prayer wearing a wimple and a mantle, with her head on cushions and a dog at her feet. There are only about 100 oak figures like these in the country, and two are a rare possession for any village.

Here three generations of Henry Smiths were rectors for over a century, from 1629 to 1736; and Robert Goodwin was rector for three years last century, his memorial being the churchyard, for he left a bequest to keep it beautiful.

The Historian in the Monastery

IT is at the abbey of St Albans, in 1217, when he was about 17, that Matthew Paris becomes a historical figure. The abbey was blessed with material and literary riches, and, although development was to be slow, the Renaissance of learning had really begun there, with Matthew as its exemplar.

Godly and gifted, he was the foremost liberal and intellectual spirit of his age, mathematician, theologian, poet, historian. When he sat down in the scriptorum to record the affairs of the world a new force came into operation; the fabulist and the brief recorder of local annals passed, and a historian of worldwide observation was here, to render superb service to his generation and posterity.

Kings, princes, and potentates came to the abbey, and Matthew Paris, who had taken up the history of the world where Roger of Wendover left it, at 1235, Boswellised his illustrious company. He travelled England, he went to Europe on romantic monastic missions, and, like Froissart in a later age, he learned from those who knew the story of events, setting it all down in his incomparable history, the Chronica Major. He made himself as familiar with the affairs of Italy, Germany, and France as with those of England. He had an eye on Spain, he noted the doings of Hungary; he knew all about King John's offering to become a Moslem if the Emir of Morocco would join forces with him against the pope.

Not content with presenting a picture of his own age, this indefatigable scholar went over earlier chronicles and turned the period from 1067 into history in his Historia Minor.

The result was a magnificent work, full of movement and event, not colourless, but breaking out at times into condemnation, whether of kings or of luxury-loving friars. He is as careful as Livy to record earthquakes, eclipses, and falling stars; and a veritable Gilbert White concerning weather, bird life, or animal life. He died in 1259, the Father of English History.

John of Gaunt's Steward

HINXTON. Its thatched cottages stand in a row not far from the shady lane where the stream winds lazily through golden meadows, and a fine timbered house nods its overhanging storey in a sort of welcome to any visitor. If we come at the right time we shall be welcomed by the call of the sanctus bell outside the tiny spire rising from a dome set in the battlements of a 600-year-old tower. The story of the church begins about 1080, and from that time comes the font and a doorway blocked up in the nave. The rest of the church is mainly 14th and 15th century, and we come into it by a door which has been hanging most of the time since then. The chancel has old benches, and there are old beams in its roof. The ancient roof of the nave is a fine mass of timbering. There is a little old glass, an old oak screen with traceried bays and a modern cornice, a fine Jacobean pulpit, a peephole in the 14th century chancel arch, and a rood stairway is cut in the splay of a window. Here we come upon Sir Thomas Skelton, steward to John of Gaunt, his portrait engraved in brass in armour as he might have been at Agincourt, with his feet on a lion, and with him are his two wives in long gowns with draped headdresses, and with dogs at their feet.

Fruitful Village

HISTON. Its roots go deep into the past, to the days of the Romans who left odds and ends to be dug up here; but Histon is modern, too, for it is one of the group of villages which come into Cambridgeshire's educational scheme of village colleges and it lies in the midst of acres and acres of fruit trees, having the great Chivers factory with 2000 people who turn out a hundred tons of jam every day and played a great part as pioneers of the English canning industry.

By the church are the remains of the moat which protected the old manor house, now gone. The medieval church itself, though much restored, has in its nave wall fragments of stones carved with zigzag by Norman masons and a pair of noble 13th century transepts. There were once two churches, but the lord of the manor, Sir Francis Hinde, pulled down one 300 years ago, using stone from it to complete his fine house at Madingley. Only within the last century has the Norman font he carried off been moved from the hall to the church at Madingley, and at the same time fragments of the old church were brought back to Histon's old church of St Andrew, to be embodied in the chancel.

There are lion gargoyles along the south walls of this cross-shaped church, and on the south transept is a gable cross too worn for its detail to be seen from below, but it portrays Christ fully robed, and without the crown of thorns. The tower rising on low arches from between the transepts, the south porch, and the fine nave arcades are all 14th century; the nave, aisles, and most of the windows, and the font are 15th. The west window and those of the clerestory were made new last century, when the 13th century chancel was extended to its original length and given its fine east window, a group of lancets under a triple arch copied from an old fragment. The transepts resemble each other with their lovely arcaded walls and their double piscinas, and specially fine are the two triple lancets under rich arches in the south transept, their centre cluster of shafts replaced by a 14th century pinnacled niche and a bracket carved with a Catherine wheel and two angels bearing Catherine to heaven. The oak seats in this transept, with their poppyheads and arm-rests of animals, were modelled in our own time from a 15th century pew in the other transept, and the cherub in the aisle, and the oak lectern of St John writing his Gospel (with his eagle on his shoulders supporting the Bible) are Norwegian work. There is an old chest with a round lid, another made from the tracery of a reredos, some old glass fragments, and an ironbound poor-box.

The Sea-Shell

HORNINGSEA. It lies in leafy meadows by the Cam, almost missed by those who often go rowing from Waterbeach to Cambridge. Its long flint church, all under one roof and crowned by an embattled tower, has some things old and beautiful. The arches on the south of the nave come from the time of our first English builders who learnt from the Normans; on the other side they are 14th century. In the chancel is a double piscina with a pillar and quaint arches, and a niche inscribed, God make us saaf. Two chancel windows have fragments of old glass, and there are remnants of 15th century benches, a font and a coffin stone 700 years old, and a very fine Elizabethan pulpit with rich linenfold, a border of flowers, and an arcaded canopy. The church was much restored in the time of John Chapman, who was 54 years vicar here last century.

An odd thing we found in the south doorway, which in itself is 600 years old, yet is but a child in time compared with one of the stones in it, for where the stone is broken at one side is revealed the fine fossil form of a sea-shell.

Old Warriors

HORSEHEATH. It was known to the Romans, and it had for a while a fine house in a great park, but both are gone. Now it has a few old houses to keep company with the wayside church, in which are treasured the brasses and monuments of lords and ladies of its greater days. They were the Audleys and the Alingtons. A fragment of old glass in the church has the shield of the Audleys, one of whom distinguished himself at Poitiers.

A brass portrait in the church shows William Audley, who was alive at the time, standing with his feet on a lion, magnificent in armour and with a very long sword. Near him is the brass of Robert Alington, who has lost his head since they laid him here in 1552. The Alingtons held the manor here, and one of them was slain on Bosworth Field. His son Giles, Master of Ordnance to Henry the Eighth, lies in splendour with his son, one above the other, both in armour, heads on helmets and feet on hounds. The son outlived the father by 64 years.

There is another Giles Alington of Shakespeare's day on an impressive alabaster monument with his wife and their six children, he in slashed breeches and armour, she in a ruff and hooped skirt. The Alingtons throve under the Stuarts and had the privilege of handing to the king his first drink at his coronation.

Most of the church is 600 years old, but the fine nave, a blaze of light from great transomed windows, is 15th century, and its lofty height is crowned by a noble roof with a great span, with massive moulded beams and carved bosses. The beautiful blocked doorway to the rood stairway has flowers in its mouldings. The oak chancel screen comes from the 15th century and has still traces of painting in its panels. The font is 500 years old, and set in the wall behind the pulpit is a fragment of Norman carving from an earlier church. There is a 16th century sundial.

Life from Age to Age

ICKLETON. The thread of continuity which runs through England's life from age to age is here in its full strength; here are our witnesses for thousands of years. Here the ancient Britons brought their Icknield Way across the Cam. Here are great monoliths fashioned by the Romans. Here the Normans built a nunnery of which something is left. Here are arrow slits which surely must be Saxon, painting on the wall which is surely medieval, 14th century arches, 15th century screenwork: so the tale of the centuries runs on.

It is fitting that in this old place the wall round the churchyard should be coped with ancient stones carved by medieval masons; we noticed on one of them a crocodile, on another a fox, on others odd figures worn by wind and rain. The church stands by the green, and has a central tower begun by the Normans and finished in the 14th century, when the little heads were put at the corners. In its spire is a cot for the sanctus bell. We open a door heavy with ironwork 600 years old to come into a nave four times longer than it is wide, planned by the Saxons. The Normans built the arches resting on massive capitals and set here four round pillars as remarkable as anything we have come upon in a village church. They are monoliths brought here by the Romans, probably for a Roman building discovered near the village last century, and taken from the ruin when the Normans came to pierce the Saxon walls and add the narrow aisles to the church. Between the top of the arcades and the clerestory windows are narrow windows like arrow slits which look like Saxon, and on two of their deep splays are ancient paintings of saints and a king. There are traces of more old painting on the arches themselves. The 600-year-old arches of the tower rest on Norman columns, and the Norman west doorway remains. The chancel has Norman fragments of masonry and medieval stone seats for the priests, as well as the old piscina. The chancel screen is 15th century and has been painted afresh in medieval fashion; so has the traceried ceiling of the tower. There are many fine old benches with flowery ends, the few remaining ones that keep their poppyheads having two cockerels beak to beak, a two-headed dragon on a bed of roses, an angel and a demon weighing a soul, St Luke's bull, and St Mark's lion.

The east window has the Crucifixion scene with charming pictures on each side: Mary with her precious ointment, and Mary and Martha in a little ship with their brother Lazarus; Etheldreda with Ely Cathedral, and small pictures of her escape from a pursuing husband cut off by the tide, and again of her dream that while she slept her staff grew into a tree. In the west window Christ is standing on the world with the four Gospel streams flowing from his feet, and round Him are Bible figures; the window is a memorial to one of our great civil servants, Sir Wyndham Herbert, who died in 1905. His father, Algernon Herbert the antiquarian, is remembered in another window, and there is a marble relief in memory of another member of the family who was a war correspondent and fell on the march to the relief of Khartoum.

Memories of Pepys

IMPINGTON. Samuel Pepys knew it well, for Impington Hall was the family mansion, begun in the middle of the 16th century by one of the Pepys family and theirs till the 19th was on its way. Though it has been enlarged, Pepys would recognise today the red brick house in the park, with the arms of Pepys and Talbot carved on an oak shield over the garden entrance. Several times he rode over here from Cambridge to see his old uncle, Talbot Pepys, noting it all in the diary, and once describing how he slept in the best chamber, walked in the orchard with his cousins discussing his uncle's will, and then went to church and listened to a good plain sermon. "At our coming in (he writes) the country people all rose with so much reverence; and when the parson begins, he begins Right Worshipful and Dearly Beloved to us." We are reminded of another vicar who used to begin "Dearly beloved Eliza" when his wife was his only congregation.

The village is among the orchards, with its church against a belt of trees, a simple little building with patchwork walls of stone and cobble, mostly from the 14th and 15th centuries but with fragments of Norman carving in an outside wall of the chancel, and with much that is new. We enter, as Pepys entered, by a charming black and white porch with traceried windows cut in oak, and there on the wall, framed in a scrollwork of leaves, is a 500-year-old painting which was probably hidden when Pepys came, for it was discovered under plaster last century. It shows St Christopher as a red-robed giant carrying his holy burden across a rocky stream. The Child holds the world in his hands; fishes swim round the saint's feet; and at the door of his cell the hermit who set the giant working for Christ in this way holds out a lantern and waves an encouraging hand.

Another old wall-painting of a small figure is in a canopied niche between two angels in the chancel, and there is another exquisite niche in a window splay, with pinnacles rising from its dainty vaulted roof, where we counted 20 tiny rose bosses. The old church roof with its bosses is hidden under a new panelled ceiling. Generations of the Pepys family were baptised at the ancient font, and there is a fine brass of 1525 picturing a family here before them, John Burgoyne with his wife, two daughters, and seven sons. The knight is in armour with many curly-tailed dogs on his heraldic tabard; his wife is charming in a girdled gown and a pointed headdress.

Impington has one of the group of village colleges founded in Cambridgeshire for the purpose of training children to live the worthy lives of country folk. The college at Sawston was the pioneer of this praiseworthy education scheme, and similar schools have been opened at Bottisham, Linton, and Histon. So in this proud county a new generation is growing up with a wider appreciation not only of the usefulness of country life but also of its essential dignity.

Buried in the Snow

IMPINGTON furnishes among its records the most extraordinary parallel to Arctic peril and adventure that English annals afford, a burial alive of a human being for eight days; from the railway line skirting the park we see a stone marking the spot where she lay.

The victim was Elizabeth Woodcock, the wife of a farmer, who, setting forth on horseback on her return from marketing at Cambridge on Saturday, February 2, 1799, was overtaken by a snowstorm only a mile from home. Something, supposed to have been a bright falling meteor, startled her horse, which backed into a ditch, causing her to dismount, and then ran away across the fields. In pursuing it she lost one of her shoes and, her foot becoming frozen, she sank exhausted near a hedge where the snow had drifted deeply. Unable to rise again, she became buried by snow, enclosed in a mound six feet high, incapable of movement owing to the stiffness of her frozen clothes and the position in which she lay. A long struggle enabled her at last to get her hands free and push the snow from her face, so that it set in a cave-like formation about her head. In the morning she found that her breath had caused a sort of tunnel to form from her head to the outer air; and she retained sufficient presence of mind to utilise this for an expedient which was ultimately to lead to her rescue.

In her struggles she had lacerated her right arm on the stout stem of a bush near her; breaking off a branch from this bush, she fixed her coloured handkerchief to it and thrust it through the hole as a signal of distress to passers-by. Soon the outer extremity of the opening was closed by the formation of a thin sheet of ice, which acted as a window, letting in light so that she was never in absolute darkness, and enabling her to distinguish between night and day. She heard the bells from clocks and belfries sound, and kept count of days and nights; she heard the cries of animals; she heard horses and carts pass, and even caught the talk of gypsies. Again and again she cried aloud, but no one heard.

Nature mercifully minimised her suffering. She felt no hunger, and thirst was quenched by her eating a little snow. Her only discomfort arose from the melting of her ice window, which caused her frozen clothes to thaw and her body to become sodden and greatly reduced in temperature. This discomfort was increased when, after six days a general thaw reduced the interior of her prison to slush. She was, however, too weak now to extricate herself. For four days and nights she had been sought by her husband and kin, but as no trace of her could be found they had sadly come to the conclusion that she had been robbed and murdered.

At last, on Sunday, February 10, eight days after her imprisonment, a neighbour taking a short cut across the fields, saw her handkerchief fluttering from its twig. Approaching, he heard the sound of laboured breathing, and, looking through the tunnel in the snow, he saw a huddled figure. He was too terrified to address her, but called up a shepherd, who cried, "Are you there, Elizabeth Woodcock?" "Dear John Stittle, I know your voice; for God's sake help me out of this place!" she said.

She was carried home, and for the next five months she battled for life, but frost and snow had done their work and she died on July 13 in the same year.

Medieval Treasures

ISLEHAM. Closed in on three sides by the fens, it is a big quarrying village known for its limestone. We see it like a sentinel in the flat countryside, with an old windmill and an imposing church helping to make the picture.

More than a thousand years old is Isleham, and here for most of the time has stood a little Norman chapel, built for a small priory founded in the 11th century and abandoned by the monks as long ago as 1254. It has narrow windows in deep splays, and an apse at the east end, and after long use as a barn is waiting for its day of restoration.

An ancient lychgate (here called the Stockhouse, because it has a small bay which once sheltered the stocks) points the way to the stately church close by, majestic enough in its proportions to be something of a village cathedral. Most of it is 14th century, but the tower with its pyramid cap has been rebuilt. We come in by a great porch with a medley of old glass in its windows.

It is a veritable treasure house of beauty and interest, the nave striking with fine arcades, the chancel with a lofty arch which saw the dawn of 15th century building. The rich font is 500 years old, and so are the stalls, with their heads of women for arm-rests and their misereres showing a king and a queen, a bishop with a fine mitre, and a woman with a garland of flowers. Fine, too, are the Jacobean altar rails, with their carved borders and very effective balusters. In the north transept are old benches with poppyheads of leaves and quaint animals.

A great treasure is the fine eagle lectern, which was found about 70 years ago in the fen dyke, where it had lain for generations, buried for safety in some dangerous time. We are not surprised that another village claimed it too, for it is so good an example of 15th century brasswork that a lectern at Ely Cathedral was copied from it. The eagle has outspread wings, and in its beak is an opening for Peter's Pence, which were taken out from the tail. Three lions guard the foot.

Other treasures are at the vicarage, cups and flagons valuable for their gold, an Elizabethan charter with the queen's seal, and a copy of the charter King Alfred gave for the building of a chapel here in 895. But the oldest of all has come from the vicarage to the church, a table black and brown with age, made by a vicar in 1918 from an oak dug out of Isleham Fen, the very wood of a tree which must have been growing nearly 2000 years ago.

Two ancient village families are with us as we walk about this fine building, the Bernards and the Peytons. The arms of both are among the carvings on the walls of the 15th century clerestory, and an inscription round the cornice tells us that Christopher Peyton gave the lovely hammerbeam roof in 1495. On a fine tomb lies the first of the Bernards to be lord of Isleham, Sir Geoffrey of the 13th century, one of the Crusaders who went with Prince Edward to the Holy Land. The moulding of the canopy above his tomb is like that of Edward's Coronation Chair in Westminster Abbey. A worn figure of a Crusader in the other transept is thought to be Sir Geoffrey's son, and another knightly figure is Sir Gilbert of 1349. The last male of the Bernards is portrayed in brass, Sir John of 1450, who fought at Agincourt and was one of those ordered to kill the French prisoners. He is shown in plate armour, with his lady in a long gown and a horned headdress. Finer, however, is the brass of Sir Thomas Peyton and his two wives, one of them Margaret Bernard who brought Isleham to the Peytons. A charming 15th century trio they are under their handsome canopy, Sir Thomas in armour with great elbow guards, and Margaret in a rare gown patterned like brocade. Also in brass is Sir Richard Peyton of 1574, a Reader at Gray's Inn, his wife with her skirt open to show the crown on her petticoat, signifying that she was a Lady-in-Waiting to the Queen.

For 300 years the Peytons were here, and we see sculptures of them on two Elizabethan tombs, knights and ladies, one perhaps the foundress of the almshouses in the village. Still another lady lies stiffly on a nameless monument on the wall. A portrait in the vestry shows Richard Thomas Robins of our own day, who read the lessons here for 50 years, and lived in a house on the site of the old home of the Peytons, St Bernard's Hall. Still to be seen is a barn from the old homestead.

One more name must be added to those of the men and women who have passed this way. It is that of Charles Haddon Spurgeon, who a year or two before he began his famous preaching ministry in London, was baptised in the River Lark near Isleham. It was the beginning of the most extraordinary preaching career imaginable.

It Stands in Beauty

KENNETT. It takes its name from the brook on which it stands, in a lovely wooded corner near to Suffolk. The woods enfold its old church like a mantle, furnishing it with a setting which surprises and charms us by its unexpectedness. It is a church in which everything pleases, and we come into it through a Norman doorway above which rises a medieval tower, shaded by trees.

Very effective is the 600-year-old arcade with its great strength, and charming is the elegant tower arch seen from the chancel, making a perfect frame for the rich medley of colour in the west window. The east window is a group of three tall lancets, all of one height, their deep splays framed by arches on slender shafts with lovely bell capitals and with stone heads of bishops set between. The double piscina in the chancel is a gem, with grape clusters at the ends of the richly moulded arches and with fine pillars and flowered drains.

The oak chancel screen is 15th century and has richly carved bays with roses in the spandrels. We noticed that William Godfrey, lord of the manor, was rector here for the last 65 years of last century.

The Seven Works of Mercy

KINGSTON. It was a fine old market town with a fair when its church was built on the banks of Bourn Brook. Now its market, its fair, and its importance have gone, but the treasure laid up in the church remains with the old mass dial on its walls. An ancient door brings us to it, opening into an interior with white walls and a flood of light, its stately array of lovely arches crowned by an ancient black and white roof. The arcades are 15th century like the tower, the chancel is 13th and 14th and is odd for being lower than the nave, and for its patchwork of walls with filled-up arches of rosy stone. On the north side is a charming arcaded niche of three bays, perhaps a reliquary for saints; on the south side a window has a piscina in its splay, and a sill forming the sedilia. There are two charming niches also by the west window, one of them new with the names of three men who gave their lives for peace.

On the chancel walls are the oldest of the ancient paintings which are one of this church's fine possessions. On the north wall is what is thought to be part of a 700-year-old picture of the Conquest of Evil, showing two knights in chain armour fighting an enemy with spears. Over the chancel arch is a striking 15th century painting of six white angels on a red background, their wings outlined in black, and in the most fascinating of all the pictures we see the Seven Works of Mercy. They are in a great wheel above the west window, with figures of seven people between the spokes, and below are remains of the Seven Deadly Sins, suggested by a fine horned demon, and the head of a dragon. There is a tiny Jacobean pulpit, an old chest, a 15th century chancel screen, and a 600-year-old font like a solid block, its base shaped into arcading with richly carved arches; and the east window has a little old glass with flowers, and a roundel of a stag lying in the shelter of trees.

Henry the Eighth's Chancellor

KIRTLING. It has the quiet charm of so many corners of our countryside with that group of characteristic English beauty—a church tower peeping through the trees, a gabled house of bricks mellowed by Time, and ducks on a pond by long thatched barns. It has a house that is famous in story, the great Kirtling Towers by the Roman Catholic church, making a fine picture as it rises from lawns surrounded by a deep embowered moat covered with a green carpet patterned with forget-me-nots. The house we see was new last century, but it has the red brick gateway with four turrets through which Queen Elizabeth passed to the house that was here before. Here she was entertained in great magnificence by the son of the builder of the house.

It was the first Lord North who built it, Chancellor to Henry the Eighth; he lies in a fine slate tomb richly adorned with shields, the second lord, the son who entertained Elizabeth, lying under a huge canopy borne on six pillars and crowned by painted figures. Lord North is a fine figure in black armour tipped with gold, his head on a helmet and a griffin at his feet. The third lord died in the year of the

Great Fire of London and has a floor stone in the chapel; it was he who discovered the springs at Tunbridge Wells, and he was a notable figure at Charles the Second's court. On a small brass is a portrait of Edward Myrfin kneeling at a prayer desk. He died in 1553 after a life of travel. There were not many Englishmen of his day who knew more of the world.

The glory of this medieval church is its splendid south doorway, its arch enriched with zigzag and resting on pillars with carved capitals. The door swings on ancient hinges and there is a Norman window by the porch, and guarding this entrance are two heads under a very fine tympanum carved with Our Lord sitting on a rainbow. The interior is charming with grey arcades and rose-coloured walls. The south arcade has three Norman arches, and the north has a fine row of 15th century bays. The chancel is 13th and 15th century, and in the roof of the chapel and the north aisle are bosses of flowers, the corbels being heads of men in caps, bearded men, and draped women. Below the chapel roof are two quaint oak figures.

Here is one of those pathetic memorials unique in our generation, a wooden cross from a grave in France. It is that of Frederick Bowyer, a boy of 19 who fell in the last British attack on the German line in 1918, and sleeps at Cambrai with 400 of his comrades.

K NAPWELL. Its farms, church, and thatched cottages stand by a belt of woodland in which are ancient earthworks, and near them is a spring which bubbles a slight red tinge due to the iron in the water, so that it is called the Red Well, scene of miracles in superstitious days. A long line of chestnuts brings us to the small church with a nave and chancel which fell last century and were rebuilt. The 15th century tower remains, with a gargoyle of a lion and a fine arch opening from it to the nave, all that remains of the old building except for a relic as old as itself—the font, with heads of animals and roses carved on the bowl, which is set on a panelled stem.

Francis Bacon's Chaplain

L ANDBEACH. The thatched barns among the meadows keep company with its church, a patchwork of new and old stone and a veritable treasure house of medieval glass and woodcarving of various ages.

Gargoyles grimace from the 14th century tower, with its little stone

Linton

Sawston

Bottisham

THREE VILLAGE COLLEGES

Linton   **Thatched Cottages**

Linton   **The Old Guildhall**

spire, and two crude fellows in flat caps look down from the old porch; but it is the angels we remember. Some support the old roofs of the aisles, and others appear as oak figures with painted shields, carrying on their backs the weight of the 15th century nave roof with its massive beams carved with leaves and cherubs—a magnificent sight lit by clerestory windows. Yet another oak angel rests on a pillar with arms upraised and wings outspread to bear the lectern Bible. This and the pedestal pulpit were made from fragments of rich woodwork bought by a rector over a century ago, some of them thrown out from Jesus College. Part of the original chancel screen helps to make up the pulpit, a screen from the west end taking its place. There are medieval stalls with carved misereres of dragons and roses. The altar table has more beautiful old carving let into it; a Jacobean chair has serpents for arms and on its back two grotesque feathered creatures with entwined necks; and an ironbound chest has outlasted generations of churchwardens. The 14th century added the lofty arcades, built the rich canopied recess in the north aisle and gave the 13th century chancel the east window, with its glowing medieval fragments and its portraits of Henry the Seventh's grandparents, the first Duke of Somerset shown reading in a red gown, and his wife majestic in mauve against a yellow background. Others are here with them in excellent glass, and we wonder who is the little old man standing before a castle with an arrow through his eye.

Under a floorstone by the font lies the rector of Landbeach who was chaplain to Francis Bacon while he was Lord Chancellor. It was this rector, William Rawley, who prepared Bacon's manuscripts for publication, and when Bacon died (leaving Rawley £100 and his polyglot Bible), he brought all his unpublished papers to Landbeach, edited them, translated his English works into Latin, and wrote the memoir which all subsequent writers on Bacon have found indispensable. In 1666 the old rector read the funeral service over his wife and his son, both victims of the Great Plague, and a year later he followed them to the grave.

Four John Cottons

LANDWADE. No two families left a more treasured heritage to Landwade than the Roman who settled here 1600 years ago and the Cottons who arrived in the 15th century. The Roman built his villa where a winding stream would water his garden and supply his bath, and then he laid down the mosaic pavement which we have seen in the Sedgwick Museum at Cambridge, the only Roman pavement preserved in the county. The Cottons built the great house in the park and the 15th century church beside it, where a fine array of monuments keeps their memory green, though their brass portraits have been stolen off one rich canopied tomb. Among them are four Sir Johns. Sir John of 1593 is sculptured as a knight in gauntlets at prayer with his wife under the canopy of their painted tomb, a dog at the feet of the lady, whose scent case hangs on a long chain. Sir John of 1620 lies in armour on an alabaster tomb in the vault he built, his sword at his belt and one of his three wives on a ledge below him, her finger in a book. The alabaster figure of Sir John the Third of 1689 reclines under an arch adorned with cherubs; his hair is long and curly, but he is armed for war. Sir John of 1712 and his wife appear on medallion portraits between their two children.

The church where they lie is a squat little building in a hushed corner, reached by an avenue of pink chestnuts, with a little bridge stepping over the deep water moat of the hall close by. Worn outside and white-washed inside, its chief interest apart from the Cotton monuments is its medieval glass and the delightful stone corbels supporting the old roof beams, some full of character. Here are heads of men and women, and there is a lion, and in the chancel are the best of all, a monk and a bishop, a king and his lovely queen with her hair gathered in a flowered net. The piscina and an exquisite niche are flowery, too, and the old poppyhead benches are carved with roses. Remains of canopied niches jut out from the pillars of the old oak screen of fine tracery. From the 13th century come parts of stone coffins. The old glass includes shields and saints, Margaret appearing twice among them with her dragon, once in the south transept and once in the north. Other saints stand on a tiled floor in a nave window, and another is with angels in the east window.

Tony Lumpkin

LEVERINGTON. We found a windmill still working in this pleasant spreading place among the orchards, and beauty and interest in abundance safe in the medieval church. So lovely is its ribbed spire, rising to a height of 162 feet on a majestic tower, that when it showed signs of wear after 700 years it was rebuilt stone for stone with all its dainty gabled lights. The tower and its spire are masterpieces from the 13th century; the two-storeyed porch is a masterpiece from the 14th. It has a pierced crest of wavy carving along its gable ridge, with stepped buttresses niched for statues, heads on its vaulted roof, embattled columns between its four windows, and old doors with a wicket through which we enter.

The doors open into a nave with graceful arcades from the 15th century, a beautiful leafy tower arch, and a font in isolated loveliness. It is one of the best 15th century fonts, with eight saints seated under canopies round the bowl, angels under the bowl, and eight figures standing round the stem, while odd corners are filled with flowers and animal heads. A lofty 15th century tower arch opens into the chancel, and above the old door to the vanished roodloft are stone heads of Edward the Third and his Queen Phillipa. The sedilia and the three arches opening to the side chapel are 13th century. Stone corbels look down from the roofs, a woman in a horned headdress and a demon among the old ones, queens and clerics among the new. The stout altar rails are Jacobean, and there is a curious old oak lectern with six lions crouching below an eagle painted red and gold.

Flowing medieval tracery fills the east windows of the chancel and the chapel, and the third east window has a Jesse tree in 15th century glass, brilliantly restored at the end of the last century. The branches curl round over 60 figures in white and gold, and half of them are original. In a chancel window is more fine old glass given by Sir Lawrence Colville 500 years ago. His arms are here and a picture of Our Lady of Pity mourning the Son lying on her lap, while round them kneel knights and ladies praying. There is more medieval glass with saints under canopies in another chancel window.

A queer and familiar name looks out from a wall memorial here to Captain Anthony Lumpkin, who died in 1780, seven years after Oliver Goldsmith had produced She Stoops to Conquer. It is said that Goldsmith stayed with his friends the Lumpkins here and it is considered probable that he took the name of Tony Lumpkin from Anthony. The suggestion has been made that he may have written some of the play under the village mulberry tree, and it is curiously interesting to reflect that the captain named on these walls may perhaps have been the original of Tony Lumpkin whose figure has so long been familiar to us on the stage.

The Endearing Old Houses

LINTON. Furze Hill raises its chalk down behind the mile-long street, the River Granta flows slowly at its feet, and it has more endearing old houses to the mile than perhaps any other place in the county. They enchant the eye in the street, a timbered inn, a gabled house with raised plaster work, and thatched cottages standing out from comely neighbours. In all the quaint touches of this straggling little place is nothing more charming than the group hidden from the highway with the old church, the dreaming old Guildhall, now a house, and the little bridge over the stream. Near by at Little Linton is the Grange, a small Elizabethan house within a moat. In the field beside it we found one of those ancient clapper stiles with bars which fall at a touch to let us pass over and then slip back again. There is one in a lane where Shakespeare used to walk, at Charlecote in Warwickshire. Here also (at the church) are kept two of those old fire hooks, fixed on their poles, which were used for pulling burning thatch from houses.

The fine church is mostly 500 years old with crude gargoyles on the nave, a sundial on the battlements, arches resting on Norman pillars, and clerestory windows of the 15th century. The two porches are the same age, but in one is a holy water stoup which may be Norman. There is a little old glass with roundels of Bible scenes, a peace memorial window with St George and St Michael, a chest with Jacobean carving, and more Jacobean carving in the sanctuary. The font is 15th century. There is a brass portrait of Nicholas Paris of 1427 in armour with a lion and a sword, and a curious 17th century family group in marble with a man holding his wife's hand over a skull while she leans on an hourglass, a daughter in black and white above, and, below, 11 children kneeling in quaint rows, five of them chubby figures in nightgowns, and six ghostly draped figures.

Linton has one of the village colleges started by Cambridgeshire as an experiment in education, the idea being to educate children over eleven for the lives of country folk. They are drawn from a number of villages round each college and may learn craftsmanship of every kind, needlework and cookery, with all facilities for music, drama, dancing, and films. The building at Linton is a long low white building with all the chief rooms looking out on the playing-field. It was the third of these colleges opened in the county, the first being at Sawston and the second at Bottisham. The Linton buildings are by Mr S. E. Urwin, the county architect.

News in a Window

LITLINGTON. Here is a thrilling piece of news of 400 years ago, scratched in Latin on the stonework of a window in the church. These few faintly-seen words tell us that Francis Drake was about to set sail on the voyage which took him round the world and marked the start of England's greatest adventures on the sea. In 1580 he returned, to be knighted by Elizabeth at Deptford, having circled the world in three years.

A thousand years before that many adventurers from overseas had settled at Litlington. Under Limlow Hill they lie, buried with invaders of still earlier days, and many more were laid to rest near the church, the bones of one unknown soldier being found beneath a little heap of Roman coins. One of these Romans had a handsome residence here, and we have seen fragments of his tesserae floor in the Cambridge Geological Museum.

The lower part of the church tower recalls invaders of a later day, for it is Norman. The upper part was finished in the 13th century, when the nave arcades were built with clustered pillars and heads of women in quaint square headdresses. More heads look out from the ancient south doorway, and angels and lions are round the medieval font. In the roof are left some of the old bosses carved with flowers and heads, and one with a brass Crucifixion showing Mary and John. The chief interest of the oak screen spanning the noble chancel arch is its age, for it is earlier than most of our ancient screens, coming from about 1400. A broken stone coffin with its lid is outside by the tower.

Many a prisoner must have looked through the iron grille of the old lock-up, a red brick cell. Here during the Commonwealth came a Puritan priest who preached himself into prison over and over again. He was Francis Holcroft, who started his ministry as a voluntary priest here. He was ejected from Bassingbourn, but in spite of constant imprisonments he had preached in nearly every village in Cambridgeshire before he died worn out at an early age, having done more than any other man in this county to promote independent religious thought.

LITTLE ABINGTON. Little it may be, but its many thatched cottages and its charming corner group of timbered houses make it more of a show than Great Abington across the Granta. Through buttercup meadows a shady lane brings us to the 600-year-old tower of the church with a peep of Abington Hall. The porch has been made new, but its medieval timbers shelter a Norman doorway, simple, deep, and narrow, closed with an ancient door. From still earlier Norman days come the north doorway patterned with stars and a blocked window. For the rest, it is a simple place, with a transept and a font of the 13th century, fragments of stone coffins, some pews with old ends and backs, and a plain old chest. A 15th century screen spans the chancel arch, which has a peephole in one of its pillars. The chancel has a charming double piscina with Norman carving, and in one of its windows are the Wise Men in rich glass. A tiny low window in the north wall has long been a puzzle.

Old Door and Old Windows

LITTLE CHISHALL. Both Great and Little Chishall are new-comers in Cambridgeshire, having crossed the border in 1895. This one brought with it a squat church from ancient days, a little nave and chancel. For 500 years its door has been opening and shutting in its porch, but much of what we see was here before it, for the tower is 13th century (with a pyramid roof just topping the nave), and there are Norman windows. The east and west arches are 15th century; the font was carved by medieval masons. There is a fine old coffin lid under an outside recess in the chancel wall, and in the windows are fragments of ancient glass. The east window has tiny scenes of the Annunciation, the Nativity, and the angel appearing to the shepherds, with a big picture of the Crucifixion. Here the lord of the manor at the end of the war set up the reredos in memory of his son Richard Douglas Crossman, who fell in action at Cambrai 14 days before the Armistice.

Sir Christopher's Uncle

LITTLE DOWNHAM. Little only in name, this village has an ancient church at one end, the remains of a magnificent palace at the other, and Ely Cathedral within three miles.

The palace was built by Bishop Alcock of Ely at the end of the 15th century, and we found all that is left of it serving as storerooms for a farm; but we may see the great brick oven and a smaller one where the bishop's bread was baked; we may look through his windows and stand under a carved archway through which passed more than one famous bishop, the last of them to a long imprisonment in the Tower. He was Matthew Wren, Sir Christopher's uncle, who was arrested here, after Laud's impeachment, as a supporter of the fallen archbishop; he was put in the Tower and languished there for 18 years. Long afterwards, being warned by Charles the Second as to his conduct, Wren answered in a moment of great boldness that he knew the way to the Tower.

Much of the church was already old when the palace was new. The small tower with its thick walls is mostly Norman, and best of all is the beautiful doorway in the south porch from the time when Norman ideas were changing to English. Its shafts and capitals and slightly pointed arch are a mass of crude carving, zigzags and faces and beaked animals (one of a two-headed cat), and in it hangs a noble old door with fleur-de-lys hinges.

It brings us into a plain clerestoried nave of the 13th century, with a simple arch leading into a 14th century chancel. By some of the windows are the heads of a king and a wimpled woman, a hideous dragon, and a graceless boy sticking out his tongue. The tall graceful font with a tapering bowl cut with roses is 500 years old; the fine chest cut with pomegranates is getting on for 400. We noticed that one rector, Thomas Jones, outspanned all the others on the list by serving for all but sixty years of the 18th century.

LITTLE EVERSDEN. It has a barn and a church that have seen the centuries go by, the barn with a thatched roof longer than the church itself. For 500 years two quaint little men have looked down from the west window of the church tower, and a serious old man is looking out from under its battlements. Inside the arch stands the ancient font. The fine timbered porch is 15th century, with a doorway a century older, and in the chancel the stone seats for the priest, the piscina, and the little aumbry are all 14th century. The big stalls and the lofty arcaded panelling at the back of them come from Queens' College Chapel, Cambridge.

LITTLE GRANSDEN. Its church stands on the hillside looking down on thatched cottages and the 20th century almshouses, and over the valley to Great Gransden's church a quarter of a mile away across the border in Huntingdonshire. The church belongs to all the great building centuries, mostly 13th with 14th century nave arcades and a 15th century tower, and there are windows of all these times. The font is 600 years old, but the medieval-looking screen, bright with paint and with seven winged angels, is modern. A poor old chest has three locks.

A Cart For the Gallows

LITTLEPORT. This busy little town beside the River Ouse, where sea plants grow and cockle shells are found six feet below the peat, was a very different place before the fens were drained. So inaccessible it was that men declared in those days that it was as rare to see a coach in Littleport as a ship in Newmarket; and bitterly the fenmen opposed the change, for the draining of the marshes meant the enclosure of common land and the cutting down of their food supply of fish and wildfowl. Here at Littleport their smouldering discontent took flame, they sacked the houses of the well-to-do, extracted money with violent threats, and then, made bold by success, marched on to Ely and held it to ransom at the point of punt guns mounted on a waggon. But the troops were called out, 70 fenmen were sent to prison, five were transported, and five were hanged. But none would lend a cart to take them to the gallows, and the bishop of Ely (who then governed these parts with heart as hard as Pharaoh's) had to pay five guineas for one.

An opening in the church tower once led through to a footpath above the floods which frosts now sometimes turn into an ideal place for skating. High above fens and floods rises the splendid tower, a landmark for miles, the finest possession of the spacious church which has little to show within its crazy stone walls except attractive pictures in two windows. In both we see St George slaying the dragon, one in the delicate colouring of Christopher Webb, the other above a richly glowing scene at Emmaus by Martin Travers, who also shows us St Crispin cobbling shoes while his brother Crispian attends to a customer. Two fine records are on the walls, that of Frances Wise who taught in the Sunday School for over 60 years, while Benjamin Arber was completing his 60 years as bellringer. We read that he and his wife died the same year; she went in the height of summer; he when the leaves were turning.

Norman and Saxon Too

LITTLE SHELFORD. It lives in a secluded world with the Granta between it and Great Shelford, with two bridges and two big houses, all that remains of the charming Shelford Hall and the dignified manor house, with its avenue where the rooks are always cawing. One of many hidden ways leads past the manor and the farm where the river slips through a wood and kingfishers streak over an ancient mill pool. The way to the church is plain, for it stands by the crossroads with 13 fine limes and an ancient cross with a new head.

It has a tiny spire on a 600-year-old tower, and stones from all our great building centuries, Norman and Saxon, too. There are stones carved with Saxon plaitwork below a tiny Norman window, a carved coffin stone which may be Saxon in the porch, and in the chapel are four more stones which are probably Norman, like the queer animal with human arms propping up the 13th century chancel arch. The chancel is 14th century. The small sacristy entered by an ancient door in a rich arch is 15th century, and has holes of three piscinas in a windowsill. The arcaded oak pulpit is Jacobean. The font is 600 years old. The stalls have on them the arms of the Frevilles, whose 15th century chapel (up three steps) has some fine stone ornament on its piscina and on a canopy over the figure of a saint, with fragments of old glass in its windows.

Some of the Frevilles who died before their chapel was built appear in the chancel in stone and brass. Sir John, an alabaster knight with an inscription in Norman French, is here from the beginning of the 14th century, and from the end of it, in brass, are Robert and Claricia, with a greyhound and two dogs at their feet as they clasp hands, their son Thomas holding his wife's hand near them in a brass of 1405. A 15th century rector, John Cate, has another fine brass portrait. The shadow of the sword falls on three tablets telling of General Sir Charles Wale, who survived many battles to die at Little Shelford in 1848, of his son who fell at Lucknow, and of his eight grandsons and great-grandsons who gave up their lives when half the world was turned into a battlefield.

Every Hour of a Century

LITTLE WILBRAHAM. It shares with its Great namesake the honours of antiquity and a famous Saxon cemetery in which about 200 graves have been found. Some of them may be seen in a chalk pit.

The most interesting possession the village has preserved since those days is a fine little brass portrait of one of its priests whom we see kneeling at prayer in his robes, holding a rosary. It has been in the chancel floor since 1521; his name was William Blakwey. The church was old when William Blakwey came, for it is 14th and 15th century and has a 600-year-old tower which projects into the nave at the west end on three very pointed arches, the tall eastern arch singularly striking as it stands between segments of arches at each side looking like flying buttresses. There is a peephole in the chancel arch which, like the font, is 15th century. By the porch are two steps with the base of the old cross on them, and by the gate lies an old lady who lived through every hour of the 18th century, Elizabeth Hobbs.

Runnymede in His Memory

LODE. Here where the pastures glide into the Fens was the landward end of the Bottisham Lode, the waterway for the fenman's barges. Here it left its cargoes, and gave the village its name. The village has a group of thatched cottages, and, hidden in trees, the fine Elizabethan house called Anglesey Abbey, with a vaulted room remaining from its Norman days.

The village has long been one of the homes of the Broughtons, and it has a thatched village hall with golden walls given in memory of Urban Broughton MP, who was granted a peerage but died before he could receive it, so that it was conferred on his son, who became Lord Fairhaven. In his memory his widow and children gave the village hall, and in memory of his sister they gave to the simple 19th century church two great silvered candlesticks richly wrought with leaves. They also gave to the nation the meadow of Runnymede by the Thames, scene of the sealing of Magna Carta.

By the Roman Road

LOLWORTH. We may stand on the Roman road and see its medieval tower rising above its thatched cottages. It looks down on a field called Burnt Close (from a fire which burnt down most of the village and the aisles of the church 600 years ago). It has been a small place ever since, never recovering, but it sent a score of men to the war, and in memory of three who did not come back it has restored the church and the old tower. In the tower an ancient door still opens to the belfry, latticed with fine old ironwork. There is a 600-year-old font, an ancient coffin stone, a 14th century wall-painting with small figures of Unbelieving Thomas, and engraved in alabaster in the chancel are two ladies of the Langley family of long ago, their hands at prayer. They wear belts with their low-necked gowns and have butterfly headdresses.

The Village With Two Churches

LONG STANTON. Off the Roman road from Godmanchester to Cambridge, it is long enough to have two parishes, each with a church of its own.

By a charming group of thatched cottages and an old windmill that has lost its sails stands the simple church of St Michael, framed in chestnuts and roofed with thatch above the nave. A 15th century porch brings us to the great stone arcades two centuries older. One of the windows in the chancel has a little old glass in black and white, but the chancel itself was made new last century. The treasure of the church is a fine oak chest with two roundels on the front. It was a centenarian long before Thomas Burgoyne knew this church; he was its patron in the 15th century, and the chest has a brass plate to his memory.

The noble church of All Saints has been much changed but its tower and spire are 15th century, the nave arcades are 14th, and a 15th century arch opens into an older chancel made new. A niche in the wall is perhaps the oldest thing in the church, 13th century. The very fine font is 600 years old, elaborately carved with pinnacles.

There is an old box-pew of the 18th century which was used by the Hattons, who bought the manor from Queen Elizabeth and were here during three centuries. They turned the transept into their chapel, and on an elaborate tomb lie the alabaster figures of Sir Thomas and his wife with six sons and daughters kneeling round them, all dressed as in the days of the Commonwealth. The father has long curling hair and is in rich armour; the mother, with a hound at her feet, has a bead bracelet, a kerchief round her head, and holds her handkerchief and a book. The manor passed to the Hattons after Elizabeth seized it from Bishop Cox, the first Protestant Bishop of Ely. It was not all the queen took from him, and the story goes that when the poor bishop was driven to complain the imperious Elizabeth retorted, "Proud priest I made you and I will unmake you."

The Five Battles

LONGSTOWE. It is scattered along its quiet lanes within ghostly sound of the tramp of Roman legions down Ermine Street.

The hall in the park was old when the Cage family bought it in Queen Elizabeth's day; they left it long ago, bequeathing their ashes and their monuments to the church in the shade of the great trees. It has been refashioned, like the hall which keeps it company.

On a table tomb lies the alabaster figure of Anthony Cage, who died the same year as the great Elizabeth. He is in armour, and his wife has her tiny head set round with a wide ruff. A monument of 1679 shows the curious figure of Sir Ralph Bovey rising from the tomb to grasp an anchor let down by a hand from heaven. A window of St George carrying a lance is in memory of Colonel Frederick Sharp, who fought through five battles of the war and fell in 1916.

A Cambridgeshire Vision

MADINGLEY. Its name brings up a vision to every Cambridge man, and not to them alone, for who can forget the view from this wooded hill of the towers and spires of Cambridge rising from the trees against the background of the Gog Magog Hills? Well may Rupert Brooke ask:

> Is sunset still a golden sea
> From Haslingfield to Madingley?

From a pretty corner where the ways meet we see the sloping park with the beautiful hall where Edward the Seventh lodged as a student, and where Charles the First is said to have hidden. Built by Justice Hinde in Tudor days, it was altered by his Elizabethan descendant Sir Francis, who pulled down the old church at Histon for building material and stole its Norman font. Not till our own day did the house give up this font, a great treasure rich with Norman carvings, but now it is for all to see in the medieval church by the fine iron gates of the park, where a thatched and timbered lodge and a lake with a Japanese garden add to the picture.

Three ladies from the big house are also to be seen in the church, one of our own day and two of long ago. Annie Heycock, who died at the hall in 1923, looks out from a pleasing medallion; Jane Hinde, who married Sir John Cotton and died in 1692, reclines in alabaster on a cushion in her lace-trimmed nightcap and gown; Mrs Jane Cotton, an odd figure of 1717, kneels on her cushion. A father and son of the house have memorials carved with signs of their calling. Both were naval commanders, Sir Charles Cotton the father commanding the Channel Fleet on the look-out for Napoleon. A curious sculpture shows a bonny baby wrapped in a coverlet with angels watching over him.

The north doorway, the graceful arcade with bell capitals on clustered pillars, and the slender tower with pillars and capitals to match, are all 14th century. The south porch is 15th and has a door 100 years older. An ancient mass dial is on a wall. The rich balustered altar rails are Jacobean and come from a Cambridge church. Medieval windows fill the place with light, one showing Mary Magdalene in beautiful modern glass, others with fragments of old glass, a golden medley and a rich patchwork in which Mary and John are seen at the foot of the Cross in front of a charming town of gabled houses, turrets, and spires. Saints and the pious pelican are in two panels of Flemish glass, and six old paintings on wood show Christ's first followers. Ten headless oak figures on the tower wall were once in the roof of the chancel; and also brought down into the church for us to see is a bell made 600 years ago by a Bedfordshire man. It was found when men were rebuilding the short spire on the tower, which was new when this bell was made for it.

The Church With 200 Angels

MARCH. Among the disappearing fens, the high ground crowned by Ely Cathedral is part of an archipelago of islands, on one of which stands this capital of the Isle. Till late last century it was a hamlet of Doddington; now it is a busy little market town and a railway junction, with a long straggling street and buildings befitting its grown-up importance. Three of the four parishes into which it has been divided have each a modern church, St Mary's, St John's, and St Peter's; but Old March, away from the stir of the official capital, treasures the beautiful medieval church. A few dwellings gather round it, and a thatched farmhouse near by has 1658 on its chimney stack. A long avenue of venerable elms runs along the road which brings us to it, and at the foot of one of the trees is the square base of an old cross, carved with roses and shields of arms and set on a flight of steps.

The old church was built about the middle of the 14th century as a chapelry of Doddington, and given the rare dedication of St Wendreda, an obscure Saxon saint of whom little is known, but whose relics are said to have been taken in a golden shrine, at the request of King Ethelred, from here to Ely. Fine battlements adorn the walls of this church, except for the new gabled chancel. The parapets of the 15th century aisles have quatrefoil tracery, and a band of quatrefoils runs round the plinth of the aisles and the old south porch, which has big windows, stone seats, a gable cross, and a stoup. There are grotesque gargoyles, and by some of the windows are human and animal heads, one of a woman in horned headdress. The sanctus bell still rings in the bellcot on the eastern gable of the nave, which has a striking 15th century clerestory of nine windows on each side, richly patterned in flint and stone. Crowning it all is a fine tower of about 1400, from which soars a graceful spire with canopied lights. The tower stands on two open arches with a vaulted passage between them, preserving a right-of-way existing here before the tower was built.

The medieval windows which light the fine interior are set in walls carved with arches at the top of which are human figures and angels. Lofty arcades divide the nave and aisles, the north aisle 600 years old and the south side 500. Exceedingly lofty, dwarfing the arcades, are the arches of the tower and chancel, the tower arch having a good Jacobean ringer's gallery halfway up.

The great glory of the church is the magnificent double hammer-beam roof, whose equal it would be hard to find. It is all richly carved by 15th century craftsmen, with an amazing array of angels hovering over the nave from the arches and the hammerbeams, as well as from the corbels, which support saints standing in niches between the clerestory windows. There are nearly 200 angels in this heavenly host, all with outstretched wings, some with musical instruments, some with shields, and others with emblems of the Passion.

It is thought that William Dredeman, who died in 1503, gave this lovely roof, and two small brass portraits in the floor of the nave, now very worn, are believed to be of him and his wife. Under the tower is another brass with 16th century kneeling figures of Antony Hansart in armour and tabard, his feet gone, his wife in kennel headdress and girdled gown, their small daughter without a head. Below them is their shield, and above them is a striking and unusual Annunciation showing the Madonna kneeling at a desk, the Archangel Gabriel kneeling before her, and a vase of lilies between them.

There is an ancient font, and a modern pulpit with a vine border and figures of the Good Shepherd and the Four Evangelists. A richly coloured window of the south aisle has St Michael, St Etheldreda with her abbey at her feet, and St Wendreda holding her church. The most striking of the windows has a setting of seas and mountains, and a child with a bunch of flowers looking into the sky, where Our Lord is receiving two men at the gate of Heaven. A stone by the chancel door marks the grave of John Wyldboar, who lived through the hundred years from the middle of the reign of Charles Stuart.

What Happened by the Old Stump

MELBOURN. The road to London runs through its fruitful orchards, and on it we notice the stump of a great elm tree which we are told was flourishing in the days when the villagers gathered round it to chase Charles Stuart's ship money collectors with pitchforks. The stump still sends out new shoots each spring.

The village has a reputation for independence and courage; it has one of the oldest Nonconformist churches, the old Congregational chapel having been founded in 1694. It is still in use as a Sunday School. On the village green is a cross to the men who did not come back from the war and an oak seat to a villager with a good village motto carved on it: Kind words are the music of the world.

Melbourn was an important place in the Middle Ages, and has several old moated houses and a medieval church to keep company with its cluster of thatched cottages. The imposing 14th century tower is crowned with a tiny spire, and opens into the nave of the church with a richly moulded arch. The 600-year-old porch has turret stairs leading to an upper room, and the fine doorway brings us into a medieval interior with stately arcades of the 14th century, a 15th century clerestory over them. A 600-year-old chancel arch leads us into the sanctuary, which has three notable possessions: a 13th century double piscina and two aumbries which have managed to preserve their original doors. There is an Elizabethan chalice, a Bible of 1611, a delicate traceried chancel screen of the 15th century, and some old stalls, but only a few fragments are left of the glass, which filled the windows in those days. The oldest possession of the church is the crude Norman font with a crack in it which was strengthened centuries ago by iron clips. A crested memorial of 1760 tells us of Dame Mary Hatton whose Tudor home remains here. There are old and new heads carved in stone, a king and a bishop by the elegant doorway of the vestry, and a queen and a bishop with St Peter and St Paul among the new stone heads in the nave, where angels support the carved beams of the fine roof.

Andrew Marvell's Father

MELDRETH. Here the men of the Bronze Age left a hoard of axes, spears, and swords, but today it is a place of peace enbosomed in orchards, with thatched houses peeping out from the blossom, and shady trees overhanging the brook on its way to the Rhee. Fame has passed it by except that it was the birthplace of Andrew Marvell, father of the poet of the Commonwealth and himself a very good preacher. He was master of Hull Grammar School and also of Charterhouse, and he died tragically in crossing the Humber.

He would know this church, for the tower was begun 800 years ago and has been finished 600 years, and there are three Norman windows. The north doorway is 12th century, and a blocked arch is a century younger. We come in by the 15th century porch, in which still hangs an ancient door opening to a lofty bare interior. The elegant arcade, the clerestory, and the font are all 15th century, and the beams in the roof and over the chancel arch have traces of medieval carving and painting. Twelve stone angels support the roof. The church has an ancient ironbound chest and a great coffin stone, and it keeps as relics two great firehooks which were used for pulling burning thatch off cottages. A little old glass in the window has a complete figure of John the Baptist in camel hair with a tiny kneeling figure in front of him.

March   St Wendreda's Church

Melbourn   **The 14th Century Tower**

St Wendreda's, March

St Mary Magdalene's, Ickleton

By the chestnut on the green where three ways meet are the old stocks and whipping-post, and the stump of a wayside cross.

Ireton's Way

MEPAL. Here the Isle of Ely dips down to the fens and New Bedford River and Old Bedford River run side by side cutting across the great loop of the Ouse like a chord of an arc. They mark one stage of the work of draining the fens. When the island was held for Parliament in the Civil War General Ireton, wanting a road for his troops, made the Causeway which begins at Mepal and now bridges the two rivers; it is still called Ireton's Way.

The little church has been here 700 years but is much made new. In it we found a tablet to James Fortrey, a refugee from Brabant who lived at the old farmhouse. We are told of him that he was bred in court and in camps, was page to the Duchess of York under Charles the Second and groom to her husband, James the Second, but that he did not follow his royal master into exile for reasons of his health.

The Widow Comforted

MILTON. It has thatched cottages leading to a church in a lovely bower of trees, with quaint gargoyles on its 13th century tower. The nave has old tiebeams and bosses in its roof, and 14th century arcades leading into aisles lighted by windows with flowing tracery and fragments of medieval glass, Flemish roundels of St Margaret and St Catherine among them. The chancel has a Norman arch, a double piscina with a pillar crowned by a floral capital, and lovely sedilia with slender pillars between the rich canopies and the head of a woman at each side. The lovely 17th century altar rails and the stalls with figures of a bishop, a man, and lion heads on the armrests are said to come from King's College, Cambridge. The oak door of the vestry has Jacobean panels. Among the old monuments are a coffin stone, a Flaxman sculpture of two draped women in memory of Elizabeth Knight, and a Chantrey memorial to Samuel Knight with a descending dove. But far the finest is a 16th century brass set in a floorstone, showing Sir William Coke in his judge's robes and mantle, his wife with a pretty flowered headdress and a gown with puff sleeves, two sons, and three daughters. Another 17th century brass on the wall is in memory of John Harris, and shows four sons in tunics and three girls dressed like Little Red Riding

Hood; all these children passed away before their father, but the inscription tells us that the widow still had ten others to console her.

In Memory of Two Wars

NEWTON. It is recorded that one summer's day in 1746 a fire here burnt down most of the village and roasted the apples as they hung on the trees. Today it has a few cottages at the cross roads, a pleasant village hall and handsome farmhouses, a great house in Georgian style, leafy lanes, and green pastures.

Great chestnuts spread themselves against the 14th century tower of the little cross-shaped church. Here is something from four of our building centuries, a fine font from the 12th, transept arches from the 13th, a nave arcade of the 14th, and a clerestory of the 15th, when the old timbers were set in the roof. Perhaps the best thing of all is the graceful tower arch, with continuous moulding.

Here are two memorials of the last great wars in Europe. One is to Christopher Peach Pemberton, who witnessed the most terrible day in the modern history of France, for he was at Sedan. He was there to record the events of the war, and fell towards the close of the battle while advancing with the staff of the Crown Prince of Saxony. The other memorial is to Alexander Rogers, a devoted friend of the village who gave his life for his country in 1915. The name of Rogers comes 12 times on the peace memorial among those who served, all 12 related, and three of them did not come back. By the plain pillar to their memory is a drinking trough.

The Medieval Doorways

NEWTON-IN-THE-ISLE. It lies near Wisbech and looks over the wide flats of the fens, but its stone church is apart among fine trees. We come into it through two medieval doorways, one with a king and queen on each side, and the other in a porch with an unusual Nativity scene in a window; it shows a woman and two noblemen with sword and dagger, bringing their gifts, while two angels hold a curtain behind. Like most of the church, the tower and spire are 14th and 15th century, but the round pillars bearing the nave arcades may be Norman. The clerestory is 15th century, and so is the chancel arch, in which is a richly carved modern screen with a vaulted canopy supporting a roodloft gallery with traceried bays.

It is reached by the old rood stairs. In the sanctuary floor is an ancient coffin stone carved with three crosses.

Three Graves

OAKINGTON. It has a little garden which has become a shrine. In it are no gilded canopies, no sculptured arches over marble tombs, but three brick graves with iron railings round.

They are the graves of three Puritan ministers, spiritual fathers of Cambridge Nonconformity, Francis Holcroft, Joseph Oddy, and Henry Osland. All three lost their livings for their preaching, and one of them his liberty; and here all three were laid within 25 years from 1687, three men who, in their own words, bowed not down.

Francis Holcroft was one of the victims of that intolerant era when our ancestors were certain that with their little plummets they had sounded the depths of the universe, and each religious party persecuted another as power and opportunity arrived. Cambridge sent Francis Holcroft forth an MA, fellow of his college, a clergyman but a Puritan. A profound scholar, he had no secular ambition, but laboured modestly first at Litlington and then at Bassingbourn, until in 1662 he was ejected, and fronted an almost friendless world, implacably hostile to the Church which had shattered his life and ruined his fruitful ministry. Preaching stealthily up and down the county to those who held steadfast to Puritanism, he was seized, tried for unlawful preaching, and actually banished the realm. The intercession of Lord Anglesey, who approached Charles the Second on the matter, prevented the fulfilment of this terrible punishment, but Holcroft was thrown into prison as an insolvent debtor.

Compelled thus to suffer as criminally responsible for the poverty persecution had brought upon him, he was kept in gaol until his debts were paid, being generously assisted by Archbishop Tillotson, who had been with him at Cambridge. After the Revolution he was able to return to his work, taking general charge of a chain of congregations in his native county and over the border. His earlier sufferings, however, told upon his health, which broke down, and he died a victim of melancholia, to be buried here in 1692. He is still remembered with honour throughout Cambridgeshire, where in every village he preached the gospel as he understood it.

The church near the little graveyard has a 15th century tower with gargoyles under the parapet, and a 13th century doorway opening on an interior with arcades that have been leaning about 700 years. The sanctuary has Jacobean panelling, and a canopied niche at each side of the east window. The font and a piscina are 700 years old, so are three coffin stones, one carved with crosses. In one of the windows are fragments of old glass with the head of a golden-haired man.

A Precious Stone

ORWELL. Over the hills and far away runs the Roman road to Akeman Street, and here runs another road, a narrow invisible way that passes round the world and none can see. It is the imaginary line of the meridian of Greenwich. We found here also an interesting field of one acre which from time immemorial has been the freehold of the parish clerk, providing him with his entire emolument except for his ceremonial fees. It appears to have been left for the purpose long ago, and those who will remember the delight they took in their childhood in hearing the parish clerk's Amen will like to know that his green acre at Orwell is known as Amen Field.

The church has a very precious stone as old as the 13th century tower of the church, rising where the ancient Britons built an earthwork before the Romans came. It is what remains of a small stone Calvary, with traces of colour and still perfect figures of Our Lord and St John. For three centuries this Crucifixion was hidden from sight in the wall of an arcade, where it was buried to save it at the Reformation. It is 700 years old.

The glory of the building is the fine 15th century chancel with grey walls and lovely windows with embattled transoms. The east window reaches nearly to the wagon roof with fine painted bosses of the shields of county families, and faces peeping out of foliage. There are 15th century stalls and quaint heads of a hooded man and a wimpled woman on the arches of the nave above which rise 15th century clerestories. The pulpit is Jacobean and the altar Elizabethan. Peeping out from a niche in the chancel wall, as if behind a pulpit, we see the head and shoulders of Jeremiah Radcliffe with his square beard. He is at prayer and wears a red gown, and above him are two books by which we are reminded that he was one of the translators of the Bible.

Orchards by the Ouse

OVER. It lies among the orchards, but the fishermen know it well, for the wayward Ouse broadens out where the ferry takes us over the border to a delightful little inn. But Over will not let us hurry away, for it has a handsome church which the centuries have filled with interest without and within. Its sanctus bell has hung in the bellcot for 600 years, and all that time the spire has been pointing the village folk the way to Heaven. The tower is older still, a landmark in this valley since the 13th century. Its fine west doorway has a niche at each side, and above it a sculpture of Our Lord in Glory.

It is the 14th century porch by which we come in, through a splendid entrance archway with deep mouldings and shafts. The porch has beautiful open windows at each side, fine buttresses with embattled cresting from which rise tall pinnacles, and under the battlements trailing ballflowers which run along the aisle with a fine array of gargoyles. Among these is an owl, a lion, men with great heads and open mouths, and a woman emptying a pitcher.

The church is full of light, and old stone seats run round the walls (so that the weakest went to the wall), and the arcades and clerestories have stood 600 years. Between the arches are kings, bishops, and people, and from the mouldings of the capitals peep out little heads, one of them with three faces. Above it all is an old roof with kingposts supported by 14 oak figures in niches. A 13th century arch leads us into the 15th century chancel, through the original oak screen, which has lost its vaulting on the west but keeps it on the east. The chancel windows are set under arches, and the piscina has a pretty drain with six holes and a rose in the middle. Some of the stalls are old, with seats carved with grotesque animals, flowers, and heads, while on the arm-rests are quaint carvings among which we noticed a horse with a head like a hippopotamus, a little bearded man wearing a kilt and a big hat, a griffin with a pig in its claws, and a dragon eating a man. The fine Jacobean pulpit stands on a 600-year-old pedestal, and has a richly carved and vaulted canopy. The 15th century font has angels round the bowl, the old chest has a gabled lid, and there are traces of wall-painting in which a kneeling figure can be seen.

The Remarkable Group of Trees

PAMPISFORD. A pretty village among fine trees has grown up where once men dug a ditch to close the gap between forest and marsh. All that is left of this ancient defence is the Brent Ditch running between Abington Park and Dickman's Grove, most clearly seen in the park of Pampisford Hall. In the park is a remarkable collection of fir trees from Japan, Mexico, China, California, Austria, and the Pyrenees, and worthy of them all is another village tree, the cedar shading the lawn of a house by the church, itself bowered in chestnuts and with a charming porch hewn from oaks rooted in medieval England.

The porch shelters a simple Norman doorway with a curious arcaded tympanum, and its ten small arches filled with crude carvings, perhaps the story of John the Baptist, for we see the block and the head of the figure lying on the floor. John the Baptist, carved by modern hands appears again with Christ as a finial for the old domed cover of the Norman font.

The 600-year-old tower has a tiny spire and its pleasant arch opens into a massive arcade from the time when Norman styles were changing into English. The 15th century chancel arch is screened with delicate oak tracery of the same age.

A Benefactor of the Nation

PAPWORTH EVERARD. Its white walls lie along the Ermine Street of Roman Britain, but the fame of Papworth belongs to our own 20th century, for the white walls are those of a little world apart, where hundreds of men and women are fighting adversity, busy with a multitude of things by which they hold their own.

Here there is little of the 14th century now left—two doorways, the plain font, and the chancel arch on its clustered columns; for the rest, the church (which has a short spire) is yet a long way off from being a centenarian, but even when the young church has reached old age Papworth will be remembered for the part it has played in the health and well-being of our people.

This place in the green heart of Cambridgeshire is the self-supporting colony of hundreds of people with tuberculosis, the low buildings of their hospitals and the sanatorium are set in lawns and gardens on the hillside with a church among the trees on the ridge looking down on it all. In its short life Papworth has stored up a record of man's helpfulness to man as glorious as that of any ancient foundation. It is the model village for receiving men and women afflicted with the white scourge of tuberculosis. It contains within itself their homes, their hostels, their hospital, their sanatorium. It sustains them in their illness, it gives new life to them, new faith, new hope, and its mainspring is charity. From its modest beginnings the Papworth Village Settlement has risen to the height of a national undertaking.

Papworth is a barrier against the spread of tuberculosis. When the patient can leave the hospital here he does not go back to a life and work where he is almost certain to relapse. As his health begins to improve he is trained by gradual stages for one of the 11 trades which form Papworth industries. No workshops in the world are more cheerful than these. When he is yet more fit the patient may take his place as one of Papworth's permanent workers or settlers, the quality of whose handicraft the outside world has had opportunity to appreciate. They will do printing for you, or write your signs, or make you a travelling trunk or a portable building.

One of the best testimonies to Papworth is its appearance, trim and spick and span and newly built from end to end; but a stranger coming on it unawares would never know it for what it is. He might take it for some model village built by a philanthropic and far-seeing manufacturing firm for its working folk. He would see a playground full of children at play, and would find a swimming-pool. Among the trees and gardens he would discover bright modern cottages. The hostels would be quite in keeping.

A number of chalets in a tree-shaded row would be the first thing to give him pause. What are they for? They are the open-air bedrooms for the patients when they first come to Papworth. They are part of the cure the hospital begins. But all the rest that the visitor sees are the progressive steps upward from them: workrooms where trades are learned and practised, separate hostels for the unmarried workers of both sexes, cottages where the married workers live with their families. It is one of the highest tributes to the efficacy of the Papworth system that no child born there while a member of the community has contracted tuberculosis.

The Bright Yellow Flower and the Blue-Green Leaf

PARSON DROVE. A few years after the war we came here in search of the last woad mill in Cambridgeshire, believed to be the last in England, but, alas, we came to find only a plant of bright yellow flowers and blue-green leaves growing in the corner of a garden. It was all that was left of acres of woadplants which grew here almost to the beginning of our century. The woad mill was no more. It had fallen to pieces and been removed, together with the balls of woad pulp the mill crushed, to Wisbech Museum, where we may see it as a rather melancholy relic.

It was Julius Caesar who first instilled into the minds of civilised people the fact that some of our ancestors dyed their skins with the blue dye obtained from the woad plant. In his Gallic War we read that " without exception all the Britons stain themselves with woad, which produces a blue tint; and this gives them a wild appearance in a fight." There is little doubt that Caesar libelled the brave race which so vigorously resisted his legions; if woad was used for staining the bare skin of the warriors it was used quite as much in giving a brilliant colour (rather like a natural indigo) to their clothes. It was the beginning of brighter fashions in dress.

Woad dye was obtained from the crushed leaves of a plant which grows still in many gardens, the botanical name being Isatis tinctoria. Growing from one to six feet high, it has branching flower-stalks with yellow blossoms and small pods. It was from the blue-green leaves that the dye was obtained.

Many people still in Cambridgeshire remember the woad crops of their fertile soil. For over 2000 years the industry thrived until modern discoveries and modern machinery killed it. The young woad plants were delicate and needed much care, and men and women crawled along the field removing the weeds with a tiny spade fitting into the palm of their hands. When the plant was picked the leaves, having been crushed to pulp in a primitive horse-worked mill, were moulded by hand into balls, which were laid out in sheds to dry, and after three months the balls were mixed with water and put in a dark chamber to ferment for about six weeks, when they were ripe for despatch to the cloth manufacturers.

The woad-mill village lies on one of the roads which are so straight hereabouts that we only lose them in the distance, and the church tower, rising in the trees, is like a beacon in the flat countryside. It is a 15th century tower with bosses of roses and men's heads in the vaulted roof, and a great panelled arch reaching the full height of the nave.

We may come into this light church by a 13th century or a 15th century doorway, both sheltered by massive porches. The nave has striking 15th century arcades of seven bays, with an east window where an arch opened to a chancel till it was swept away in a flood 300 years ago. There is a little old glass set in the clear windows. The font is 15th century and the pulpit Jacobean, and a silver paten with an engraving of the head of Our Lord is the only piece of Communion plate in the county left untouched by the Reformation.

PRICKWILLOW. The fens stretch round it like a sea, and in its great fertile fields we found cabbages, rhubarb, and potatoes growing round the church. The 17th century bell hanging in the spire of the central turret once rang in Ely Cathedral, and from that lovely place came also the font elaborately carved in Italian marble from designs by Sir Christopher Wren. The bowl is carved with four great shells, and has four cherubs linked together by small sea-shells and a rope of beads. We understand that the church, like the vicarage, is set on piles, and we gather that one of the steam engines working here to drain the fens discharges 150 tons a minute into the River Lark.

The Priory Roof

RAMPTON. A fragment of its ancient village cross still stands on the green, and its charming church behind the orchards is old enough to have had its walls not built but rebuilt 600 years ago. Part of the tower is 15th century, and so is the doorway, which brings us to a narrow aisle, separated from the wide nave by a low arcade 700 years old. The chancel arch is 12th century, and looking down on it all is a fine black and white roof with queenposts, thought to have been brought from Barnwell Priory when the monasteries were dissolved.

The chancel has a tiny low window, a double piscina, and an aumbry with its ancient door. The east window, for a long time unworthily debased, has been restored to beauty in memory of those who fell in the war, and also in memory of two rectors, one of them

Charles Evelyn-White, a historian of the county. Back again in the window is much of its fine tracery of 600 years ago, which came to light with a collection of carved stones now in the east wall. Another window of the same period is that at the east of the aisle, with some 14th century glass including a small headless figure in blue and red and gold.

The canopied pulpit is a fine little example of Jacobean art, and the font is a Norman bowl standing on a small complete font of the 15th century. There are several old bench-ends, fragments of the medieval screen in the new one, traces of an old wall-painting said to be St Christopher, and much painting of a later time. A dark stone in the floor has a cross and a Lombardic inscription to Sir Nicholas de Huntingdon, of 700 years ago, and a sculpture of a knight drawing his sword is perhaps a monument to Sir Robert de Lisle, who held Rampton in Henry the Third's day. His family built a fortified house on Giant's Hill near the church, and its moat can still be seen.

The Devil's Dyke

REACH. Its long wide green is fair to see with cream and rose-walled cottages round it, and it has the ruined wall of an old church keeping company with the new church. But its interest is not in these things.

Here we are carried into ages past. Here the past has been like a river, depositing now something older than history, now something Roman, now a Saxon weapon or two, and at times the peat-cutters here have brought to light the fallen giants of a submerged forest; one was an oak 130 feet long. Here has been found also a wild bull's skull with a flint axe embedded in it; we have seen it at the Sedgwick Museum, Cambridge, where it arrived perhaps 2000 years after the blow was struck.

Here lived those subjects of Queen Boadicea who rose as one man at her call, so that we can picture the warriors of Reach rushing south to destroy the Roman city of Colchester. They were the Iceni, a warlike people who were also mighty engineers, and they left a great monument striding away from this village to Wood Ditton. It is the Devil's Dyke, running straight for about six miles and filling the gap between fen and wooded heights.

Beginning here, and constructed with remarkable exactness, it was carried across country at an average height of 18 feet above the level of the plain. With a ditch at the foot, the rampart, 37 feet wide at the base and 12 at the top, rises 62 feet from the bottom of the dyke, with a slope of 50 feet on one side and half as much on the other. It kept war out and peace in for the Britons; in later ages it served the Saxons as part of their boundary between the kingdoms of Mercia and East Anglia. British and Roman relics have been found in it, with Saxon weapons and implements in the ditch.

Chalk is quarried today at Reach as it has been for thousands of years. It was one of the inexhaustible stores of flints, the tools which made man master of the world. The Romans found another use for the chalk, building from it a fine villa whose remains lingered to fill another chapter in the history of the village; and it was chalk from here which formed a lady chapel in Ely Cathedral.

The little inland port seized by the Saxons from the Britons became a centre of trade which survived the Conquest, and King John is said to have granted the villagers the right to hold a yearly fair. The fair still continues, and here every year come the Mayor and Corporation of Cambridge to proclaim it open, and to distribute new pennies.

The Village College

SAWSTON. It has in its annals an exciting page of the story of the past, and it is working out a hopeful page of the story of the future. The tall chimneys of its paper mills stand out in the fields, a midway mark between a house of Tudor stateliness and a light and airy building which was our first village college, to which children from all the villages round come for a practical education for country life not obtainable at the ordinary village school.

It was to Sawston that Mary Tudor came to take refuge with the Huddlestons at the manor house in the anxious days when the reign of the young Edward the Sixth had ended. The house served the Roman Catholics well, for when the Protestant wind blew again a priest's hiding hole was made in it by Nicholas Owen, the Jesuit dwarf who was nicknamed Little John. He made hiding places all over the country with incomparable skill and industry, and in the end he was caught himself and paid for his work with his life.

The church, which stands by the house, has an impressive exterior and an interesting collection of brass portraits within, new and old.

The tower is 14th century, the arcades are 13th except for three Norman arches at the west end of each, and the porch, the clerestory, and the chancel arch (with a peephole at each side) are 15th. There is a double piscina 700 years old. Two charming little Jacobean figures in black gowns and white ruffs kneel on their wall-memorial; they are Gregory Milner and his wife. There is a fine canopied tomb in which lies the wife of Sir Walter de la Pole who died in 1423.

Four brass portraits show a man of about 1420 with an inscription to someone else (the inscription having been found in the manor moat a century ago), a knight in 15th century armour, a couple of about 1500 in shrouds with their five daughters, and a Tudor priest from Norfolk, William Richardson. The John Huddleston who gave shelter to Mary Tudor has no portrait, but an inscription remembers him as "once Chamberlayn unto Kinge Phylipe and Captaine of his Garde, and one of Queen Maryes most honorable Privie Counsel." His family remained on here, and three 19th century descendants have their portraits on brass, Richard drawn in medieval fashion, Edward kneeling in a long travelling cloak, and Sarah with a fringed cloak over her gown and a draped headdress.

On one of the Norman pillars in the nave is a stone figure of Our Lord set here in memory of the men who went out to the war. In memory of them the old market cross has been restored. The market is no more, but an old custom of picking peas continues, and in due season all who will may go with their baskets to an acre of land left by a rich man long ago to grow peas for the poor.

The educational idea born at Sawston in our time may prove to be one of the most potential factors in the transformation of our countryside. The conviction behind the movement, which began in this village, is that the English heart beats best in its villages and that our people should be encouraged to stay there. It was the Director of Education in the county, Mr Henry Morris, who gave the idea practical shape in the formation of a college for training children in rural life and rural work. The college was opened in 1898 by the Prince of Wales, who planted 50 trees, and this light and airy set of modern buildings, built round a great quadrangle, centralises education for children over eleven from the villages round about. There are carpentering and engineering shops, kitchens for teaching cookery with all kinds of stoves, needlework and art rooms, libraries and reading rooms, and, of course, a college hall in which one of the most popular functions is the midday meal, served for a few coppers. It is intended to cover Cambridgeshire with ten such colleges embracing all its villages, and similar colleges have already been set up at Linton and Bottisham and Impington. The buildings are all in keeping with the modern note in school architecture, and the idea is to give abundant facilities for music, dancing, drama, and films. There are acres of playing-fields about each college, and indoors and out the buildings are delightful. The Sawston college was designed by Mr H. H. Dunn.

The Ride to a Reign of Terror

HISTORY has few scenes as dramatic as that of Mary Tudor fleeing in the guise of a market woman to win the proudest crown in Europe. Daughter of Henry the Eighth and Catherine of Aragon, she had been a pawn on the chessboard of her father's tyrannical career. Kept in confinement and poverty, she had at the peril of her life refused to abandon her faith; and at last had been restored so far to favour that Henry had declared her in the succession to the throne. And now, unknown to her, Edward the Sixth had died, and Lady Jane Grey had been acclaimed Queen. The Duke of Northumberland, desiring to imprison Mary, had sent word to her that the king wished to see her, and Mary had set out from Hunsdon, but a secret messenger, coming apace from London, met her by the way and revealed the truth. She immediately changed her route, and riding hard, arrived at Sawston late the same night. A member of the Huddleston family gave her shelter at the risk of her life, for the Protestants, while sympathetic to Mary as a wronged princess, shrank from the thought of a Roman Catholic queen.

News of her arrival travelled through the night, and a force of her enemies marched in the morning to assail the old hall in which she had found shelter. Escaping in disguise, Mary hastened away, but, pausing on the Gog Magog Hills she looked back and saw the hall in flames. "Let it blaze; I will build Huddleston a better," she exclaimed, and the present building is proof that she redeemed her promise.

Reaching Kenninghall in safety, she sent letters to London claiming her rights as queen; and then moved to a strong place in

Framlingham Castle. There the Roman Catholics flocked to her aid, and soon she had an army of 14,000, reinforced by the nobles and their followers who, sent to arrest her, followed the example of the fleet in suddenly defending her cause. The plot of the Duke of Northumberland, with its disastrous consequences, collapsed at once, and Mary's march to London was an unbroken triumph. She entered the capital as a wronged woman vindicated, welcomed by the people.

There were to be bitter lamentations, for the queen was to burn alive 300 of her subjects who did not accept her faith. But she was at her best in those Sawston hours, infirm of body but indomitable in spirit, aware of her deadly peril, yet high in hope, and in her extremity mindful of her obligation to the man whose house was burned over his head for having sheltered her.

The Old Moat

SHEPRETH. Charming it is, with lovely groves of trees and murmuring brooks and thatched cottages dotted about the lanes. Here was a Roman house, of which traces have been found; today there is a comfortable Georgian house where the ways meet, a cross with ten names on the little green shaded with limes, and at a secluded end of the village a moat still filled with water.

By the moat is the neat little church, which takes us back to Norman days. The Normans built its chancel arch, and its font is by the English masons who learned their work from Normans. In one of the recesses by the chancel arch is open window tracery through which we peep to the altar.

We come in through a 12th century doorway, but the clustered columns of the nave, and the chancel itself, are 14th century. The old chest is crumbling with age between its iron bands.

A low pyramid cap covers what is left of the massive old tower of the 13th, 14th, and 15th centuries; the stones that were once at the top have been used in the churchyard wall.

From the Great War

SHUDY CAMPS. A little group of houses by the park in a far-away corner of the county, it has sad memories of war and two visible things to stir us, linked with the catastrophe which tore the world to pieces. Its curious name may come from the vanished earthworks raised when a village did battle for itself. It gave six of its sons for freedom when all Europe was turned into a battlefield in our own time.

Two things we see here from this vast field of war, a wooden cross from the grave of one of the vicar's two sons who lie in Flanders, and a small bracket which comes from the ruins of the famous Cloth Hall of Ypres. The hall is in the background of the east window which glows in memory of all the men of Shudy Camps who did not come back.

The reredos below this window is an old oil painting of the women at the tomb, and is interesting because it is claimed as Vandyck's.

It is a plain and simple little church, but it is 15th century, and in the spandrels of the west window are carvings of the Madonna and a warrior. The south porch has a medieval roof and a door still hanging on its ancient hinges.

A Scene at Westminster

SNAILWELL. From a dark pool here the Snail creeps forth to become a sluggish river winding to the fens. The pretty little village dreams among fine trees, elms and chestnuts shading the tiny green and keeping company with the creepered walls and rose-bowered porch of the church.

A very curious thing we found in this small shrine of St Peter, a tiny jewelled box on the altar with a few grains of sand in it from Jerusalem. On the wall also hang four Great War medals of Sir Kildare Borrowes, whose brother was vicar here.

The church has one of the two Norman round towers in the county, just topping the high-pitched roof of the nave. The rest of the church comes from the 14th century, but it has been much restored. There are two medieval oak screens, pews with old poppyheads, a 600-year-old font, a jumble of old glass in the modern porch, and a lovely old relic of stone carving set above an arch; it is a stone cross delicately pierced and set in a roundel. The beautiful hammerbeam roof has three rows of carving in its wall-plate, and on the ends of the beams are six old wooden figures, three bishops and three men with shields. A medieval gravestone in the churchyard is that of a 15th century priest. It was found in the wall of the church. On the wall is a memorial to James Baker, who was clerk for 50 years.

From this small place William Flower went out to die for his faith in 1555; he was martyred in St Margaret's churchyard, Westminster. It was a bitter sight, for, his hand having been struck off at the stake, he was then knocked down into the fire, there not being enough faggots to burn him.

Cromwells Begging their Bread

SOHAM. It was one of the English cradles of Christianity, where Felix of Burgundy came to found his abbey on high ground above the plain. Here they laid him to rest, and a few years later St Etheldreda founded her abbey at Ely, and both abbeys flourished till both were destroyed by the Danes. Soham Abbey was never raised again, but the little town has a fine view of the cathedral which grew out of Etheldreda's abbey at Ely, standing on the hill at the end of the five-mile Causeway built to link the two towns soon after the Conquest.

The fruitful orchard land of what was once Soham Mere lies to the west. The sails of a windmill turn at each end of the straggling town and between them lies the splendid church built nearly 800 years ago. Its oldest remains are still its chief glory within, but it is to the 15th century that Soham owes its grand tower, rising above the fenland like a symbol of faith that many waters cannot quench. It rises 100 feet high, with lovely battlements and pinnacles, and looks down on two beautiful medieval porches. The aisles have cornices carved with roses, and there are heads at the south doorway. There is an impressive array of arches inside, four of them believed to have supported the central tower of the 12th century church. The western arch has rich mouldings and capitals of that period, and most of the simpler arches of the nave are of the same age. The tower arch soars impressively, and an arch of the 15th century, leading into a chapel, has two rows of flowers in its mouldings, embattled capitals, and grotesque animals on each side. The chancel has 13th century walls, the south transept has a 13th century piscina, but the richly carved sedilia is 14th. A brave array of angels, sitting and kneeling, praying and holding shields, looks down from the grand old roof.

In one of the chapels, to which we come by an ancient door with iron bars and a massive lock, is an old stone altar, and medieval glass with angels, birds, and flowers. Among a wealth of ancient woodwork in the church is a 15th century screen, its tracery tipped with

Swaffham Prior   **The Two Churches**

Soham   **The Beautiful Tower**

Soham

Sutton

TWO CAMBRIDGESHIRE INTERIORS

roses, animals, and grotesque faces; an eagle and a queer man are peeping out above the entrance. There are 15th century benches with carved heads on which is an angel, a bishop, and a flying lizard, and on some 600-year-old stalls in the tower are carved seats with the quaint fancies of the medieval craftsmen. On one of the walls is an old painting of a bishop, and hidden behind the organ is the 16th century monument of Edward Bernes, showing his 15 children kneeling; he and his wife are lost. An inscription in the chancel tells of John Cyprian Rust, "scholar and friend of children," who shepherded his flock here for 53 years.

In the churchyard lies a very old man whose inscription says curiously, "Dr Ward, whom you knew well before, was kind to his neighbours and good to the poor," and not far from him is the grave of Elizabeth D'Aye, unknown to most of those who come into this churchyard, yet a woman of much interest, for her mother was the only grown-up daughter of Cromwell's best son, Henry. Elizabeth had come down in the world. Her mother, Elizabeth Cromwell had married an officer in the army, William Russell of Fordham, who lived far beyond his income, kept a coach and six horses, and gathered so many creditors about him that it was said to be fortunate that he died. His widow, so far from trying to retrieve the shattered fortunes of her family, struggled to keep up appearances, and it is recorded that she took as many of her 13 children as she could and went up to London, where she died of smallpox caught by keeping the hair of two of her daughters who had died from it.

Her daughter Elizabeth married Robert D'Aye of Soham, who also spent a good fortune, and was so reduced that he died in the workhouse. Richard Cromwell's daughter appears to have come to widow D'Aye's assistance, but she died in the grip of poverty, leaving behind her still another Elizabeth, who married the village shoemaker of Soham, a man of honesty and good sense who rose to be a high-constable. Well may the biographer of the House of Cromwell be moved by the thought of his descendants begging their daily bread. "Oh, Oliver," says he, "if you could have seen that the gratification of your ambition could not prevent your descendants in the second and third generation from falling into poverty, you would surely have sacrificed fewer lives to that idol. How much are they to be pitied!"

There was born at Soham in 1748 a leather-seller's son named James Chambers, who must have broken his father's heart by choosing evil ways and living the life of a ne'er-do-well while trying to be a poet. He lived to be nearly 80, when he died at Stradbroke, and for most of his life he appears to have been a roaming gipsy, making acrostics of people's names if they would give him a meal. He wrote some of his verses in Soham workhouse, but none of them are to be matched with the fine work that has come from many of these houses of adversity. There are references to him in old books and papers, but he has been forgotten as a good-for-nothing, and the best reference we have found to him was written by Mr Cordy of Worlingworth in Suffolk:

> *A lonely wanderer he, whose squalid form*
> *Bore the rude peltings of the wintry storm:*
> *Yet Heaven, to cheer him as he passed along,*
> *Infused in life's sour cup the sweets of song.*

Mr Cordy made an appeal for him and found him a cottage, which was furnished so as to encourage him with his poems. But it was no use; in a month or two he was off again, preferring a bed of straw to a couch of down.

The Chalice from the Grave

STAPLEFORD. Before the Romans came to England, before even a hut of mud and wattle appeared beside Stapleford's long street at the foot of the Gog Magog Hills, the fortress of Wandlebury Camp was dug on the crest of the ridge, commanding the ford of the Cam at Hauxton and Grantchester with Fulbourn Fen supporting it on the north. Though its threefold ramparts have been partly levelled by time, it is still imposing, a raised circle 1000 feet across, in which coins of Nero and British kings have been found. The Romans took possession of it, and close by is an overgrown Roman road. A clear day brings a glimpse of Ely Cathedral.

The church, circled by trees in a quiet lane, may have Saxon stones in its foundation, but the tower and the tiny spire and most of what we see are from the beginning of the 14th century, the chancel arch alone being Norman, a lovely thing with zigzag ornament and fine capitals. The chancel has been rebuilt, but keeps its old lancets and its double piscina, and from the past comes also the ancient font, the 13th century coffin lid, a fragment of crude carving, a chest latticed with ironwork 500 years old, and the small brass portrait of William Lee, vicar for 43 years in Shakespeare's day. In the church is the stone coffin in which an earlier vicar was buried with the pewter chalice and paten beside him which we now see, worn and broken, in a glass case.

STEEPLE MORDEN. It lies among orchards and meadows by the Hertfordshire border, with little dormer windows peeping from deep thatched roofs and flowers bordering the cottage walls. It has lost the steeple which gave it half of its name, for it fell in a storm 200 years ago, and the tower was replaced by a low one of red tiles with a shingle spire above the 14th century porch. The nave arcade has clustered pillars and capitals of about 1300, the font is about the same age, and there are a few fragments of ancient glass. In one of the aisles is a Jacobean altar, and there is a plain old chest.

The Baron of Dundalk

STETCHWORTH. Once it was a town, able to bear a considerable share in the draining of the fens 300 years ago; and the church in the park, where a fine avenue of elms leads to Stetchworth House, has a statue of the man who for 20 years managed this important business of reclamation. He was Lord Gorges, Baron of Dundalk, and he appears in his armour and wig with his wife on the monument to their 19-year-old son Henry, who died in 1674 and is lying before them in an elaborate kilted dress, the white figures very striking against a black ground.

Many faces from the past peep out from the walls of this rather plain church, a mixture of medieval styles with a small Norman doorway, a great arch framing the dim 13th century chancel, and in the nave a 15th century font carved round with heads and shields. More faces come between the 15th century arches of the nave arcades, and others support the old tiebeams in the roof, one laughing under the strain, another pulling his mouth awry. Under windows in the aisles are four brackets from which odd little men and women look out. Here William Thorpe served as vicar for half of last century.

The Man Who Set the Stage to Rout

STOW-CUM-QUY. Quy Water rises from the springs in the chalk above the flat land, flows past the houses and cottages, turns the wheels of the old mill, and gives its name to this island of the fens. On the high ground, standing finely and alone by the busy highway from Cambridge to Newmarket, is the flint church with a tower seen for miles round. It is five or six centuries old, and the tower arch opens into a 14th century nave with clustered pillars. We go up a step into the chancel, through a 15th century oak screen carved with growing flowers, birds, and grotesques. The medieval font is supported by angels. In the floor by the chancel step is the brass portrait of John Ansty in armour of the 15th century, with four daughters in horned headdresses kneeling at prayer, and a remarkable group of 12 sons kneeling in double file, all in tabards with the Ansty arms. On the wall of the north aisle is a black brass of last century with the portraits of Thomas and Helena Martyn.

The village had two vicars who became archbishops, and remembered on a tablet is the famous Jeremy Collier who was born here in 1650. A fiery believer in his own opinions, he had a remarkable career. Son of the parson-schoolmaster, he was educated at Ipswich and Cambridge, entered the church, and after holding various livings, was appointed lecturer at Gray's Inn. A Tory High Churchman and very nearly a Roman Catholic, he was unshaken by the wrongdoing of James the Second, and refused allegiance to William and Mary. He roused anger by rejoicing over British military reverses, and set the country ringing with indignation when, accompanying to the gallows two men who had planned to assassinate the king, without a word of contrition uttered by them, he pronounced absolution, as though to murder King William was not a crime. He had already been imprisoned for treason, and now fled into hiding and was outlawed. An outlaw he remained for the last 36 years of his life, but the Government acted magnanimously, ignored his presence in London, and permitted him to publish volumes of essays and history.

The one thing that justified his existence was his magnificent Short View of the Profaneness and Immorality of the English Stage. With all the wits, the Tories, and the Jacobites arrayed on the side of the dramatists who since the Restoration had made the stage a sink of infamy, this little outlaw routed them all, not merely the petty purveyors of obscenity, but Vanbrugh, Wycherley, Congreve, and Dryden himself. He put them in the dock, tried them by their writings, and convicted and scourged them to shame and silence.

Westley Waterless
Sir John Creke, 1324

Wisbech
Thomas Braunston, 1401

Horseheath
William Audley, 1365

Hildersham
Henry Paris, 1427

Stow-cum-Quy
John Ansty, 1460

Cambridge (St Benedict's)
Richard Billingford, 1442

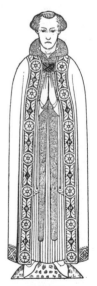

Fulbourn
William de Fulbourn, 1391

OLD CAMBRIDGESHIRE BRASSES

There were half-hearted replies, but the outlawed parson returned to the attack each time and completed the rout. He made vice, grossness, and immorality no longer a marketable commodity in the theatre because they were dressed in wit; he opened the door to honest comedy and decent drama. He was such an influence as is needed on the stage in our own time.

That was his life's work, and it brought him his monument, Macaulay's immortal essay.

The Cross on the Roman Road

STRETHAM. We see its spire and the white sails of its centenarian windmill from afar, and in the middle of its highway, which the Romans called Akeman Street, its splendid cross stands 20 feet high (on a newer pedestal). On a wall in the village hangs one of the old fire-hooks used for dragging thatch from burning roofs.

A noble cedar stands in the rectory garden, and in the churchyard a mighty yew grows with other trees said to have been planted when the church was made new in the 14th and 15th centuries. Much has been altered since, but in the south porch are fragments of a still older church, stones carved by Saxons and Normans, and part of a coffin lid with a maltese cross. Inside are two ancient coffin stones. Women wearing wimples look down from between the arches of the medieval north arcade; women would be wearing wimples when the 15th century chancel screen was made, with its projecting arches. There is also an old chest shaped like a travelling trunk.

The lancet tower arch makes an effective frame for the graceful west window, and the glass in another window is a modern masterpiece in memory of two women, showing two souls entering into heaven between Prudence, Piety, and Charity, and a knight fighting a flaming demon. A stone under a canopy in the chancel tells of Nicholas de Kyngestone, a rector of 600 years ago, whose brass portrait has been stolen; but Joan Swan's remains, a fine big picture of this woman who died in 1497 and whose two sons, John and Richard Riplingham, followed each other as rectors here.

Monk John's Road

STUNTNEY. It was the first Bishop of Ely who gave it its name. He conceived the idea of making a road across the fens and found a monk named John to plan it for him. Monk John hit on a steep island rising sharply from the fens and used it as a stepping-stone for his road to Ely, and Stuntney Causeway it has been for eight centuries and more. The old legends tell us that the place for the road was disclosed by St Edmund in a dream, the saint wishing to travel by it to visit St Etheldreda at Ely's Saxon abbey. So it was that many pilgrims came this way, and as the centuries rolled on there came this way a man of sterner dreams, for the old hall, which is now a gabled house in a cluster of farm buildings, was the home of Cromwell's mother, and Oliver inherited it from his uncle. Here he spent much time before he became MP for Cambridge, and we think of him looking across the fens to Ely.

The last two generations have turned a fine little Norman church into a plain place with a saddleback tower and a timber arcade. The few remnants of Norman days are in two zigzag doorways, the fine font with a bowl like a water-lily, the walling of the chancel, and the disused chancel arch with its beauty hidden by the organ. There is fine wood carving on the stalls and at the altar, with tiny heads of animals and grotesques.

The Beautiful Tower

SUTTON. Like a beacon above the valleys of the Ouse and the Cam rises its magnificent tower, with a big and then a little octagon on the top of its three buttressed stages, finished with pinnacles and a tiny spire. It is one of the county's most beautiful towers, and a grand church it guides us to, for it was largely rebuilt by two Bishops of Ely at the end of the 14th century, when the peak of medieval architecture was in sight. They were Bishop Barnet and Bishop Arundel (who crowned Henry the Fourth). Their arms and a fine portrait of Bishop Barnet appear with a king, a woman, and grotesque animals as bosses on the vaulted roof supporting the porch room. Inside the tower is another vaulted roof, but of oak, and here angels, animals, and men (one with his tongue out) are among the bosses.

Set in the lofty spaciousness of the nave are many stately arches: the two arcades, the tower arch, and the chancel arch, while the arcaded walls frame the lovely windows of the aisles. The east window is between two canopied niches which have modern statues of St Etheldreda and St Andrew; in the battered niche over the elegant piscina in the south aisle is a broken Madonna. At the east end of the south aisle is a charming oak reredos, and here we found two kneeling children by the altar, one a boy, the other a girl in a wide-brimmed hat, both carved in oak by a modern craftsman. One pathetic thing there is here also, a wooden cross from Flanders, scarred by shrapnel. It was set up on the battlefield over the grave of the two boys the vicar gave to his country.

There is an old brass eagle, some old pews with poppyheads, a stone bench running round the church, and a massive 15th century font with a string of flowers. But even more interesting for its story is the small stone bowl by the font, for, though chickens were feeding out of it on a farm here only a few years ago, it is now thought to be one of the few relics of Burystead Monastery. Other traces, including a traceried window with a monk's head carved over it, exist in two houses beyond the end of Sutton's long street, where are remains of the fishponds and the moat; and the earth has yielded up tombstones of fenmen who brought their babies to be baptised at this small bowl seven hundred years ago.

He Made Way for Darwin

SWAFFHAM BULBECK. It has a lovely corner with cream cottages roofed with thatch and pantiles, an oast-house among long barns, and a farm with walls made up from the ruins of a nunnery, founded by a Norman who gave his name to this place and whose family may have bequeathed to it its greatest treasure. The treasure is something we have rarely seen, a magnificent cedarwood chest made by some Italian craftsman five centuries ago as a travelling altar. Its lid is carved inside so that it can open to form a reredos, and the carvings show the three crosses on Calvary with the multitude pressing about them on horseback and on foot, another scene of the Resurrection, and one of the Assumption. The front of the chest has a frieze of angels and Old Testament scenes.

The church which houses this treasure is mostly built of chalk that has stood 600 years, with a tower a century older still. The beautiful medieval windows, crowned with a clerestory, fill it with light, so that we can examine in detail the quaint creatures carved on the poppyheads and arm-rests of the 15th century benches—birds and animals, camels and mermaids and griffins, one fish caught swallowing another, and fishes with feet and heads of animals. The beautiful chancel has tracery in its windows like butterfly wings and an elaborate sedilia near which is an old coffin, its broken lid carved with a cross.

One of the vicars here was a remarkable man who lived through all but seven years of last century, known for 71 years as Leonard Jenyns and for 22 as Leonard Blomefield. He had something to do with the way the career of Charles Darwin went, for he was a first-rate naturalist and was offered a post as such on the voyage of the Beagle. As it would have taken him from the village for five years he could not go, and recommended Darwin in his stead. When Darwin came home Blomefield wrote the volume on the fishes Darwin had discovered, and many walks had they together in the countryside, observing life in aspects common to them both. He was a disciple and an editor of Gilbert White, and could almost recite White's Selborne by heart. His own chief book was a volume of British vertebrates, but he wrote a charming autobiography and many scientific papers. He lived till he was 93 and was buried at Bath, having seen his younger friend Darwin laid to rest in the Abbey.

Pictures in the Windows

SWAFFHAM PRIOR. It has two windmills and two churches. One windmill is working, the other has done with work; one church has a nave but no steeple, the other has a tower but no people. The two churches stand in one churchyard, side by side. The 18th century nave of the church of St Cyriac and his mother Julitta is derelict, but its 15th century tower still stands, its top with eight sides seeming to overhang the square base, an illusion arising from the fact that the pilasters rise from carved corbels. St Cyriac's serves as a place of worship no more, but its bells call the people to St Mary's, whose nave has been in ruins but is now itself again.

St Mary's own tower, once the model for St Cyriac's, begins square, rises to an octagon and then to a lantern with 16 sides. The lower part is Norman lit by round-headed windows, the top stage is 13th century with pointed lancets, and then comes an abrupt end where the steeple was pulled down after being struck by lightning. From inside its arch, six feet thick, we can see that the tower is now but a shell, with a quaint turret stair and a medley of medieval glass in one window. The medieval arcades and their embattled capitals have been patched up. The old font has been brought back from a garden rockery. Some coffin stones have found sanctuary here, and five portrait brasses have survived from three centuries. The oldest shows John Tothyll of 1463, with his wife and dog. Next comes Richard Water with his wife; then William Water and his wife and seven sons; then a charming couple of 1530; and last Robert Chambers, in the top boots and long cloak fashionable in Charles Stuart's days.

Belonging to our own day is the pleasant chancel screen with a vaulted loft and the charming gallery of stained glass, every window with six scenes, original in conception and softly coloured. Two windows sing the hymn of praise in scenes of all Creation, the volcano and the glacier, light and darkness, the shadow of the Moon eclipsing the Sun, and the sea with whales. Some may recognise among the scenes Sedge Fen at Wicken, others Mount Pilatus. Edward the Seventh is here among a group of natives. The windows in the north aisle tell the story of the war, the Zeppelins and the aeroplanes, tanks and guns, men fighting and dying, munition makers and ambulance men, and peace at last, with the men back at their work in the countryside. Two swords hanging on the wall recall wars of other days. With one Colonel Allix, descended from Huguenot refugees, fought at Waterloo in the British Army; the other belonged to an officer who was with Lord Roberts in one of the dramatic scenes of the Boer War, when Cronje surrendered.

A Great Array of Woodcraft

SWAVESEY. Every Cambridge student knows Swavesey, for here the fens hold out their first invitation, and when Lent term begins with frost here is excellent skating. But for those who come in summertime there is the charm of thatch and cottage gardens, and opposite the old manor house is one of the handsomest medieval churches in the county, an amazing collection of creatures new and old sitting on its array of benches.

Of the priory founded by Alan de la Zouche only a few banks and ditches are left, and it is the church which now dominates the long straggling village, its warm-tinted stone shown to perfection by the dark cedars. The imposing tower has three 13th century arches inside, but is mostly of the 15th century. A great porch has sheltered for 700 years the richly moulded entrance into the spacious interior, where stately arcades divide the clerestoried nave from its aisles, some of their arch mouldings resting on slender shafts, others continuing to the floor.

Though the wonderful bench-ends all look old, most of them are skilful 19th century copies, and only the block in the north aisle is medieval, so low that these old seats seem to have been made for children. Both old and new ends have edges carved with flowers and all have striking poppyheads, no less than 154 in all, with animals, saints, and angels among them. Some of the animals are fighting, angels are playing fiddles; there is a dragon with two heads, a snake attacking a lion, a pelican swallowing a fish, a boar with its baby, an owl with a mouse in its beak. Passing through the 13th century chancel arch we find more entrancing stalls, again new and old, with men and animals on the arm-rests and poppyheads, one delightful poppyhead showing Aesop's stork filling the pitcher with stones so that Master Fox can lap the overflowing water.

There is also exquisite stonework in the sedilia and piscinas of the chancel and south chapel, the heads of a 14th century man and woman by the canopies of those in the chancel, and still daintier 15th century carving elaborating the arches over those in the chapel. The graceful traceried font is 500 years old. There is a medieval stone altar with the old consecration crosses, several coffin lids, and one stone coffin. All the oak screens are modern, but one of the altar tables is Jacobean, and much old woodwork is left in the roofs, six small angels bearing up the chancel beams and two men doing the same in the south chapel. The big chest was a thankoffering from the villagers for help when floods in 1876 threatened to drown them all. A big monument of 1631 to the wife of Sir John Cutts shows two women opening a door and boasts a long genealogical inscription in which John Kempe, Cardinal Archbishop of York, figures.

Next Door to Bedfordshire

TADLOW. It is only a step into Bedfordshire from this scattered little place, with a moated farm called Tadlow Bridge and a small cobbled stone church with two cedars overtopping its 500-year-old tower. A block of stone with a socket hole set in the walls of a farm is all that is left of its ancient cross. In the 13th century church is another stone with traces of the lost portrait of Margaret Broggrife, whom they laid to rest here in 1493. Only a few lines of her skirt are left, but a drawing in the church shows us the outline of Margaret's figure and the picture of her six children before they were trodden away by many feet.

Knight of the Civil War

TEVERSHAM. It is sheltered by trees and surrounded by great fields of the plain; from the trees a tower peeps out calling us to the little church it crowns. It stands in the place of one founded by a man who fell fighting the Danes. Its tower is 15th century, with the original painted roof with red and green shields and flowers. The lovely 13th century arcades have delightful capitals at the east end shaped like a slender wineglass and carved with sprays of foliage. The chancel is five and six centuries old, with beautiful seats for priests elaborately canopied. There is a tiny peephole in each pillar of the chancel arch, and across the arch is a 15th century oak screen. The panelled roof above it all has bosses of flowers and a cornice of angels wearing crowns and holding ribbons. There is a fine Jacobean pulpit, a plain old font, and a medley of old glass in the west window. The battered figures of Sir Edward Styward and his wife lie on a table tomb, he in chased armour as he would be seen in Charles Stuart's day, she in a ruff, a gown with a hooped skirt, and a bonnet. They lived through the exciting years of the Civil War.

Long, long, before them men were fighting here for their existence, for life went on at Teversham in prehistoric days. Even before man and the woolly rhinoceros came to it Time bequeathed to this place some witness of life, for in the gravel men have found fossils of shell fish long extinct in England.

THETFORD. A tiny hamlet near Grunty Fen, it has little for us to see except a few thatched cottages, and a little lowly church with a roof like a mantle of moss. Although it is 600 years old the church has lost much of its antiquity, but it keeps its old font, the heads on it worn by time, and it is interesting that it should be here, for it has been in the river and was rescued last century. There are angel corbels supporting the roof of the chancel, and in the bell turret hangs a bell which tolled for the little chapel at Ely Place,

Holborn, the chapel of the bishops in the garden which grew the strawberries King Richard calls for in Shakespeare.

An Island's Thousand Years

THORNEY. Thorney's natural beauty is all the more enhanced because of its place in the plain fenlands. Its lanes are perfect bowers of greenery, gabled houses are everywhere, and there is a fine green space by the church in which the village is passing rich, both for itself and for its story. For this is holy ground, and this island in the fens, once an oasis in a wilderness of marshes, is a witness of the thousand-year struggle of Englishmen for their altars and their homes.

Grand as it is today in its simplicity and strength, the Abbey Church has come through much change of fortune to be but a fragment of its old self which was five times as big when the Normans left it, and it is the only part extant of the monastery founded here for anchorites in 662, though traces of foundations of the monastic buildings have been found. Its story begins when Wulpher, King of the Mercians, went to Peterborough in 662 for the consecration of the minster. Saxulph, the Abbot, told him that some of his monks wished to live the hermit's life, and the king granted them permission to retire to dreary Thorney Island in the marshes. There they dwelt in huts and built themselves a chapel, and though little is known of them their names are not wholly forgotten. Tancred, Tortred, and their sister Tona were for ever remembered for their renunciation, and sleep as canonised saints somewhere beneath the stones of the once great Abbey Church.

Other saints found the same sanctuary, but not all can be said to have rested in peace, for the Danes swept down on the monastery, burning and pillaging, and the monks took refuge in the woods. In 972 it was refounded by Ethelwold, Bishop of Winchester, and King Edgar endowed it. A hundred years later the monastery suffered at the hands of its friends, for when Hereward the Wake made his stand against the Conqueror Thorney Island was one of his fastnesses, and suffered in the attack.

Then, in the last years of the Conqueror's reign, a change took place in its fortunes. Thorney was born again. The old Saxon church was taken down and a new great one raised in its stead, and with its new foundation there was born a new vigour in well-doing. William of Malmesbury paid a tribute not merely to the piety of the monks, but to their courage and industry in coping with the fenland. A very paradise bearing trees, he called it, extolling the vines and apples of this wonderful solitary place for monks of quiet life. The abbey buildings were enlarged from time to time, and a chapter house was built early in the 14th century where the vicarage is now, and the abbey gateway was renowned in the same century for being "one of the hundred celebrated places in England." The place grew in fame, and its mitred abbot sat in the House of Lords till the Dissolution, when the monks were driven away, the lead of the roofs was stripped and melted down in fires fed perhaps by the woodwork of the Abbey Church, and of its stones 140 tons were taken for building the new chapel of Corpus Christi College. The fruitful fields went back to marshland and desolation.

Nearly a century passed, and there was another turn of fortune's wheel. It began with the great adventure, led by the Earl of Bedford, of draining the fens, and one of the chapters in that story included the restoration of the remains of the Abbey Church in 1638. Inigo Jones is said to have been the architect.

Gone are the six aisles, the central tower, and the spires which crowned the western towers of the Norman church, which was nearly 300 feet long, but it stands majestic in the shape of a T formed by the old nave with its splendid west front, and transepts added at its eastern end last century. The Norman masonry gleams light and lovely in contrast with the 19th century's rust-coloured stone. The five great bays of the Norman arcades now in the side walls are magnificent, some of the round arches on clustered pillars. Under the arches, and in the Norman triforium above them, the later windows are set. The imposing west front is mainly Norman, though later turrets crown the two Norman towers which flank it, and are now 83 feet high. A smaller window lights the west wall, set in an earlier arch which rises to a fine gallery of nine saints in niches, who are thought to have either lived at Thorney or to have been buried here. The third in the row, from the right, is Tatwin, a hermit here who took St Guthlac in a boat to Croyland when he was finding a site for his hermitage.

The east window is a great lancet without tracery, about a century old and striking with a rich mosaic of roundels in purple tones glinting with gold and greens, representing the miracles of Thomas Becket. It is a copy of a window in Canterbury Cathedral. Other windows have old shields of the Duke of Bedford, John of Gaunt, and Henry the Eighth and Catherine of Aragon, and lovely Flemish panels with scenes of Bible story, among them a fine Pieta, the Upper Room at Emmaus, and Christ receiving the saved from a tomb, with a demon trapped under His feet and another demon fleeing.

A tablet on the wall gives us another strange chapter of Thorney's story. It is a French inscription to Ezekiel Danois of Compiègne in France, the first minister of the Huguenot colony which fled to England to escape persecution and settled here. He was a worthy successor to Thorney's saints, and we read that "in unwearied zeal, learning, and strictness of life, he was second to none; a great treasure of literature was here hidden from the world, known to God and himself, few besides." Twenty-one of his 54 years of service were spent at Thorney Abbey, and he was buried here in 1674. It is one of the strangest episodes in Thorney's history that Huguenot pastors continued to minister here till 1715.

The Fate of the King

THRIPLOW. Its smithy and its cottages gather about the green, and on a hill on the edge of the village, with a 17th century thatched cottage close by, the church looks down on peaceful fields which came into history for some fateful hours of 1647. It was the time of the first dispute between the Long Parliament and the Army. The army commanded by Cromwell and Fairfax had been ordered to disband, and the angry soldiers assembled on Thriplow Heath threatened to march on London. As a practical gesture of defiance of the Parliament the army sent Cornet Joyce with a troop of horse to carry off the King from Holmby House in Northants. Three weeks later Thriplow Heath saw another act in the momentous drama of King and Commonwealth, when Charles was brought back on Midsummer Day across these very fields.

The church has a central tower which can be seen for miles, six or seven centuries old, resting on four arches adorned with quaint faces. It has old painted roofs, an oak chancel screen of the 14th century, a Norman font, and a sculptured family group with Edward Lucas and his wife kneeling with their four children, subjects of Queen Elizabeth.

The Fanatic

TOFT. On the edge of this village of demure cottages is a cunningly thatched house near a church rising with stately grace from the meadows.

Here came the fanatic Dowsing on his destructive round of the churches of Suffolk and Cambridge, and he left the alabaster reredos a mere fragment of lost beauty. St Christopher's hands are gone, and St Hubert has lost his head, but is a delightful little figure still, in a white gown lined with red and touched with gold, still carrying the key St Peter gave him to cure hydrophobia. His dog is licking his shoe, and by him is a hart with golden horns, for he was the huntsman converted by a vision of the Cross between a hart's antlers. Dowsing smashed the glass saints, too, but fragments have been saved in the east window of this 15th century church, made new last century, when the north aisle was added and the tower was rebuilt in memory of Edward Powell, rector for 49 years. Two oak angels guard the tower arch and 12 stone ones support the old nave roof. There is a plain old font and an oak pulpit of Tudor linenfold.

The Brave Blind Man

TRUMPINGTON. It is in modern poetry (in Rupert Brooke and Tennyson) and it has a place in the history of our medieval craftsmanship. Many a Cambridge man since Chaucer has taken the way past King's and Peterhouse which begins as Trumpington Street and ends two miles away at Trumpington Church; and some, like Rupert Brooke, have passed by Chaucer's mill, where the Cam divides Trumpington from Grantchester:

> Beside the pleasant mill of Trumpington
> I laughed with Chaucer in the hawthorn glade.

Tennyson brought it into the Story of the Miller's Daughter:

> From the bridge I leaned to hear
> The mill dam rushing down with noise
> And see the minnows everywhere
> In crystal eddies glance and poise,

But here is something which stood in England long before our

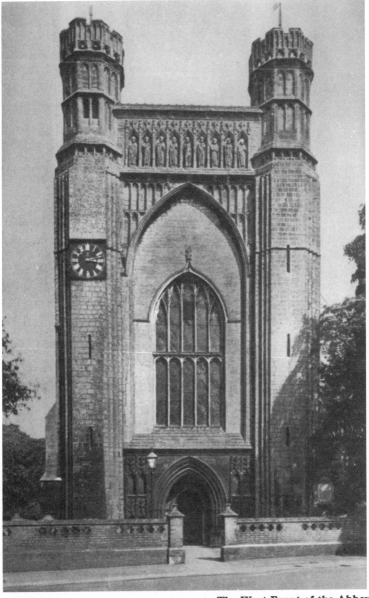

Thorney   **The West Front of the Abbey**

The Via Devana, a Roman Road

The Devil's Dyke, a Prehistoric Defence

ANCIENT CAMBRIDGESHIRE

poetry began, long before the great medieval brass of Roger Trumpington was made. On the way to the village from Cambridge is the first milestone set up in England after Roman times. It was put here in 1729, when milestones painted with the crescent of Trinity Hall were set up by the College far and wide; but this first of our milestones for over a thousand years is an actual Roman stone. Old as it is, there were roads here before the Romans, trackways of Iron Age Men who lived and fought and were buried here with their weapons and their pottery, much of which is to be seen in Cambridge Museum.

Between the slow-moving river and the fast-moving traffic of the London road are Trumpington's old houses and trees, and a medieval church still beautiful though much restored. The grey walls, the delicate clustered pillars, and the lofty arches make a stately picture as we see them from the sanctuary, the arcades soaring up to a clerestory of trefoiled lancets on one side and round quatrefoils on the other. Very charming are the windows of 14th century tracery, with a medley of medieval glass in the east window and two headless saints with more fragments in another. The heads of 15th century folk are carved with angels round the bowl and stem of the font, a king, a bishop, and some odd-looking fellows among them. Only the base of the 15th century oak chancel screen is left, but it has some good carving, coloured and gilded. The pulpit is Jacobean and there is an older ironbound chest like a family trunk.

The most precious of all the possessions of this church is the great brass portrait of Sir Roger de Trumpington, who went with our future Edward the First on the Crusade which so nearly ended in Edward's death by an assassin. There is only one brass portrait in England earlier than this, that of the Surrey knight Sir John D'Abernon at Stoke D'Abernon. Sir Roger here is portrayed as a crosslegged knight six feet four inches tall, with his sword in a dog's mouth and his head on a helmet secured by a chain to his girdle. He lies on a 14th century canopied tomb, with a rich arch from which the heads of men and women look down on him.

The block of stone under the tower arch begging us to pray for the souls of John Stockton and his wife is all that is left of the wayside cross they gave the village 500 years ago. Where it stood on the main road is now a striking cross to 36 men killed by war, its shaft carved with the Madonna, St George, and St Michael, and a Tommy trudging along while shells splinter the trees round him.

Most of the 36 must in their youth have been thrilled with the tales of G. A. Henty, who made of war an adventure far different from their experience. This Victorian best-seller was a Trumpington man, born here 1832. Many of the wars he wrote about he had witnessed, first on active service in the Crimea, and later as a war correspondent with Garibaldi, Lord Napier, with the French starving in Paris during the Commune, with Lord Wolseley in Ashanti, till his health gave out and he settled down to writing adventure books for boys, about three a year. In 1902 he died on board his yacht in Weymouth harbour. Another writer here before him was Christopher Anstey of Anstey Hall, who delighted our great-grandfathers with his new Bath Guide, written in the days of Beau Nash. At Old Mill House lived the traveller and naturalist Dr F. H. H. Guillemard, who loved to tell how his ancestor came over from France, not with the Conqueror but in a wardrobe, a Huguenot escaping persecution. The wardrobe was here when he died in 1934 and may be here still. We can only imagine how he used to regret the pile of three-cornered Cape stamps which he collected as a boy and which his mother burned during spring cleaning. She could scarcely foresee that one day they would be worth a small fortune.

In the churchyard sleeps another famous man, Henry Fawcett, the blind reformer of Mr Gladstone's day, his life summed up in these words on his tomb, *Speak unto the people that they go forward.*

Nemesis overtook him as he was entering on his career; it came in a moment. Out shooting, he was struck in the face by two pellets from his father's gun, and each pellet took an eye. His father himself was short sighted, and now, in an instant, the son was totally blind. In ten minutes he had formed a resolution. He resolved never to complain and not to permit the accident to cause any deviation from the career already planned for him. He took up his fellowship at Trinity Hall, Cambridge, and in a few years made his name as a professor of economics, and author of a book on that subject which attracted wide attention. At 32 he entered Parliament, a brave and independent figure, subject to no party servitude, but unswervingly devoted to reform. His enlightened interest in Eastern affairs won him the title of Member for India. In 1880 Mr Gladstone made him Postmaster-General, an office in which he was a brilliant revolutionary, giving us sixpenny telegrams, the parcel post, and postal orders.

All through his parliamentary career of over 20 years he was one of the most progressive spirits, a blithe and gallant soul, who insisted that his fellows should treat him on terms of equality. "Do not patronise those who are blind," he used to say to his friends; "treat us without reference to our misfortune; and, above all, help us to be independent." He lived valiantly up to his precepts. He enjoyed life to the full; in his blindness he was a successful fisherman, a finished and fearless horseman, a tireless pedestrian, and a remarkable skater. In company he was the merriest of the party, a wit, a romp, a delightful companion. It was a point of honour with him always to speak of having seen this or read that. He had the good fortune to meet and marry Millicent Garrett, who lived for her husband and their home but won fame as one of the first advocates of votes for women. She came of an old Suffolk family at Aldeburgh, and is remembered as one of the most brilliant women of her generation.

Richard's Pillar

TYDD-ST-GILES. Its sister Tydd St Mary lies over the border in Lincolnshire; all the tale of the Cambridgeshire Tydd is told in its church, which captures attention at once by the fact that its tower stands 50 feet away. It has stood for 700 years, though its upper stages were rebuilt in brick 500 years ago. Its triple lancets are now blocked up, and so are two of its arches. Under the other two we can walk. The rest of the church is the old nave and aisles, with arcades running the whole length from east to west, and with a richly moulded chancel arch framing the east window. The 13th century arches are crowned with 15th century clerestories, and their capitals are of great interest in showing the growth of ornament from the conventional scallop and leaf to the natural foliage and drooping leaves. The finely carved font is 500 years old, and a coffin stone in the floor of an aisle is 700. On a pillar is a worn inscription in old French, saying: "This pillar Richard the Priest first began; pray for him."

Tydd St Giles claims Nicholas Breakspear as a curate. It is a resounding claim, for he is the only Englishman who ever sat in the chair of St Peter, becoming Adrian the Fourth.

Remembrance of Things Past

WATERBEACH. The River Cam flows near this pleasant village, and sometimes on the ear "drops the light drip from the suspended oar" when a boat comes down so far from Cambridge. Between Waterbeach and Landbeach runs the Cam Dyke built by the Romans to keep back the fenland waters.

A fragment of ancient sculpture in the church, on which is one cherub blowing a trumpet and another keeping him company, is from the monastery which stood 800 years ago on the farm of Denny Priory, two miles away. The farmhouse has risen from the ruins and the farmyard is on the site of the cloister court. The house has parts of the chapel with a fine arch built by the monks in Norman days, and a great barn which was their dining hall. There is a legend of a lilac bush still growing here which says that somewhere under it sleeps Agnes Countess of Pembroke, who took the old priory and turned it into a home for nuns of St Clare. Monks, Knights Templars, Nuns of St Clare, and the pious Countess of Pembroke passed by these fields, heard the murmur of the river, and have gone.

The church which keeps the cherubs from the vanished priory is five and seven centuries old, with white arcades and cream walls. It has fragments of old glass, an ancient coffin stone, and a modern altar with eight disciples in panels, with mosaics around it of Our Lord and the Madonna, saints and prophets, and on the pulpit are scenes of Paul at Athens and the Sermon on the Mount.

We understand that a 14th century chalice was found in the walls of this church and sold to South Kensington Museum.

WENDY. It shelters off the Roman Ermine Street, a cluster of cottages and a church of last century overtopped by a cedar. It has for a neighbour the once important place of Shingay, an old home of the Knights Hospitallers of which nothing is now left but a dry moat and a row of limes which led to it. The arms from Shingay's vanished chapel are over the doorway of Wendy's church. It is a simple aisleless place with floral paintings covering its walls from floor to ceiling, and the best thing it has is the fine hammerbeam roof of the nave with tracery in the spandrels; it was brought from an old church in Cambridge.

In the churchyard we hear the splash of a natural fountain in the vicarage garden, one of the many springs in the neighbourhood.

The Sculptured Monk

WENTWORTH. As we go from Sutton to Ely it is worth while turning aside to the small church of modest little Wentworth, for it has something to show of the four best building centuries in our history, from the 12th to the 15th. Its church has still the two doorways through which the Normans came, a fragment of Norman carving in an outer wall, and indoors a wonderfully preserved piece of sculpture which is a veritable treasure. It is set in the chancel and shows a monk in a simple robe holding a book in one hand and in the other something like a great key. He stands under a round arch on carved pillars, and in the background is a quaint castle with little windows and pointed roofs. He is evidently meant for St Peter. The chancel, except for its modern arch, is 13th century; in the arch is an oak screen with fragments of the medieval screen worked into it. We noticed that Richard Wakeling was rector here for 55 years to the end of the 18th century.

The Portrait of Lady Alyne

WESTLEY WATERLESS. Ducks swim leisuredly at the gate of its unpretending little church, which has a great treasure in a brass standing high in our national gallery of brass portraits. Though only 17th in order of age, it has one of the very earliest brass portraits of a lady. It is one of two fine big portraits set in the floor, showing Sir John Creke and his wife Lady Alyne. Here they have been for 600 years (since 1324), he in elaborate armour with lions at the shoulders and elbows, a very fine helmet like a mitre, and a curious coat worn at the time reaching to the knees behind and only to the waist in front. Lady Alyne has her hair platted under her veil, and is wearing a wimple and a graceful gown fastened with a cord, and has a dog at her feet.

On a low tomb not far from them lies the stone figure of a civilian they may have known, with long hair and a tunic reaching to his knees. The simple church lost its Norman tower last century, but the inside, gleaming with white arcades and golden walls and roofed in black and white, is pleasantly surprising and ancient too. The nave and aisles are 14th century and the chancel is 13th, and at the crudely carved font the village children have been christened since the church was new. The fine niche by the east window is 600 years old, and the fragments of old glass are of the same time.

Old Brasses

WESTON COLVILLE. It is sheltered by fine woods, and its church is set among chestnuts, having for company in the churchyard part of the 15th century cross with a kneeling stone, two coped and ancient coffin lids, and a sundial which has counted the sunny hours since the Great Plague year. What is left of the old church is mainly 14th century, with a chancel arch on clustered shafts, two piscinas, and an aumbry. We come in by a door 200 years old, hanging in a 14th century doorway. The chief possession of the church is a pair of brasses; one of Robert Leverer of 1427, a knight in armour with flowers growing about his feet, his wife in a graceful gown and flowing headdress and their son between them; the other of Abraham Gates of 1636 kneeling with his wife at a prayer desk. Their brass is adorned with cherubs and skulls and an angel racing away blowing a great horn.

WEST WICKHAM. It looks over the Suffolk border from its lovely hill, and has a simple church to which its people have been coming 600 years. All this time the heads of a man and woman have been looking down from niches by the east window. The same old rafters are in the roof, the children are christened at the same old font, the medieval rood stairs are still here, and the south door has its ancient latch and ring. There are parts of an old screen in the tower arch, two medieval benches with carved ends, a chest with three locks, and Jacobean pilasters on the reredos.

WEST WRATTING. As if the gardens of the thatched cottages were not enough, there is a garden for all by the wayside, a riot of purple and gold when we stopped to read the invitation on its gate: Let all enjoy; let none destroy. Chestnuts make a green bower of the road to the church, which regained last century a little of the attraction it lost 200 years ago when Sir Jacob Shafto brought the 14th century building up to date. Sheltered by the old roof timbers of the porch is a 15th century stoup with a panelled back and an arch matching the two piscinas in the nave and the niche by the chancel arch. A few massive old beams remain in the modern nave roof with its bosses of flowers and leaves. Here we found an old painting showing Christ before Pilate and labelled Titian.

Medieval Tower Above the Trees

WHADDON. From ancient Ermine Street we catch sight of its roofs and its medieval tower above the trees. The tower and the fine north doorway have weathered 500 years, and the rest of the church is older, mainly 14th century, with a cornice of odd faces round the outside of the nave, and heads of medieval folk by the windows of the embattled aisles. Inside are stately arcades and two noble arches, the one to the tower framing a wide west window, the older one to the chancel spanned by a 15th century screen. Two rude people put out their tongues at us from the tracery of this screen, and others gape down open-mouthed from the roof, which has fine bosses carved with flowers and animals. Fragments of old glass are in the top of a window. An angel blows a trumpet on an organ said to have come from Manchester Cathedral. Grace Pickering is remembered for the Black Letter Bible she gave to the church in 1688, and Robert Hurlock for his 55 years as vicar. He died in 1852. The 500-year-old font bears the arms of the Deschallers, the last of whose men lies here in a tomb very worn and with its brass portraits gone. The only trace of their old home are some stalwart oaks.

The Old Man at St Paul's

WHITTLESEY. Willows fringe the road that brings us to this northerly isle of the fens, the River Nene flows slowly past, and wild fowl settle among the rushes and the low pastures of Whittlesey Wash. It has been a market town for seven centuries and its market house is still in the middle of the square. It is an ordinary little town, flanked by the tall chimneys of brickyards rising in mass formation, but the bells ring out melodiously across the fens calling us to one of the loveliest steeples in the county. It is the tower of St Mary's, raised in the 15th century, and beautiful with fine windows, panelled walls, and a doorway worthy of a small cathedral. Its splendid arch and its lofty vaulted roof rise up to panelled battlements with pinnacles from which spring flying buttresses to support the soaring spire.

The church comes from the three great building centuries, the chancel arch and the north arcade of the nave from the 13th, the chancel and the south arcade from the 15th, and the rest of the old work mostly from the 14th. The oak altar and the reredos are in memory of our heroes, one who died near Ypres, and those who came home safe. In a modern window glowing richly with purple, green, and gold, are three English saints, Edmund with the arrow of his martyrdom, Etheldreda with a model of Ely Cathedral, and Guthlac with the scourge. There is a bust of General Wakelyn Smith, a surgeon's son who sleeps in the cemetery here, having fought at Waterloo and lived to be Governor of the Cape in 1847.

Whittlesey has another medieval church, St Andrew's, with an imposing exterior and a fine tower. Slender pillars support the old nave arches, and there are grotesque corbels under the open timber roof. On each side of the 15th century arch are quaint figures of a man and a woman. The oak altar has a stone supported by four angels against a background carved like richly patterned brocade, and another angel is holding the lectern desk on the tips of the wings and fingers. The oak pulpit with a figure of the Good Shepherd is in memory of a soldier who fell in France.

Here was born a boy who became Archbishop of Canterbury in 1368. It is thought that the pope desired a mild archbishop and chose William Whittlesey, who settled down in the old Bishop's Palace at Otford in Kent and lived quietly there, but was tempted one day, by the pressure of heavy taxation of the clergy, to make his way slowly to London and protest from the pulpit of St Paul's. He walked into the pulpit but had only just begun his sermon when he swooned and fell into the arms of his chaplain, and was carried out of the cathedral, put into a boat and rowed down to Lambeth Palace, where he lingered for a few months and died.

A Story of the Centuries

WHITTLESFORD. There was a welcome for travellers here seven centuries ago in the Hospital of St John, and there is a welcome today by its ruins, at a timbered inn with quaint carvings on its rafters. It is thought that the inn may have been part of the hospital in its later days, and we may still see close by the lancet windows of the 14th century chapel, with the ancient piscina and the recess in which the priest would sit.

For thousands of years there must have been an atmosphere of

New Bedford River

The Little Ouse
SCENES IN THE FENS

Wisbech   **The Beautiful 16th Century Tower**

Wisbech   **The Monument of Thomas Parke and his Wife**

Wisbech   **The River Bank**

Wisbech   Clarkson Memorial   **Whittlesey**   Medieval Church

Ickleton   **Village Street**

Wicken   **Village Pond**

holiness here, for on what are called Chronicle Hills the men of the Iron Age buried their dead with high ceremony. They were borne from afar on the ancient trackways, along the green lane to Thriplow or past Whittlesford Mill, close to the church. On the bridge over the Granta was once a hermit's cell. Today the old church stands in its green solitude with its story told in paintings set in oak panels, once as the church was in 1022, then as in 1390, then as in 1904 when it was in danger of falling, and again in 1922 on its 900th anniversary, when it was restored as it had been in 1470.

The tower, about 600 years old, has quaint gargoyles of animals and men, and under the parapet is a group of Norman windows, a stone in the head of one of them carved with a queer animal whispering into a man's ear. The old timber porch has three little heads cut on the beams of its roof, perhaps 600 years old, the nave has a 13th century arcade, the lofty chancel has arches and doorways blocked up, an old oak stall with poppyheads, a medieval screen across two arches, Jacobean panelling and a Jacobean chair, and an oak chest eight feet long held together by a mass of iron bands with five locks. The font is 13th century. There are beautiful fragments of the medieval alabaster reredos kept in a case after being hidden in a chancel wall, and on a wall of the tower are traces of old painting.

Two fine figures in a modern window show two old friends of the village, Henry Ciprian holding a model of this church that he helped to build in the 14th century, and a village bowman of the time of Crecy. Here we come upon three fine modern men who are remembered: Walter Dixon, a scientific pioneer who served in the navy during the war; James Robertson, "a father and friend in home and school and village," master of Rugby and Harrow and Haileybury, and vicar here; and Patrick Moore, a boy of 20 who gave his life for us in the days before Armistice, and of whom we read, "Praised be God for his proud and cherished memory."

The Thrill of History

WICKEN. We are in the presence of mighty names, and the thrill of history here, where all may see the fen as Hereward the Wake saw it, as the Saxon monks of Thorney Abbey knew it when they cut their reeds from it, as the first Bishops of Ely encountered it when laying a causeway from isle to isle across it. Black dykes flow between the acres of thick impassable rushes, the reed warblers trill among them from dawn to dusk in spring, the late cuckoo flits over them when autumn approaches, and Montagu's Harriers, the eagles of the marsh, flap heavily from bog to dyke in search of prey. Rare bird visitants are finding in Wicken and in Burwell Fen a sanctuary the National Trust preserves for them and us, and here we may see one of the rare expanses of a vanished or vanishing England.

A mile from the village is Spinney farmhouse, built from the stones of the ancient priory, and once the home of one who can only narrowly have missed a great page in history, for he was the best of all Oliver Cromwell's sons, Henry. Here when the Stuarts came back and he had lost his lands he came to settle down, and the story is told that Charles the Second, returning from Newmarket, took it into his mind to visit Henry Cromwell at this farmhouse. He found him farming contentedly, and a lord who was with the king thought it a merry jest to seize a pitchfork and carry it before Farmer Cromwell, explaining that he had been mace-bearer when Henry was Lord Lieutenant of Ireland.

Henry Cromwell lies in the little church standing lonely by the wayside, and a brass plate tells us that the oak chancel screen was given in this century in memory of him and his wife Elizabeth. A floor stone under the altar is to Oliver Cromwell's sister Elizabeth, buried here in 1672, and another stone in the chancel floor has the name of Oliver Cromwell the Protector's grandson, who was brought here in 1685. Here also were born two other grandsons of Oliver, Richard who died in London in 1687 and William who died in the East Indies in 1662.

There are two dainty treasures in brass, portraits of Margaret Peyton of 1414 in a graceful gown and mantle with a dog at her feet with bells round its neck, and John Peyton of 1520, a slim figure with long hair wearing a simple mantle with loose sleeves.

The church has little to see except its memorials. It is chiefly 15th century with something of the 13th, and is a simple structure with a tower crowned by battlements and pinnacles. It was the first church known to Isaac Barrow, whose nephew taught Isaac Newton and is in Poets Corner, and to Andrew Fuller, first secretary of the Baptist Missionary Society, both of whom were born here.

The Best of Cromwell's Sons

HENRY CROMWELL was laid to rest here on March 22, 1674, He has been overshadowed in history by his renowned father, by his brother Richard, who failed to hold the position of Lord Protector to which their father had nominated him, and by the earlier Thomas Cromwell, Earl of Essex; but Henry Cromwell was decidedly a man of mark who deserved lasting respect. Holding high office, in situations of great difficulty, he invariably showed himself to be a man of strong character, sound judgment, breadth of outlook, fitted for fine national service, and, as Carlyle calls him, "really an honourable figure."

He was 14 years old when the Civil War began. When he was 19 he was serving as a captain under Fairfax and later under his father. When he was 22 he was sent as a colonel with reinforcements to Ireland, and took part in the final movements of his father's campaign there. Three years later he was nominated as a representative of Ireland in the Barebones parliament, and next year was sent to Ireland again to report on the new Government there.

It was a delicate piece of work, for the Lord Deputy at the head of the Government was his own brother-in-law, Lord Fleetwood, who had married Bridget Cromwell, Henry's sister, and Henry came to the conclusion that the army was playing too big a part in the government of the country and that it would be an advantage to have Fleetwood recalled to England. He suggested this course to his father who was now the Lord Protector, and Oliver, in one of the most charming of his letters, responded by explaining to Fleetwood that he needed his assistance in England. Fleetwood accordingly left Ireland, though for some time he retained his appointment nominally as Lord Deputy in Ireland. Henry Cromwell became Commander-in-Chief of the Army in Ireland and a member of the Council. He believed in Ireland having a more constitutional form of government and was much hampered by the Parliamentary generals who favoured domination by the Army. More than once he offered his resignation, but spontaneous protests from Ireland reached the Protector, who eventually agreed that his son should be the Lord Deputy there. The fact is that Henry was a popular Englishman in Ireland. He was voted land worth £1500 a year, but declined to receive it on the ground that Ireland was poor.

When a movement was started to make Oliver king, Henry urged his father not to accept that "gaudy feather in the hat of authority." He resisted attempts to tax exhorbitantly those who had Royalist sympathies. When the Protector died Henry welcomed the succession of his brother Richard. He was himself appointed Governor-General of Ireland, but wished to resign and return to England to express his views on Irish affairs. He was openly opposed to the restoration of the Stuarts. When his brother was deposed he resigned his office in Ireland, reported himself to the Council of State in England, and retired into private life, as Carlyle says, "in a very manful, simple, and noble way." He lost his share of his father's forfeited estates in England, worth £2000 a year, but was allowed to keep Irish estates worth £600 to £700 a year, which he had purchased.

A number of Royalists, including Clarendon, used their influence to check those who sought vengeance on all who bore the name of Cromwell, and Henry lived quietly for the remaining 14 years of his life at Spinney Abbey, where he died at the age of 46, "a man of real insight, veracity, and resolution (said Carlyle), very fit for such service" as he had undertaken. He entered the war, as he himself said, "by natural duty to his father." While he was quite young he found himself bearing heavy responsibilities in a land where few men have won untarnished honour, and with sound public spirit and independence of judgment he curbed the spirit of military despotism, developed no personal ambition, and almost single-handed became a welcomed ruler. It is a rare sight from those troublous times, and betokens a rare man.

Bronze Age Weapons in the Fen

WILBURTON. Its life was going on far back in the mists of time, and sometime in the Bronze Age men tipped into the fen of the Old Ouse near Wilburton a great collection of swords, spears, and axes. We may hope they had no more use for them. Three thousand years later this strange rubbish heap was found and some of its treasures are now in our museums. The church, with a tiny spire on its tower, is young compared with all this, 500 years old and much restored, but we come into it by a porch with something of a Norman arch left in its wall, and Norman stones in its roof supporting an upper room. There are lofty arcades and great nave windows, and the east window has a carved niche on each side. In the peace memorial window are the two warrior archangels with their dragons, and another window has St Etheldreda with a model of Ely Cathedral. The twisted altar rails are Jacobean. The old wall paintings are fading away.

On the last pilgrimage to Etheldreda's shrine at Ely the rector here, Thomas Alcock, entertained Henry the Seventh and his young Prince Hal at the rectory, and the three cocks from the Alcock shield appear in the fine old roof, with six more over the opening of the rich medieval chancel screen, which has dragons in the tracery, rude faces in the spandrels, and a new vaulted canopy. Thomas Alcock's predecessor, Richard Bole, is on a fine brass in rich robes, under a pinnacled canopy, and another brass has on it John Hyll of 1506 with his two daughters. William Byrd of 1514 has his family of nine with him on another brass, and inscriptions tell of the Markwell family, who made a record in the belfry, each ringing the six bells for 50 years.

A hero of the Great War, Albert Pell, has a monument in medieval style, taking the shape of a little tomb under an arch. He lived at the big house designed by Pugin in the park, where also stands the red gabled manor house built for a London alderman in the last years of Queen Elizabeth. It was long neglected, but has been restored and is a charming home again; on the way to it we pass a venerable oak six yards round the trunk.

Lovely Roofs

WILLINGHAM. The fighting tribes of Britain knew Willingham and its way across the fens, and, by an odd turn of history, their earthwork ring on the rising ground above the marshes is called Belsar's Hill, named after the Norman commander who came this way towards Ely in search of Hereward the Wake.

The village with its windmill lies among the orchards, and is proud of one of the finest churches in the county, abounding in interest, well restored, and with two special treasures among its roofs. For 600 years this tower with its flying buttresses has been a landmark in the Ouse valley, crowning the embattled walls of a building that is chiefly of the 14th century. Fragments of Norman carving are in the spacious porch, which has windows and a big niche and carvings of its own, among them a blindfolded man and a head with a finger on one eye. The porch shelters a shaft piscina, and a finely moulded doorway by which we come inside.

It is a place to linger in, for good things are everywhere as we walk about. Here in the chancel are very beautiful sedilia, and modern figures of the Madonna and St Etheldreda in rich canopied niches. Here is a font made about the time of Agincourt, a carved pulpit just as old, and the ancient altar stone still in use in a chapel. There are three screens with much medieval woodwork and some of their old colouring, that of the north chapel having a pattern of green parrots on a red ground. There are medieval stalls with heads of kings and bishops; aisle roofs with bosses of flowers; and a chancel roof fine with angels.

But the crowning glory of the church is the grand 15th century roof of the nave, a roof of the double hammerbeam type. All its beams are carved or moulded, the spandrels pierced with tracery and in it are 30 angels, some at prayer, some with musical instruments, and some holding symbols of the Passion. A dozen others are on the wall-plate each side, bringing the number of this heavenly congregation up to 54.

The other lovely roof is in a charming chapel now used as a vestry. It is 14th century, and is an example of a rare treatment of roof arching in stone. The arches spring from brackets and grotesque corbel heads, and in their spandrels are leaves and quatrefoils with tiny rose cusps. Also in the chapel are a pillar piscina, a Jacobean cupboard, and some fragments of oak carved 500 years ago.

Paintings by medieval artists are still to be seen on these walls though they are mostly blurred and patchy. Over the chancel arch is painted a big consecration cross, and with it is part of a 14th century Doom scene, one of the demons being in a corner of the nave beside a clear 15th century Visitation, in which the two figures are in blue and white on a red background. Over the arcades we can make out St Michael with sword and scales, St Christopher crossing the stream, and a man at his side; and by an aisle window are two figures in red and gold, one headless.

The Queen Mislays Her Jewels

WIMPOLE. Its park lies between two Roman roads, great gates with a stone lion and unicorn opening to it from one part of Ermine Street, and a marvellous avenue running from another and crossing Akeman Street on which the village lies. The avenue is a double one of elms, like a nave and an aisle, 100 yards wide and more than two miles long, and is an approach to the hall built three centuries ago by Sir Thomas Chichele, enlarged by the Earl of Oxford, and made bigger again by Philip Yorke, Earl of Hardwicke. Here Queen Victoria was entertained soon after her marriage, and the story is told how, having by mistake mislaid her jewels, she came down to dinner with a wreath of roses in her hair, someone saying (we doubt not with truth) that not all the jewels in the world could have made her look so queenly.

The great house and the church stand together, linked by association down the ages. The church was made new with brick walls in 1749, but it has kept its Chichele chapel with a great display of monuments in stone and brass. On a big alabaster tomb lies Sir Thomas Chichele of 1616 in gilded armour, at his feet a dog with a bone, and round the tomb six children, one a wide-awake babe in a cradle.

The little collection of brasses on the chapel wall includes a fine portrait of Dr Thomas Worsley in his rich Tudor vestments, an unusual picture of the Madonna and her Child, and a very attractive figure of Edward Marshall who was parson here and died in 1625. We see also a graceful woman in a little cap, and a group of six girls in kennel headdresses. In two of the chapel windows there is 14th century glass, with many old shields of lords of the manor, and a figure in brown disguised as a monk. One attractive window shows Our Lord in Glory, and another the Madonna and St George in memory of a soldier of the Great War and his mother. A third window is interesting for its story rather than for the highly coloured glass which tells it. It is to Victor Yorke of the great house, who died of heart failure in 1867 while giving a penny reading when he was the guest of the Rothschilds. We see him as an officer reading to a little group, among them his host and the daughter of the house, whom he was going to marry.

There is a huge monument to the Earl of Hardwicke, with figures of Britannia and a woman with lilies, and a plaque of himself and his wife. Famous as a lawyer who did much for that part of our law known as Equity, he became Lord Chancellor and presided over the trials which followed the rebellion of 1745. Another monument has a portrait of his son Charles Yorke, who was Lord Chancellor too, and there is a handsome marble figure of the 3rd earl, reclining with a sword and a book, wearing the rich regalia of the Order of the Garter with a pendant of St George slaying the dragon. Other family memorials are in classical style with cherubs, plaques, and figures of women by urns.

A Great Reformer

PHILIP YORKE, the great Lord Chancellor Hardwicke, was the son of an obscure Dover lawyer who sent the lad to his London agent. An industrious apprentice, he studied so hard that, without university training, he was a barrister at 25, Solicitor-General at 30, and four years later Attorney-General.

During this period his foremost patron, Lord Macclesfield, was impeached for corruption. Friendship prompted Yorke to defend him; duty bade him prosecute; and Parliament had a heart and excused the younger man this ungrateful task. At 43 Yorke was Lord Chief Justice and Baron Hardwicke, and at 47 Lord Chancellor.

For twenty years he occupied the Woolsack, a model of probity and impartial justice. The custom of the age permitted him to grow rich from fees and perquisites, a system abhorrent to modern minds but then accepted.

For years his wife would not hear of his accepting an earldom, observing that, though no suitors would expect more than £10,000 with the Misses Yorke, they would expect £20,000 with Lady Elizabeth and Lady Margaret. A thrifty woman was Lady Hardwicke. The Great Seal of the Lord Chancellor is enclosed in a rich case of embroidered velvet renewed every year, and, twenty of these falling to the Lord Chancellor, his wife had them made into bed hangings.

Hardwicke presided at the trial of the leading rebels in the Stuart rising of 1745, pronounced their doom, and enacted a law forbidding the weaving of tartan as the national dress of Scotland. He was a powerful advocate of the reform of the calendar, reformed the marriage laws, and struck a salutary blow for justice by abolishing hereditary judgeships in Scotland. He died in 1764 rich and honoured, his son Charles succeeding to the Woolsack but dying without enjoying the office.

The Town of Great Transformations

WISBECH. It has seen great transformations, for time was when the tides swept over it, coming up the River Nene winding through the fens. It has seen the sea go back, for it was once four miles away and is now eleven. No town has prospered more from the marvellous reclamation work begun by the Romans, continued by the Dutch, and finished by Rennie and Telford, snatching thousands of square miles of fenland from the grip of the sea.

It is the second town in the county, and, its river being navigable for ships of 1700 tons, is busy with merchandise, for it has become the metropolis of the flower gardens and fruit orchards of the Cambridgeshire Fens. Those who would see what the reclamation of land can do should come this way in springtime, when the country round about is like a patchwork quilt. For weeks it is a veritable fairyland ablaze with tulips, and in due season comes the apple blossom, a wondrous sight. As for the great canning industry which has expanded so surprisingly in our time, Wisbech is one of its great centres and the figures of its canning factories (the first in England) are almost astronomical. Hundreds, thousands, millions, seem unequal to the strain.

It may be that the proudest memory of this fenland town is that of the man who struck a mighty blow for human freedom, Thomas Clarkson. His father was headmaster of the grammar school for 17 years. The school carries on in a new building after 600 years of history, but part of its old buildings may be seen; it has given an Archbishop to Canterbury, Thomas Herring. Born here in 1760, Thomas Clarkson looks down on the life of his old town from a monument 68 feet high to the top of the spire which crowns his canopy. He stands near the bridge which takes us over the river to Wisbech St Mary, and on the base of his fine monument (designed by Sir Gilbert Scott), are reliefs of a fettered slave, and of his friends William Wilberforce and Granville Sharp, Wilberforce with whom he worked throughout his life, Granville Sharp who won the historic decision in the courts that slaves cannot breathe in England. "They touch our country and their shackles fall," wrote William Cowper, but it was Granville Sharp who made it so.

Thomas Clarkson is the most famous man of Wisbech, and rightly the town has given to him the noblest monument in its streets.

The subject of human liberty engaged his attention in his early days at Cambridge, where an essay of his was received with great applause in the senate house. He made friends with Granville Sharp and William Wilberforce, and joined a committee on May 22, 1787, to work for the suppression of the slave trade. Within a year the matter was being discussed in Parliament, where it was revealed that rarely less than 50 and often more than 80 in every 100 Negroes died on their voyage into slavery. He once boarded all the ships belonging to the navy at Deptford, Woolwich, Chatham, Sheerness, and Portsmouth searching for a witness on the horrors of the trade. He travelled all over the country to keep up the hearts of the reformers after Wilberforce's defeat in Parliament. He interviewed the Tsar of Russia, helped to found the Anti-Slavery Society, and saw the triumph of the cause. When he was 73 years old he was going blind, but he had 13 years to live, and an operation on his eyes brought back his sight after a short period of total blindness. At 79 he was made a Freeman of the City of London, but perhaps his best recognition is in Wordsworth's sonnet, which begins *Clarkson! it was an obstinate hill to climb*, and goes on:

> *Duty's intrepid liegeman, see, the palm*
> *Is won, and by all nations shall be worn!*
> *The bloodstained writing is for ever torn;*
> *And thou henceforth wilt have a good*
> *   man's calm,*
> *A great man's happiness; thy zeal shall find*
> *Repose at length, firm friend of human kind.*

Wisbech has lost its ancient castle, built by the Normans and made into a palace of the bishops by Cardinal Morton in the 15th century. It covered four acres and was protected by a moat 40 feet wide. It was within the old walls that King John heard the bitter news that his jewels had been lost in the Wash, and here in the troubled days of religious persecution two famous men were held in captivity, Thomas Watson, a great scholar and supporter of Mary Tudor, and John Feckenham, the last Abbot of Westminster. The history of the castle ended in Cromwellian days, and Cromwell's Secretary of State, Thomas Thurloe, pulled down the walls and built himself a new house with the materials, Inigo Jones designing it for him. Thurloe was one of the men to whom Oliver was much attached, and with whom he would lay aside his greatness. When Cromwell was raised to the Protectorate Thurloe sent out the order to the sheriffs to proclaim him, and it was his marvellous system of secret intelligence which made it possible for a member of Parliament to say in the House that Cromwell carried the secrets of all the princes in Europe at his girdle. Cromwell was truly a hero to this secretary, and Thurloe wished him to accept the crown. After the Restoration he was charged with high treason, but released; it is said that he remarked that if he were to be hanged he had a black book which would hang many that went for Cavaliers.

On the site of the old castle moat now stands the museum, which claims the distinction of being one of the oldest in the country. It has a fine collection of coins, glass, and pottery from Celtic, Roman, and Saxon England, a valuable display of fenland birds, relics of the slave trade and little things associated with Thomas Clarkson; charters of the 16th and 17th centuries, a manuscript written by 12th century monks which Pepys is known to have looked at, many autographs and over 3000 coins, the Dickens manuscript from which Great Expectations was printed, a number of early atlases, specimens of Whieldon ware, and a wonderful little head of Buddha about 1600 years old. Near the museum is an old inn with structural fragments of the 15th century, and we understand that its wine vaults were part of an underground passage to the castle.

In one of the two marketplaces stands the octagon church, a modern chapel of ease, and there is a modern church of St Augustine; but the only ancient church in Wisbech is that of St Peter and St Paul, a remarkable place with three nave arcades built in three centuries. This spacious church with a quaint array of roofs and over 30 windows, has a double nave and a double chancel, each with its own gabled roof, and both naves with aisles. The north nave is separated from its aisle by a Norman arcade of five bays, one of the arches carved with chevron, the others plain. Above this is the 15th century clerestory. Separating the north nave from the south is a lofty arcade from the 15th century, with a Norman arch at the western end facing the western arch of the north arcade, both part of a Norman vanished tower. The arcade separating the south nave from its aisle is 14th century and has clustered pillars; it was probably built at the same time as the arcade dividing the two chancels. One of the pillars of the chancel arch is Norman. The reredos is of stone and alabaster, with a mosaic copy made in Venice of Leonardo's Last Supper; there are canopied figures of St Peter and St Paul at the sides. There is an Elizabethan altar table and a 14th century font.

The tower is the finest feature of the church, and comes from early in the 16th century. Its three stages rise to a rich crown of pierced battlements, with eight pinnacles and a leaded roof like a small spire. Under the parapet is a cornice adorned with shields, flowers, and emblems; angels with symbols are over the belfry windows, and the stringcourses are carved with heraldry. The tower base forms a north porch and shelters a handsome 14th century doorway enriched with a band of carving of animals, birds, foliage, and grotesques, among them being little men, lions, and a dragon chasing a dog. The most interesting memorial in the church is a great brass of Thomas de Braunston, Constable of the Castle in the 14th century. It is one of the biggest brasses in England, over nine feet long, and shows the knight lifesize in armour which is interesting because it illustrates the coming of full plate armour. He has a steel cuirass, a pointed helmet, and an ornamental sword and dagger, his hands are clasped in prayer, and his feet are on a lion. A Constable of the Castle 230 years after him kneels with his wife on a dingy wall-memorial of 1633. He was a linen draper named Matthias Taylor, and both he and his wife are in long gowns and ruffs. Also kneeling on a wall are two Wisbech people who must have bought linen at Matthias Taylor's shop, for they died a few years before him and left charities to the town. He is Thomas Parke, and kneels in armour and ruff at a desk, his wife being in a flowing gown with a ruff and a broad-brimmed hat, and on a panel of the desk at which they kneel is their daughter, with a skeleton as an unpleasant companion on a shelf above.

In unknown graves in the churchyard lie the two friends who died as prisoners in the castle, Thomas Watson and John Feckenham. Thomas Watson was one of Mary Tudor's leading bishops, and Roger Ascham paid a high tribute to his scholarship. It has been said that he spoke incautiously of excommunicating Elizabeth, and certainly for his boldness of opinion he was more than once put into the Tower. He was a sincere Roman Catholic, and even as a bishop was allowed to have his own Roman Catholic attendant. His last days were troubled by bitter controversy on theological matters, and he died while in captivity in Wisbech Castle.

John Feckenham was the last abbot of Westminster, the son of poor Worcestershire peasants, and was a popular preacher in Mary Tudor's reign, preaching to great crowds from St Paul's Cross during the persecution of the Protestants. Even though he could not forgive heretics his heart moved him to do his utmost to persuade them to save themselves, and it is recorded that at one time he rescued 28 people from the stake. Mary Tudor sent him to try to convert Lady Jane Grey as she lay waiting for death, but he declared himself more fit to be her disciple than her master, and after the execution a dialogue between them was published, drawn up by Lady Jane. He was with her on the scaffold, but the only comfort he could give her was to say that he was sorry for her, for he believed that they would never meet again. When he was made Abbot of Westminster he began the restoration of the abbey. It had been much neglected, shrines pulled down, relics stolen, and it was he who found the Confessor's coffin in some hidden place and returned it to the shrine with its old splendour. He preached the funeral sermon for Queen Mary. Elizabeth befriended him because he had befriended her in her unhappy days. He found his way to the Tower, however, for "railing against changes," and was then thrown into prison and finally released to live in a house in Holborn. He was a good friend of the poor and was allowed to live in peace for the last few years of his life.

WISBECH ST MARY. A modest village of the fens, it has a legacy from medieval England in its church, to which we come by a 15th century porch. Between the nave arcades are faces quaint and grim, one of a woman with a round face and square headdress, another of a woman striking a man with a club, another with a jumble of heads and legs which appear to be in a wrestling bout. On a pillar is a bracket carved with a demon's head, probably by the masons who did the carving on the ancient font. From those ancient days comes the altar in a chapel made from a chest with front panels pierced and carved, and a back made by a Jacobean carpenter. The modern windows glow with colour, among them the Shepherds, the Wise Men, and other familiar scenes, with a Calvary in the east window from which stand out fine figures of St George in armour and St Michael with a flaming sword.

Captivating Oddness

WITCHAM. It is a little place on a low hill of the fens just withdrawn off the busy road from Ely to Chatteris. Its pride is in its church, which is captivating in its very oddness, a quaint mixture of bricks and stones of all sizes and shapes. Its tower is 700 years old. Indoors the church has the air of gracious age, full of light with cream walls and clear glass, Mary in red and blue looking down from a window. There are twisted Jacobean altar rails, a simple oak screen 500 years old, a few old poppyhead benches from which the rest are copied, traces of wall-painting, and in a corner among the corbels of the roof is a hooded man with tiny legs and great shoulders, eating ravenously.

The church has two treasures, one of sixty medieval stone pulpits still left in England, and a fine medieval font. The pulpit is simple and massive and only lately have the old stone steps built in the 15th century been brought to light. The bowl of the font is carved with women in 13th century headdress, a lion and an eagle and dragons, one of these having two heads snarling at each other.

A Tale of the Conqueror

WITCHFORD. It was here that the monks of Ely to their sorrow met the Conqueror. In the absence of Hereward the Wake, the Isle's defender, the monks were prepared to make their submission, but William, the story goes, came unawares to the abbey when the monks were at their meal, and, meeting none of the custodians, placed a mark of gold on the altar and quietly departed. The perturbed monks learning of the visit from a Norman knight, hastened after the king to make their apologies. They caught him up at Witchford, where he laid on them a fine so heavy that all their church ornaments had to be melted down to pay it.

The church comes from our three great building centuries, its low embattled tower from the 13th, the porch from the 15th, and the rest of the neat little structure from the 14th. The font is medieval. There is a touch of pathos in a lonely patch of glass in a window showing the three-masted ship John Temperley being lashed by waves, its sails reefed. It is in memory of someone lost at sea in 1872.

At the End of Devil's Dyke

WOOD DITTON. When the builders before history drew the line of their defensive work of bank and fosse across the open country, known to us as the Devil's Dyke, they rested one end on the impassable fens where the village of Reach is now and the other end eight miles away on the impenetrable forest at Wood Ditton. Here we may see it, its massive proportions little changed, at the edge of a small wood by Camois Hall.

There are beautiful fields about the village now, and gracious elms and chestnuts, children of the giants of the ancient forest, shade the church, a medieval structure with its ancient door still opening and closing for us, old timbers in the roof of its old porch, its 15th century oak screen still beautiful with roses and tracery and a little colour in its panels. Here is the 15th century font, a curious piscina on the edge of a window, fragments of old glass, and ancient bench-ends carved with griffins, birds, and animals. There is a fine portrait of Henry English of 1393, a knight in armour with a steel helmet and his feet on a lion, his wife headless beside him though still with her mantle and her rosary, and with a fine dog looking up to her with bells on its collar. On an alabaster panel in memory of 30 men who did not come back is another knight, St George, shown as an old man in silver chain armour with a coloured coat, his sword through the dragon. On the panel are the words, They went forth from us and died for England.

CAMBRIDGESHIRE TOWNS AND VILLAGES

In this key to our map of Cambridgeshire are all the towns and villages treated in this book. If a place is not on the map by name, its square is given here, so that the way to it is easily found, each square being five miles. One or two hamlets are in the book with their neighbouring villages; for these see Index.

233

INDEX

This index includes all notable subjects and people likely to be sought for, and a special index of pictures appears at the beginning of the volume.

INDEX

INDEX

Goodrich, Bishop, 122, 127
Goodwin, Bishop, 122
Gorges, Lord, 195
Grantchester, 134
Gray, Thomas, 46
Great Abington, 138
Great Chishall, 139
Great Eversden, 139
Great Ouse, 3
Great Shelford, 140
Great Wilbraham, 140
Greenaway, Kate, 80
Guilden Morden, 141
Guillemard, Dr F. H., 210
Gunning, Bishop, 122

Haddenham, 141
Hardwicke, Earl of, 223–4
Harlton, 142
Harston, 143
Harvard, John, 76, 77
Harvey, William, 49
Haslingfield, 144
Hatley St George, 145
Hatton family, 171
Hauxton, 146
Henrietta, Maria, 70
Henry the Sixth, 54, 58, 59, 60, 66, 71
Henry the Seventh, 221
Henry the Eighth, 73, 74
Henty, G. A., 210
Herbert family, 153
Herbert, George, 39, 80
Hereward the Wake, 111, 142, 205
Herring, Thomas, 225
Heton, Bishop, 122
Heydon, 146
Hildersham, 147
Hinde family, 172
Hinxton, 149
Histon, 149
Hobson, Thomas, 34, 38
Holcroft, Francis, 165, 179
Horningsea, 150
Horseheath, 151
Hotham, John de, 116, 118, 121
Huddleston family, 187–9
Huguenots, 207
Hullier, John, 16

Iceni, 6, 186
Ickleton, 152

Icknield Way, 2
Impington, 153
Ireton, General, 177
Isleham, 156

James the First, 73, 130
Jenyns family, 23
Jenyns, Leonard, 201
Jesse window, 163
Jesus College, 63
John, King, 226

Kelvin, Lord, 46
Kennett, 158
Kilkenny, Bishop, 121
King's College, 54
Kingston, 158
Kirtling, 159
Knapwell, 160
Kneesworth Hall, 21
Knutsford, Viscount, 21

Landbeach, 160
Landwade, 161
Latimer, Hugh, 47, 59
Lecterns, notable:
  Cambridge, 58, 67
  Histon, 150
  Isleham, 156
  Landbeach, 161
  Leverington, 163
Leverington, 162
Limlow Hill, 165
Linton, 164
Litlington, 165
Little Abington, 166
Little Chishall, 166
Little Downham, 166
Little Eversden, 167
Little Gransden, 168
Little Ouse, 3
Littleport, 168
Little Shelford, 169
Little Wilbraham, 170
Lode, 170
Lolworth, 170
Long, Roger, 49
Long Stanton, 171
Longstowe, 172
Lumpkin, Tony, 163
Luxembourg, Cardinal, 120

Macaulay, Lord, 73
Mackenzie, Bishop, 145
McNeile, Ethel, 81
Madingley, 172
Magdalene College, 70

Mallory, George, 33
Mandeville, Geoffrey de, 26
March, 173
Martyn, Henry, 39
Marvell, Andrew, 176
Mary Tudor, 187, 189
Mawson, Bishop, 122
Mazes, 24, 100, 114
Melbourn, 175
Meldreth, 176
Mepal, 177
Mildmay, Sir Walter, 66, 76
Mill, Canon Hodge, 120
Milton, 177
Milton, John, 66, 75
Misereres:
  Balsham, 17
  Cambridge, 58
  Ely, 123
  Fordham, 130
  Gamlingay, 133
  Great Eversden, 140
  Isleham, 156
  Over, 181
  Soham, 193
Moore, Bishop, 122
More, Sir Thomas, 40, 45
Museums:
  Cambridge, 32, 81, 89, 90
  Wisbech, 227

Needham Hall, 109
Newnham College, 80
Newton, 178
Newton-in-the-Isle, 178
Newton, Sir Isaac, 73, 74, 75
North family, 159
Northwold, Bishop, 121

Oakington, 179
Oddy, Joseph, 179
Orwell, 180
Osland, Henry, 179
Over, 181
Ovin, 111, 141
Owen, Nicholas, 187

Palavacini, Horatio, 16
Pampisford, 182
Pandiana, Saint, 110
Papworth, Everard, 182
Paris, Matthew, 53, 147–9
Parker, Matthew, 53
Parson Drove, 184

238

INDEX

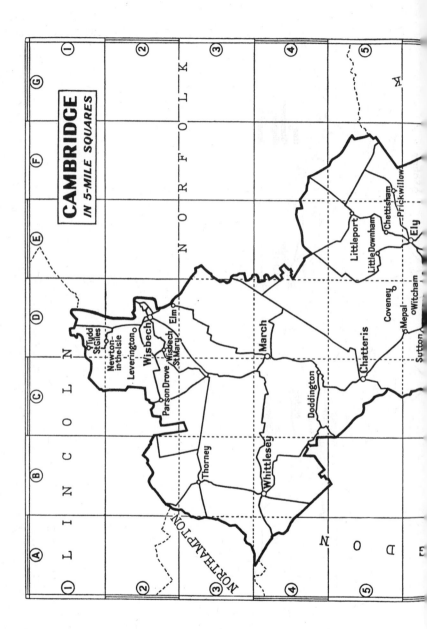

CAMBRIDGE
IN 5-MILE SQUARES